WILLIAM
HOWARD TAFT

WILLIAM
HOWARD TAFT

An Intimate History

I hope that somebody, sometime,
will recognize the agony of spirit
that I have undergone.
—WILLIAM HOWARD TAFT (1912)

JUDITH ICKE ANDERSON

W · W · Norton & Company · New York · London

Copyright © 1981 by W. W. Norton & Company, Inc.
Published simultaneously in Canada by George J. McLeod Limited, Toronto.
Printed in the United States of America

First Edition

BOOK DESIGN BY ANTONINA KRASS

Library of Congress Cataloging in Publication Data

Anderson, Judith Icke.
William Howard Taft, an intimate history.

Includes bibliographical references and index.
1. Taft, William Howard, Pres. U.S., 1857–1930.   2. United States—Politics and
government—1901–1909.   3. United States—Politics and government—1909–1913.
4. Presidents—United States—Biography.   I. Title.
E762.A56   1981   973.91′2′0924   [B]   80–27812
ISBN 0–393–01462–2

W. W. Norton & Company, Inc. 500 Fifth Avenue, New York, N.Y. 10110
W. W. Norton & Company Ltd. 25 New Street Square, London EC4A 3NT
1 2 3 4 5 6 7 8 9 0

TO
Gabriel
AND
Clarissa
AND TO THE MEMORY OF
Fawn Brodie

CONTENTS

ILLUSTRATIONS

All photographs are from the Collections of The Library of Congress.

CHRONOLOGICAL
TABLE

15 September 1857   William Howard Taft born to Louisa and Alphonso Taft in Cincinnati, Ohio

1874   Graduated from Woodward High School, Cincinnati

1878   B.A., Yale University

1880   Graduated from Cincinnati Law School

1881   Appointed to first public office: Assistant Prosecuting Attorney of Hamilton County, Ohio

1882   Appointed collector of internal revenue for Cincinnati

1883   Returns to private law practice

March 1885   Engaged to Helen ("Nellie") Herron (*b.* 1860; *d.* 1943)

19 June 1886   Married

March 1887   Appointed to Superior Court of Ohio by Governor Foraker

8 September 1889   Robert Alphonso Taft born

4 February   1890   Appointed U.S. Solicitor General by President Benjamin Harrison

1 August   1891   Helen Herron Taft born

7 March   1892   Appointed Judge of the Sixth Federal Circuit Court by President William McKinley

20 September 1897   Charles Phelps Taft born

15 March   1900   Appointed President of the Philippine Commission

July   1901   Appointed Governor of the Philippines by President McKinley

1 February   1904   Appointed Secretary of War by President Theodore Roosevelt

3 November 1908   Elected President

3 March   1909   Inaugurated as the Twenty-Seventh President of the United States

3 November 1912   Loses the presidential election to Woodrow Wilson

1913–1921   Kent Professor of Law, Yale University

1918   Appointed Joint-Chairman of the National War Labor Board by President Wilson

30 June   1921   Appointed Ninth Chief Justice of the Supreme Court by President Warren G. Harding

3 February   1930   Retires as Chief Justice

8 March   1930   Dies in Washington, D.C.

PREFACE AND
ACKNOWLEDGMENTS

One paradox has puzzled biographers of William Howard Taft as well as those historians interested in the effect of personality on the careers of American presidents: how could Taft, a man politically unambitious, be catapulted into ever higher national offices and ultimately win the presidency, a triumph he feared and dreaded? Taft yearned for only one post, a seat on the Supreme Court, yet he accepted the Republican presidential nomination in 1908 after his most enthusiastic supporter, President Theodore Roosevelt, personally chose him as his successor. Taft's major biographers allude to the influence of his wife, family, and friends on his career, but none gives them a prominent place in his decision making. When these historians come to an overall assessment of the perplexing issues surrounding Taft's attainments, they fall back on the same historically questionable explanation—it was simply his fate or destiny to become president. "The fates were, as always, pushing Taft higher and higher," writes Henry F. Pringle, author of the most comprehensive biography. Taft was, Pringle claims, the only man in American political history who can be described with complete accuracy as a creature of destiny. Allen Ragan avers that "Fate and fortune play strange tricks in the determination of the roles men are to play in life. This was especially true in Taft's history." And Taft's most laudatory biographer, Herbert S. Duffy, avoiding any speculation about the role played by his friends and family, is satisfied with the notion that Taft "seemed doomed to public life and politics from the earliest years of his career." The word "doom" may imply Duffy's sense of a peculiar incongruity between Taft's personality and his fate, but the author fails to pursue it. Alpheus T. Mason writes that young Taft "was becoming a creature of political destiny—and the wheel of fortune had only begun to spin. The fates seemed always to be pushing him higher." All of these summations suggest the existence of a question about Taft's life and career that lies beyond the range of standard historical explanation. The concept of fate begs it. A clear answer is possible if we examine in depth Taft's complex psychological make-up and intimate personal history.

Another problem about Taft's career which has perplexed historians is why he functioned so exceptionally well in the government positions he occupied prior to the presidency, but so ineffectively as president? As Champ Clark, Speaker of the House from 1911 to 1919, wrote, even Taft's worst enemies did not claim that he had failed to exhibit great ability in the important positions he had held prior to 1908. Because of this excellent record, he came into the White House supported by almost universal good-will. Yet after becoming chief executive, he earned the reputation of "Taft the Blunderer" and "Taft the Great Postponer." He spent a minimum amount of time at the White House, traveling away from Washington more often than any previous president. In office, he suddenly lost his reputation for competency and efficiency, yet several years after his defeat in 1912, he was chosen chief justice of the United States and served effectively until his death in 1930.

By concentrating on political ideas and events and paying little heed to Taft's inner life, earlier biographers bypassed or ignored important causative factors. In this book, I plan to describe the impact of Taft's numerous inner conflicts on his decision making and, in particular, on his frequent failure to make decisions at all. The result is not merely political history but the drama of a man in history—a man who engages our interest and sympathy once he is seen from the inside—as he saw and, more importantly, as he felt about himself. This history presents in nonclinical language the evolution of Taft's conflicts and extraordinary dependencies, which began in childhood, were complicated by his marriage, and exacerbated by certain kinds of success—all of which are peculiarly illuminated by fluctuations in his weight, in itself a special phenomenon. Always a heavy man, Taft reached his greatest weight—355 pounds—while in the White House yet managed to slim down to below 260 during his years as chief justice.

This book is also a portrait of a marriage. Though William Howard Taft remains the central character, his wife, Helen (Nellie) Herron Taft, whose political significance has remained largely obscured, emerges as a major force for the first time. The Taft family letters reveal the fascinating interplay between Nellie's inexorable ambition, unable to find an outlet in her own world, and the expansive, but essentially timid, good nature of her husband. We find in this narrative that Nellie's influence was not only powerful, but perhaps the most significant key to our understanding of his career. We see for the first time how Taft, of all our presidents the most reluctant to assume presidential power, was pushed into office by his indomitable wife, who became the most important influence in his life.

Another of Taft's hidden conflicts is illuminated through an analysis of his unique personal relationship with Theodore Roosevelt. Roosevelt chose his best friend as his successor in the White House then broke with him and became his competitor for the presidency in 1912. There is much that is comic here, but there is the stuff of tragedy too—tragedy for Taft himself, as he who had been so successful as a subordinate found himself fumbling and inept as president and then demoralized by the breakup of his friendship with Roosevelt. The nation may have suffered too, for when Taft turned away from the progressivism of his predecessor, he embraced the status quo policies of the conservative advisers who replaced Roosevelt in his affections.

The present study, based on hitherto under-utilized manuscript sources— especially family letters and diaries—on accounts of Taft's public and personal life recorded by his contemporaries, and on newspapers and journals of the day, provides the basis for clarifying much of the mystery surrounding Taft's destiny. One of the largest collections of the presidential series, the papers include all the correspondence between Taft and his wife. From the days of their courtship beginning in 1884 to Taft's death in 1930, he wrote steadily and copiously to Nellie on the many occasions when they were apart. "If you count the letters I have written you, you will find one for every day since I left," Taft wrote in 1892. This habit, he never abandoned. He sometimes wrote several letters a day and never felt at ease until he had told her all he thought and felt in detail, not only of important events, but also of the most trivial. He reported what he ate for dinner and what clothes he had worn one day and planned for the next. "I had a good night's sleep and a good bath. I went through my exercises," he remarked in one letter. He also revealed his innermost anxieties as he experienced them from day to day.

Nellie wrote less frequently, but her letters are no less valuable than Taft's for the understanding we seek. When Taft complained that she did not answer him either as often or as enthusiastically as he could wish, Nellie would be provoked to write. What she wrote reveals the active role she took in shaping his career. In 1917 Nellie published her *Recollections*, which, despite her guardedness, also suggests much about her deepest feelings. Most important, she describes the progression of events which led to the fulfillment of her dream of becoming first lady. Also extant is Nellie's personal diary (ignored by most of Taft's biographers), which she kept during her late teenage years. Her private ruminations disclose much about her intellectual and emotional constitution, and these revelations help considerably in explaining why she and Taft agreed to marry and why, as a consequence of that marriage, Taft turned from his great love of the law to politics. Without her compelling ambition it seems inconceivable that Taft would have forsaken his comfortable judicial bench in Ohio for the political offices which eventually brought him so much unhappiness.

A rich lode of material on the presidential years may be seen in the collected letters of Archibald Willingham Butt, personal aide to Taft in the Philippines and then, successively, to Roosevelt and Taft during their tenures in the White House. Born into a Georgian family established before the Revolution and educated at the University of the South in Sewanee, Tennessee, Archie Butt was a personable Southern gentleman much in demand at social gatherings in the capital. He remained a bachelor all his life, dedicating himself to his career in the service of two presidents. Devoted to his mother, Butt wrote her almost daily, relating in detail the activities at the White House. After his mother's death in 1908, Archie directed entertaining and informative letters to his sister-in-law Clara. The three volumes of his letters constitute a sympathetic but candid appraisal of President Taft that reveals his confusion, his mistakes, and his sufferings.

In order to explain the inner workings of Taft's mind and the numerous problems he dimly perceived but did not control, we must reach far back into his family life, especially into the relationship between Taft and his parents. And to understand better the important role Taft's mother, Louisa Torrey Taft, played in shaping his personality, it is necessary to examine her own early home environment. There is exciting evidence illuminating many puzzles, especially the major one: how the man for whom politics and the presidency were a "nightmare" again and again was constrained to decline his "heart's desire," a position on the Supreme Court, and to accept instead the highest office in the land, for which he knew he was ill-suited. The man who thought himself a "mountain of misery" while courting Nellie Herron could not have anticipated the personal agony to come. Perhaps far more than most men who have achieved high public fortune, Taft was a product and a victim of his ties to those he loved.

*　　*　　*

I owe thanks to many people for assistance, and to record my gratitude is to give, necessarily, a brief account of the writing of this book over the past decade. It began in a graduate seminar at the University of California, Los

Angeles, given by Professor Fawn Brodie. The paper from that seminar was presented in 1970 before the Los Angeles Interdisciplinary Psychoanalytic Study Group, an organization devoted primarily to exploring the psycho-dynamics of political leadership. Its members encouraged me at a time when encouragement was most wanted and gave me the benefit of their stimulating speculations. I thank Robert M. Dorn, M.D., E. Victor Wolfenstein (UCLA), Alfred Goldberg, M.D., Robert Wahl, M.D. (UCLA), Ira Carson, M.D., and Ernest Levy, M.D. Within a few years, the initial paper had expanded into a Ph.D. dissertation in history at UCLA through the guidance of my committee: Professors Theodore Saloutos (director), Fawn Brodie, and Richard Lehan (English, UCLA). Roy P. Basler of the Manuscript Division of the Library of Congress helped me secure microfilms of those Taft papers I most needed. In the course of my work I was assisted by a generous grant from the American Association of University Women in 1974–75, and by a special grant-in-aid from California State Polytechnic University, Pomona, in 1979. My deep thanks to all of these people and organizations.

I owe special thanks also to George Brockway, chairman of Norton, who has, over the past several years, saved me from many useless wanderings through the guidance of his strong editorial hand. Early on, Norton Kristy, a Los Angeles psychologist, took a friendly interest in my project and after reading the manuscript helped to clarify much of my thinking about the Tafts and their situation. I owe a great debt to Professor Edwin Perkins of the University of Southern California, who generously put his scholarship and superlative editorial skills at my service.

Fawn Brodie and my husband, Walter E. Anderson, have given me con-stant support and assistance. Both have helped see the work through several drafts, contributing much to its conception and writing. Without them the book would not have been written.

William
Howard Taft

I

TAFT IN
THE WHITE HOUSE

After watching President William Howard Taft grope his way "foggy and bewildered" through endless mazes, journalist Charles Thompson dubbed him " 'the blundering politician,' the honest greenhorn at the poker table." Theodore Roosevelt's attorney general, Charles Bonaparte, believed that Taft, as president, committed the most notable unbroken succession of "colossal blunders" in the history of American politics. Ushered into the presidency with one of the greatest popular majorities in the nation's history, Taft was hurled out of office as a result of the nastiest internal revolt the Republican party had as yet experienced. The irony of his situation was most poignant to himself; his love was the law, and he was never content except within the seclusion of the judge's bench. He was so fond of judicial work, he once said, that if he could be made a common pleas judge in Hamilton County, Ohio, he would be content to remain there all his life. He especially suffered when, as president, he was called upon to appoint another man to be chief justice of the Supreme Court, the position he desired for himself and came close to obtaining more than once before being thrust into the White House in 1909.

Taft's virtues—simplicity, honesty, fidelity, generosity—instead of saving him from bitter public attacks, created many of his difficulties. His desire to satisfy simultaneously all persons and parties led him to vacillate, and his indecisiveness consequently complicated issues in ways which brought him, and those he held closest in friendship or love, little satisfaction. He was playful, candid, ingenuous, and, above all, trusting, as countless friends and observers testified. William Allen White, a progressive Republican journalist who watched Taft closely in the White House, described him as being "large, handsome and fair with . . . the sunny disposition of an innocent child." Taft said whatever came into his mind, regardless of his audience, because he was, as journalist Charles Thompson, author of *The Presidents I've Known*, observed, "too much a child of nature. He had the innocent candor . . . of a boy under ten." He was "honest, simply honest, transparently honest," Mark Sullivan said, and "in all three hundred thirty pounds of him, not a pound nor an ounce, nor a gram was deceit." Friend and enemy alike were inspired by warm personal feelings for this immense, good-natured man. Even Arthur W. Dunn, who could scarcely talk of President Taft's four years in the White House without acerbity, admitted that personally he was a most lovable character. Although in his book *As I Knew Them* James Watson remembered Taft "as nearly devoid of executive ability as anyone of our presidents that could be named," he nonetheless confessed to loving the man: "No one, it seemed, was immune to his wholesome, warm-hearted genial charm and modest, gentle character—he was probably the most likeable man ever to hold the office of president." Conceding that he was frequently and entirely out of patience with Taft's "lumbering and ineffective" political methods, Watson still considered Taft one of the finest men who ever lived anywhere: "His impulses were all good, his emotions were all kind and his aspirations were all noble." Such impressions go a long way toward suggesting why Taft so firmly secured the approbation and confidence of Presidents McKinley and Roosevelt. Roosevelt, who had become Taft's closest friend, said, "You know, I think Taft has the most lovable personality I have ever come in contact with. I almost envy a man possessing a personality like Taft's. One loves him at first sight."

Taft was a hard worker, and his diligence vitally contributed to his success before he assumed the presidency. As secretary of war in Roosevelt's cabinet he had worked harder than any other officer. But when Roosevelt stepped aside, Taft was on his own. Once in the White House, he wanted most to please only himself, which meant, as he said to his wife in a rare sharply edged remark, he was "not going to be pushed anymore." Pleasing himself meant, however, satisfying the wishes of all factions by trying to avoid conflict and confrontation; thus in a sense, he suffered being "pushed" about more than ever before.

Within a few weeks after Taft's inauguration, Washington reporters—who had earlier hailed him as better prepared for the presidency than any of his predecessors—observed that whereas Roosevelt's administration had been like a "boiler shop," Taft's was like "changing from one of the new automobiles to a horse-cab." "It was evident," William Allen White wrote, "that the army of progress that had been moving along with President Roosevelt was camped under President Taft." If Mr. Roosevelt's administration was not unlike a continuous Fourth of July celebration, the *Fortnightly Review* remarked, Mr. Taft's was not unlike the day after. Perplexed and embittered to find himself laden with undesired responsibilities, Taft became swamped under masses of papers, and he foundered. Archie Butt, who served as personal aide to Taft as he had to Roosevelt, felt that "if the president continues to transact business as he is transacting it now, he will be about three years behind when the fourth of March 1913 rolls around."

Critical of what Taft admitted to be his "disposition to procrastinate," the New York *Sun* printed the following satirical poem:

> A solid man, both for and aft, is he who's known as Mr. Taft.
> He sits high in the halls of state, a man of most unquestioned weight.
> He has the manners of a Judge, and hence is rather hard to budge.
> If he could have eternity to make things as they ought to be,
> When time hath reached its end afar, we'd all dwell in Utopia.

Life magazine joined in with this jingle: "Teddy, come home and blow your horn,/The sheep's in the meadow, the cow's in the corn./The boy you left to tend the sheep/Is under the haystack fast asleep."

Neither lion nor fox, Taft was unable to comprehend the intricacies of the president's political role or to bully his way through like Roosevelt. He trusted almost everyone, spoke his mind freely on most occasions, and tried to be friends with everyone. The "innocent candor" for which he had always been praised became a serious liability. He openly talked of Congress, of promotions in the army, of his opinions of certain high public officers, as if his words were of no more significance than an ordinary citizen's. Henry Stoddard lamented that Taft had developed a marvelous consistency for saying and doing the wrong thing politically. Taft was, for example, dumbfounded when his remarks to Ohio Northern students about the economy caused stock prices to dive on Wall Street. Speaking about the business situation and the improbability of the rate of growth in foreign trade continuing, he said it was reasonable to suppose that "at some time within the next decade there will be some reaction or some financial stringency." "Or," he carelessly added, "perhaps a financial panic."

Most public men kept their private thoughts for their diaries, but Taft blurted his out in public. He did not care very much about the political repercussions of his words or deeds, for he felt he had done most of what others had required of him in accepting the presidency.

In contrast to Roosevelt, who was always alert to political opportunities, Taft's "bump of political sagacity was a dent," quipped Oscar King Davis of the *New York Times*. Heedless of most advice throughout his four years in the White House, he continued to say what he felt. Even his brother Horace, normally a strong defender of the president, deplored his indiscreet remarks about prominent politicians. Taft lacked the higher political wisdom which might have enabled him to avoid political disasters. He had not matured much since those days when as "champion family correspondent" he had felt obligated to relate, cordially and candidly, all he thought and did to his parents, and genuine good-heartedness could not save him from becoming the victim of more wit than any previous president. "If you put Taft and a trap in a section of land in the night and wanted to find him," Iowa's Henry C. Wallace wrote, "you would simply need to go to that part of the square mile where the trap was located and you would find him in it."

Many Republicans jumped off Taft's political wagon out of fear of his ineptitude and his indifference. Often he could not keep the names and faces straight of important supporters. To one he frankly exclaimed, "They tell me I ought to remember you but, bless my soul, I cannot recall you at all!" In contrast, Roosevelt knew the names even of the wives and children. Nellie Taft, who was a shrewd politician, often echoed the exasperation of such men as Henry Cabot Lodge and Henry Adams over her husband's "unfortunate shortcoming of not knowing much and of caring less about the way the game of politics is played." But as Roosevelt's subordinate, Taft never had needed to develop political skills.

Criticism was the one thing above all that he could not endure, and it overwhelmed him once he became president. He soon discovered that reporters no longer regarded him as simply a pleasant source of information about government programs and intentions. And when once scarred by their barbs, he became wary and viewed them as potential enemies. They were not long in recognizing the change. "The old cordiality and friendliness were gone," Oscar King Davis wrote in the *Times*, "and there was in its place a reserve that amounted almost to coldness." Within a month of Taft's inauguration reporters were complaining that Taft not only made little news, he also withheld what news he had. Archie Butt revealed that at a small gathering one night, Taft had an extraodinary burst of temper and began to damn the press—*Colliers* in particular. When the editors of the magazine requested an interview, he refused, declaring that he regarded them "as murderers and thieves, and he would, if he had his way, condemn them all to hell and eternal damnation." This was a wholly new phenomenon in his life.

James E. Pollard, author of *The Presidents and the Press*, finds Taft's difficulties with reporters a "strange paradox," since he had gotten along so famously with them when he was secretary of war. Equally surprised, biographer Henry Pringle accounts for Taft's "anxiety" as merely the usual consequence of a conscientious, well-intentioned man elevated, "by fate," to the White House. A more recent biographer Paola Coletta believes President Taft's conflicts with the press stemmed from his lack of respect for the newspaper fraternity, but there is a more subtle cause. It was easy for Taft to be friendly and expansive to newsmen as secretary of war when the responsibilities and principal criticism fell upon President Roosevelt; he could not, however, face the same men when he became their prime object of censure. Previously he had always been able to shape his life in the service of others and thus avoid personal criticism. As his mother knew, her son had no means of combatting open hostility, and she predicted that the malice of politics would wound him deeply. "If only he had a thick hide and could take it," Butt mused. "I feel dreadfully sorry for him . . . he gets so low in spirits that it is impossible to cheer him. [He] just sits silently by . . . and grows morose. He does not seem to throw it off." Smarting under his critics' jibes, Taft confessed wanly to the New York Press Club:

> There are times at the White House . . . when you get really very discouraged. Things don't go right. Your motives are misconstrued, and then you take a long walk, and you say to yourself, "There is one thing anyhow—they cannot deprive your children and your descendants of having your picture on the walls of the White House, paid for by the Congress." And then you go home, and you look at the picture of Teddy and the picture of Grover Cleveland and of Abraham Lincoln and the others you have there, and you come to the conclusion that even that isn't a consolation.

For Taft every piece of legislation that he sponsored or signed was potentially a pit into which he might fall. As he prepared to sign the Panama Canal Bill in 1912, for example, his thoughts turned to his customary regret: "I shall create enemies in signing the bill, but that is what one usually does and makes no friends. That is what politics is." He tried to derive some satisfaction from Abraham Lincoln's words, which he had photographed and framed for his office desk:

> If I were to try to read, much less answer, all the attacks made on me this shop might as well be closed for any other business. I do the very best I know how— the very best I can; and I mean to keep on doing so until the end. If the end brings me out all right, what is said against me won't amount to anything. If the

end brings me out wrong, ten angels swearing I was right would make no difference.

But Lincoln's words helped little. Everyday Taft felt the hammering over his head and concluded that simply to survive would be quite enough.

During a speech in Georgia, Taft almost apologized to his audience for being their president. Georgia had, of course, voted Democratic, and Taft told his listeners that they were therefore "innocent of choosing him as a chief executive." From the audience a voice called out, "But we got you." Taft replied sympathetically in words that suggest at the same time, though obliquely, his uneasiness over his avoirdupois as well: "Yes, and you have to carry me for about three years more, and I want to make the load as light as I can." Once out of office, Taft remarked, in an address entitled "The President" (16 November 1913), "One of the results of my observation in the presidency is that the position is not a place to be enjoyed by a sensitive man." While in office his 'comfort' in the face of criticism was that at least he had never, so far as he knew, "yielded to improper motives in any direction." But he lamented the pain. "I have had a hard time. I do not know that I have had harder luck than other presidents but I do know that thus far I have succeeded far less than have others," he wrote to Roosevelt on 26 May 1910. Recalling that Roosevelt had, in 1908, almost chosen Charles Evans Hughes as his successor, Taft with regret and melancholy made a unique confession for an American president: "The truth is, he ought to be president and then I would not have to be."

His unhappiness was sufficiently manifest to those around him. The White House staff, accustomed to a cheerful Taft lunching each day comfortably with President Roosevelt, found him much altered. Some even came to refer to the president as a "sourpuss." Of his intimates, he delighted only in Archie Butt, who rarely gave him advice and never criticized him. Because of Taft's affection, Butt was in a position to observe the president closely, and he recorded in detailed letters the changes that occurred. Butt often saw in Taft's facial expressions his deep unhappiness and bitterness. He saw his geniality give way increasingly to fits of temper.

On occasion the public also caught glimpses of Taft's changed personality. Stories circulated of his bitter denunciations of men he had come to regard, for some fancied grievance, as his enemies. His temper, the *Washington Post* observed, now showed in explosive flashes.

The chief source of Taft's unhappiness was his painful self-awareness of his limitations in the office he had assumed. "The White House is a bigger proposition than one imagines," he remarked shortly after his election; he continually ate more, as if to balance the scale. As *The Nation* observed, his feelings of inadequacy were apparent in nearly all his speeches, each one taking on the air of an apology—a complaint echoed by the *New York Times:* "What Mr. Taft does, does awkwardly and with much show of embarrassment, is to excuse himself, to present an apology for his personal and party conduct since he became President." The *Times* could not recall a comparable exhibition of such "amazing self-stultification, such innocent confession of utter bewilderment" by any man in so high a post. In the past Taft had always been able through diligence and application to earn the approval he sought and needed; as president he could hardly succeed in pleasing everyone—yet displeasing anyone was something he could not tolerate. As Pringle astutely observes, Taft procrastinated and dissipated his energies only after he rose to a position beyond his capacity.

Throughout his four years in the White House, Taft often betrayed his desire to be a one-term president, fearing he might be forced into a second term. He kept up the litany to all his friends and acquaintances: "I am not very anxious for a second term as it is, and I certainly will not make any compromises to secure one"; "a number of our best presidents have had only one term, and there is nothing disgraceful in not having two. I am trying to act as if there were not another term"; "I can afford to get along on one term." Having realized what the presidency entailed, Taft hinted that, if renominated, he would make even less of an effort in the 1912 campaign than he had during the 1908 election, if indeed anything less were possible. To Nellie, he complained bitterly about having so little vacation time in the presidency, even though he vacationed more often than any president before him. As his term wore on, as if to prepare her, he continually indicated how much he looked forward to being "out for good" by the time the 1912 vacation came around.

In public Taft often referred to his leaving office after his term was up, perhaps as a gesture of conciliation to a nation which he felt had turned against him: "I am not thinking of 1912; in fact, I don't know that I care for a renomination," he announced to a reporter from the *Independent* in December 1911, promising to "go back to private life with no heart burnings." When Taft began his term, he frequently had slips of the tongue, referring to Roosevelt as the president, much to his wife's dismay. In the election of 1912, when an Ohio town clerk at a voting booth inquired about his occupation Taft replied with a smile, "Well, just put me down as a lawyer; I want that known because I may need the business soon."

From his adolescent years, Taft's weight had increased in proportion to his discontents. First he felt family pressure to excel at Yale; new burdens arrived with various appointive offices he filled in government service, first in the Philippines and then in Washington; finally, with the manifold problems of the presidency he reached his maximum weight. At twenty years of age he weighed about 220 pounds; when he was fifty-three and in the second year of his presidency he scaled over 355 pounds. William Allen White described him as "a big blond man who had been molded between two six-foot parentheses, bulging . . . in the middle, his trousers wrinkled . . . his coat bumpy, his collar flaring; a generous short neck supported a large florid face . . . with sloping jowls." Another contemporary portrait likened him to a kind, gentle American bison. Anecdotes, jokes, and cartoons inspired by Taft's weight were innumerable. All Washington talked about the bathtub—reputed to be the size of a small swimming pool—which had to be installed for him at the White House. Several times, it was said, he had gotten stuck in the regular one, and on each occasion two men had been called in to heave him out. Taft also had a specially built Ford sedan with an extra wide door. Dentist and barber chairs also presented a hazard for him. Horace Taft recalled entering a theater with his brother one night, who, after taking his seat, looked up smiling and said, "Horace, if this theater burns, it has got to burn around me."

As he became more politically prominent, the newspapers delighted in covering his various misadventures. As secretary of war, Taft once caused great merriment in Washington by getting stuck in fresh asphalt like a giant Stegosaurus in a tar pit, and the more he floundered the worse he bogged down in the thick morass. Nearly all of America learned the anecdote of how Taft, after a horseback trip to a mountain resort in the Philippines, wired Secretary of War Elihu Root, "Stood trip well. Rode horseback twenty-five miles to five thousand foot elevation," only to receive by return cable: "How is the horse?" Many of Taft's friends delighted in twitting him about his size. James Watson was present one day to observe an exchange between the president and Chauncey Depew, senator from New York from 1899 to 1911, in which Taft for once got the upper hand.

> Mr. Depew stepped up to Taft . . . and taking liberties that I never would have thought of taking with a president, said to him, putting his hand on Mr. Taft's big frontal development: "What are you going to name it when it comes Mr. President?" It was just about that time that Taft was beginning to have some difficulty with Roosevelt, and he quickly responded: "Well, if it is a boy, I'll call it William; if it's a girl, I'll call it Theodora; but if it turns out to be just wind, I'll call it Chauncey."

After becoming president, Taft ate as never before. Apparently he was reluctant to forego this one sure source of comfort while suffering in the White House. He sensed that the heavy responsibilities were one cause of his weight problem, for he said that he would probably eat less once he returned to private life. Mrs. Parks, the White House housekeeper, described one "little" meal that the president enjoyed which included lobster stew, salmon cutlets with peas, roast tenderloin with vegetable salad, roast turkey with potato salad, cold tongue and ham, frozen pudding, cake, fruit, and coffee. Another housekeeper wrote that the president really had few preferences, "but just naturally liked food—and lots of it." His one particular weakness, she added, was steak for breakfast. He ordered a twelve-ounce steak "nearly every morning, which he would accompany with two oranges, several pieces of toast and butter, and a good deal of coffee, cream, and sugar." When not at the dinner table, she noted that he was constantly nibbling on salted almonds. James Watson, Republican Congressman from Indiana, and one of Taft's more critical friends, regretted that the president always satisfied his voracious appetite to the limit: "He kept his system so filled with undigested food . . . that most of the time he simply did not and could not function in alert fashion. Often when I was talking to him after a meal his head would fall over on his breast and he would go sound asleep for ten or fifteen minutes." Falling asleep in the midst of one of their conversations, Taft took no umbrage but "laughed heartily" at Watson's jibe that he was the "largest audience" he ever put to sleep.

Taft reacted as he had since childhood. He ate compulsively, not only from inner frustration but in order better to "fill" the roles into which he was pushed. The causes of his problem lay too deep to be cured by diet or exercise, even though he and his wife always pretended they were real solutions. Taft, ever worried over what he referred to as his "increasing flesh," undertook in February 1910 an especially stringent regimen of exercises, which Butt thought ill-advised. His appearance grew unwholesome and his temper worsened; Butt felt it was because he was wearing himself out with all sorts of gymnastics before breakfast and long walks in the afternoon. In his early years Taft saw the hopelessness of his gluttony, warning his wife as early as 1895, "I shall worry you so much with my appetite that you must gain strength to meet the trial." He put the goad into her hand and wanted her to use it. "That is my fate," he wrote to her. "You must, therefore, make yourself a thorn in my side to that end." Neither Taft nor anyone close to him recognized the psychological forces contributing to his condition.

While in the White House, Nellie tried to manage his diet, but his failure to eat as she wished only raised further anxieties. He had, thus, another incentive for escape to the countryside on his private train, where he could flee Washington and his "persecutors," and, of course, eat as he pleased. Before departure, he had his train well-stocked with all his favorite delicacies. While at home, he used the excuse of exercise to get away from his duties. He golfed and rode horseback daily with Archie Butt, who was proud to have done "something in the way of keeping him from lapsing into a semi-comatose state." Occasionally, however, Taft could not go out. "The president didn't play golf this morning," Butt noted, "he is laid up with gout . . . looking the picture of woe." Butt had suspected for some time that the president had grown gouty, and Taft resented the suggestion. Dr. Jackson, his physician, when called in to examine Taft's feet, began to laugh. The president grew red, but finally forced a smile, saying, "It is, is it?" "It certainly is," answered Jackson, "and as good a case of it as I ever saw." The result of the visit was a bandaged foot and a somewhat ruffled temper, as well as a stricter diet.

Despite the frequent descriptions of Taft as happy, jovial, cheerful, and content, and irrespective of his own occasional jokes about what Edward Cotton called his "Brobdingnagian proportions," he was neither happy nor insensitive about his condition. As his weight increased, the president suddenly became embarrassed about being seen riding horseback on the White House grounds. "Did you notice people laughing?" Nellie quizzed Archie Butt, "for he seemed to think he caused amusement." Butt understood Taft's sensitivity and instructed her to assure him that he had mistaken the natural stares and beaming of the people for fun-making. When the president made a trip to the Grand Canyon in November 1909, he decided to join some people in a horseback ride down the steep Bright Angel trail to the bottom of the canyon, despite all that could be done to dissuade him. Trying to reason with him for the fifth time, Butt was surprised to hear the president, who believed that his weight would be no handicap, retort; "See here, you go to hell. I will do as I damn well please sometime."

Taft's excessive weight actually impaired his ability to carry on the routine functions of the presidency. Butt reported several occasions when, in the middle of affairs of state, he closed his eyes and took a catnap. Once he fell asleep as Joe Cannon, Speaker of the House, was leaning over his chair talking to him. When he fell asleep in the presidential automobile, his great bulk lunged from side to side as the car turned or jolted over streetcar tracks and crossings, yet he sometimes slept this way for hours. After one dinner for cabinet members at the White House in September 1910, Taft insisted on some music on the Victrola, but he went to sleep, sitting upright, before the first piece was over. He woke up once and requested a song but was asleep again before the first note sounded. His guests were left to enjoy the music and the president's snoring accompaniment. The attorney general boldly picked out a rousing tune, saying as he put it on the machine, "it will wake anyone but a dead man." At its conclusion he whispered to Butt, "He must be dead!"

Even though Taft was aware of the humiliating consequences of his drowsiness, he was happy to escape in slumber. Nellie dubbed him "Sleeping Beauty." He merely replied, "Now, Nellie, you know it is just my way. I knew you could handle it." And she usually could.

While president, Taft discovered a number of ways to divert himself from his duties. Although he tried to treat his tenure in office as if it were a long vacation, there was nothing very incongruous in this when he is compared with most of his predecessors and successors up to 1932. Many nineteenth-century presidents had done little and had seen the office as no very rigorous challenge. Taft does appear unpresidential in comparison with the frenetic Theodore Roosevelt, but not when compared with McKinley, Harding, and Coolidge. And if one looks backward from 1932, it is Theodore Roosevelt and Woodrow Wilson who seem untraditional. Taft was an old-fashioned president, in some ways reactionary, who took office when the times had passed him by. Taft was nonorganizational and anti-bureaucratic in outlook, possessing a small-town view, which may also explain why he was most active in antitrust legislation. He disliked bigness and complexity—not unlike his chief contemporary on the cultural front, Henry Adams.

Taft disliked talk of politics. Butt learned never to discuss it and instead diverted him with gossip or any amusing story concerning mutual friends or people of interest. Taft also loved shopping expeditions. While roving in department stores, he took a childlike delight in asking the astonished clerk, "Do you know who I am?" or "Is my credit good?" If the item purchased was to be sent to the White House, he would ask with a broad grin, "Do you know the address? Do you know where I live?" He would stroll around Washington as if he were an ordinary citizen, on one occasion walking seven blocks before anyone recognized him. This delighted him. He said he felt like a schoolboy playing hooky.

Taft also regularly fled the White House by vacationing at his summer home in Beverly, Massachusetts. In August 1909, after five months in office, he took his first vacation, and once there, he was a happy man. "Mr. Taft is out of school for five weeks," the *New York Herald Tribune* reported, "and . . . playing at play with all of his might." Once when he belatedly joined Nellie at Beverly, Massachusetts, he barely allowed the train to stop before he leapt off, brushing past the Cuban and Chilean envoys who had come to the station to meet him. Suddenly recollecting himself, Taft stopped short and returned to shake their hands. But no sooner was his hand again free than he waddled to the automobile and fairly jumped into it.

When Secretary of the Treasury Franklin MacVeagh arrived in Beverly to see the president, he was asked to leave his briefcase at the gate. And the White House was told to announce that no mail was to be sent to the president during his vacation. Every morning Taft played golf; every afternoon he dozed on the veranda; and every evening he went sailing on the *Sylph*. He wished to do the same thing over and over and day after day without interruption. Taft also had a tendency to prolong vacations, putting off a complete return to Washington by making quick two-day dashes back to the White House in late September. One reporter noted wryly that the steam heat would be turned on in the summer White House at Beverly before Taft departed finally for Washington.

Even when Taft was not officially on vacation, many thought he acted as though he were. Arthur Wallace Dunn criticized the inordinate amount of time Taft devoted each day to physical recreation and each night to social relaxation. He went by automobile on impromptu excursions and took his three children, who also liked riding. Archie Butt once overheard Taft exclaim, "Enjoy this all you can, for in four years more you may have to begin to learn to walk over again."

Such diversions only increased the volume of unfinished business and the severity of subsequent criticism. *Hampton's Magazine* condemned Taft for letting other men fight for Republican legislation in Congress while the president's "celebrated smile and a large bag of golf sticks were conveyed each afternoon to the Chevy Chase Golf Links." In 1910 the *Washington Post* predicted that Taft's new private secretary, Charles Norton, would be given wider latitude than any man who had held the office in recent years and might soon become "assistant president," which proved true. The *New York Times* sneered that even if Norton fulfilled everyone's highest expectations, the people ought to expect the president "himself, and in person, to exercise a kind of supervision over the affairs of the Government." Taft's friend John Hays Hammond had to admit that Norton was by necessity "assuming unusual authority" in the White House. A cartoon in the *New York Times* (20 June 1909) showed various reporters all gathered around a mountainous Taft, slumped inertly in a chair, exclaiming, "Please Mr. President. Do something!"

Taft was rarely deterred from his accustomed daily round of golf. Embarrassed by his behavior, the editor of the *Ohio State Journal*, a leading paper in Taft's home state, sarcastically noted that the president "hardly gets fairly settled down to golf" than duties of office begin to interfere. Taft grew impatient with congressional wrangling over the tariff, in part because it cut into his vacation and forced an early return from Beverly. He consoled himself, however, with the thought of all the golf he could play in Washington while the battle raged. Taft's golfing proved most annoying, since at this time the man in the street generally considered it an aristocratic and frivolous pastime. Taft had taken up the game while president-elect; before that he was accustomed to little else than hard work. After his inauguration, Taft convinced himself that exercise on the links was a requisite for his health and weight reduction. "My time," he once proudly announced to Nellie, "is being pretty well filled up now, especially as I insist on taking the whole afternoon for golf." Taft tried to deflect criticism by depreciating the quality of his golf game. It is merely of a "bumble-puppy order," he asserted, but golf experts told reporters that he played every stroke in good form. "The beauty of golf to me," Taft confessed to Butt, "is that you cannot play if you permit yourself to think of anything else." Anyone approaching him on the links with political or departmental matters soon learned not to repeat the performance. When Assistant Secretary of State Francis Huntington Wilson once requested that Taft meet the president of Chile, who had just arrived, Taft angrily replied, "I'll be damned if I will give up my game of golf to see this fellow." As the *Washington Post* observed, Roosevelt had also left the White House office early each afternoon for exercise, but unlike Taft, he came back, often laboring along with his aides and clerks until two in the morning.

Senator Nelson Aldrich, the proponent of the high protective tariff bearing his name, was portrayed in one cartoon stuffing the tariff down the mouth of the GOP elephant while Taft stood in the background, playing golf and looking idly on. Wounded by such jibes, but unwilling to forego the activities which provoked them, Taft began sneaking off to the course on the sly. More than once the White House staff became frantic because no one knew what had become of the president. Golf, while a necessary diversion for Taft, was not sufficient. Peter Finley Dunne's sage creation, Mr. Dooley, quoted Taft to the *New York Times*'s readers as saying, "Golf is th' thing I like best next t' leavin' Washington."

In order to escape from the anxieties of his office, Taft accepted unimportant invitations to travel away from Washington, the farther the better. In his biography of Taft, Edward Cotton noted that the president was happiest when traveling on his special train. Scarcely installed in office, he went "on the road for all the world like a traveling salesman," leaving the annoyances of Washington far behind. In one two-month period in 1909 he went to New Haven for a Yale Club dinner; to Philadelphia for a Union League dinner; to Petersburg, Virginia, for the unveiling of a Confederate general's statue; to New York City for the Cottonseed Crushers' Association banquet; to Norwich, Connecticut, to celebrate its 250th anniversary; and to Boston for the Boston Merchants' Association Dinner. He also attended numerous college commencements, class reunions, state fairs, and miscellaneous banquets. Once after traveling six hours to a Methodist Chatauqua meeting and six hours back, Taft was hard put to explain why he had accepted the invitation.

"I don't know why I went," he wrote to his wife, "unless it was that there was a Yale man at the head of it." Taft made so many excursions he humorously concluded that the major part of the work of a president was to increase the gate receipts at fairs.

But several short journeys were nothing compared to the long ones Taft took in order to seek sustained relief from his anxieties. Extended tours of the country became his specialty. "I want to get in as much traveling," Taft admitted privately, "as I can during these four years for after they are over I do not know when I will get another opportunity." By rationalizing that traveling was one of his official duties, he could put off work without feeling guilty. Within a few months of his inauguration he began to plan a trip across the country, ostensibly to learn what the people thought and to give them a chance to see their new president. No "seeing-all America" tour, the *New York Times* marveled, could have been so well designed to embrace all points of interest as Taft's itinerary. One critic jibed that Taft exploded the maxim that large bodies moved slowly, for he moved faster and farther than any statesman in American history. Any future president who wished to surpass his record, he added, would have to put wheels under the White House.

From September through November of 1909 Taft made a swing around the whole country and was feted at banquets everywhere the train stopped. He looked forward to Boston codfish and beans, Chicago steaks, Kansas short ribs, Colorado cantaloupes, Montana venison, Seattle salmon and oyster, New Mexico chile con carne, Texas wild duck, New Orleans red snapper, Mississippi corn pone, and Virginia wild turkey. In addition, his wealthy friend John Hammond had donated the services of his best cook. Taft "ate his way into the hearts of his country men," the *Times* mocked, looking on the president's trip as primarily a gustatory venture. Reporters traveling with Taft noticed that no matter how tired he seemed at the beginning of a banquet, the smile that had made him famous broadened perceptibly before the sherbet. One cartoonist depicted a corpulent Taft sitting at a gigantic table shaped like the United States, entirely covered with dishes of food.

Having enjoyed his first tour so greatly, Taft planned another two years later. It was to be, according to the *Independent*, the longest trip ever undertaken by an American president. He traveled 13,436 miles, surpassing by five hundred miles his previous record. Reporters commented on the appearance of Archie Butt and Taft's personal secretary, Charles Hilles, both of whom looked bedraggled and spent at the end of the presidential journey. In contrast, Taft swung down from the train fresh and smiling, saying jauntily, "I travel so much that I feel like a railroadman." His brother Horace was only one among many who were astonished at the way traveling restored him. Horace questioned the president about his motives, but the answer he got did not satisfy him, despite its simple truth. "He just grins," Horace wrote, "and says he'd rather do that than stay at home."

What detracted from Taft's enjoyment during these journeys were the speeches he was compelled to make along the way. (He informed fellow alumni in New Haven that, if he did not have to make a speech every time he came to a Yale meeting, he would come to a great many more.) To render speechmaking less troublesome, Taft decided to prepare several standard addresses and alternate them as he went along. Staff ghost writing was a practice initiated by Franklin Roosevelt. At Tacoma, Washington, he explained to a crowd that he had written six or eight set speeches, but was very glad to find that none was required of him there. In Richmond, Virginia, at the conclusion of his first nationwide tour, he admitted that after being gone so long "your conscience begins to prick you and then your duties grow mountain high so that you cannot look over them at all. That is my feeling now. It is a somewhat strenuous life to eat and talk and talk and eat, but there are other things . . . even more burdensome."

Taft's biographers have been troubled by his wanderlust. Paola Coletta feels that Taft hoped to gain the people's support for his programs if he presented them in person. But this conclusion is unsupported by Taft's own travel accounts. He confessed to the Massachusetts Press Club that leaving Washington had one great advantage: when everyone was criticizing him and he was feeling blue, it was pleasant to go to another city where he would be cordially welcomed. "I am mighty glad to see you," he told a crowd in Montana, "and the reason why I am glad to see you is . . . that you are glad to see me." He told an assemblage in Ohio, "It is a pleasure to come to one's home, especially when you have been in Washington and have been chided . . . for your shortcomings, and to snuggle up close to those who are fond of you, who have respect for you whatever happens." Moreover, the president stated, "When you are being hammered . . . not only by the press, but by members of your own party in Washington, and one feels that there isn't anything quite right that he can do, the pleasure of going out into the country, of going into a city that hasn't seen a president for twenty years and then makes a big fuss over him, in order to prove to him that there is somebody that does not know of his defects, is a pleasure that I don't like to forego."

Angered by the absentee president, the Eastern press attacked. Many Congressmen also were irritated by his journeys. After his first long trip had exhausted the president's $25,000 traveling allowance for 1910, Congress hotly debated whether or not to increase it. Representative John Fitzgerald of New York warned sternly that "the country does not approve of this wanderlust which has filled its chief executive." Political cartoonists exploited their opportunity: a cartoon picturing a Christmas tree covered with mechanical toys, one of which resembled Taft, read, "Travels on the slightest provocation"; another portrayed Taft looking at a picture of the White House inquiring, "Where have I seen that place before"; still another, drawn on the occasion of Taft's second long tour in 1911, depicted the president at a White House which had been refashioned into a locomotive engine with a bell and a smoke stack. The caption read; "The President Comes Home: One Way to Keep Him There."

II

THE EARLY YEARS
1857–1884

Taft's grandmother Susan Dutton Torrey was known in Millbury, Massachusetts, as an "eccentric" individual but "splendidly so." Many neighbors long remembered Susan Torrey as the woman who decided to remodel her Grecian-pillared home and took an ax to smash down the walls herself. Susan enthusiastically studied astronomy, logic, and philosophy at Amherst Academy and upon graduating in 1823, became a public school teacher. She warned Samuel Torrey, her prospective husband, that she doubted whether she was suited to marriage. As the new Mrs. Torrey, and eventually the mother of four daughters, Susan became a superior homemaker but remained a dissatisfied woman. On many occasions she expressed discontent over the restricted role women were expected to assume. She revolted, at least in spirit, by engaging in a series of "furious" activities which included studious reading, landscape painting, and suffragette politics. She was determined to bring up her own daughters with an uncommon degree of education and freedom.

Delia, older sister of Taft's mother, Louisa, recognized their mother's domestic frustration. "Mother," she wrote her sister, "is very ambitious and ambition in a woman is synonymous with unhappiness. She has great mental and physical activity, and there is not a man or woman in town with whom she can have any satisfactory intellectual conversation." Susan Torrey did her best to see that her daughters' education provided them with more alternatives than she had known. Fortunately Samuel Torrey indulged his wife and daughters and gave them the freedom to pursue a liberal education, even though the avenues available to women seeking independent careers in the mid-nineteenth century were severely limited. Samuel Torrey's easygoing attitude toward his wife and daughters was perhaps the result of his neurotic expectation, at age forty, of imminent death. His doctor in Boston had urged him to move immediately to Millbury in the hope of prolonging his life. There he met Susan and later died—at the age of eighty-eight.

Delia and Louisa attended Miss Mary Lyon's Female Seminary at Holyoke, founded in 1837, the first permanent American institution for the higher education of women. When they were not in school, the girls traveled freely between Millbury, Worcester, and Boston, visiting friends and attending cultural events. They also received instruction from lyceum celebrities. Horace Greeley, Oliver Wendell Holmes, and Lucy Stone were among the lecturers Susan Torrey invited to her home whenever they visited Millbury. The sisters even made several unchaperoned trips to New York and Washington.

Louisa and Delia soon found the girls-school atmosphere too constraining and decided to spend two years with their aunt Harriet Dutton in New Haven. There they studied philosophy and natural science by attending lectures at Yale. Delia was rather scornful of the men she met and seemed to prefer a single, and thus independent, life that might better satisfy her ambitions and serve her dignity. "Ladies of strong minds seldom marry," Delia declared. Meanwhile Louisa, not so confirmed a marriage-hater, was captivating many of the Yale students. "This is owing," her Aunt Harriet supposed, "partly to her musical gifts and also to her fine figure and manners."

Both girls, however, soon agreed to relinquish the close company of college men in order to teach and travel together. "Tell everybody," Louisa wrote Delia in January 1853 "that I have come to the same conclusion as yourself—viz.—not to marry." For several years the girls did precisely as planned, with full approbation of mother and aunt. By teaching they earned money for traveling, to such places as Niagara Falls, Quebec, and New York. But they were never financially independent, since they relied on money from home to supplement their incomes.

The girls' traveling and life style finally proved to be too great an expense for the family. "I think," Louisa wrote confidently to her mother, that "if I am thrown upon my own resources I shall not be obliged to teach as I can support myself very comfortably with my pen." Although she did publish some articles in magazines, an independent living did not materialize. "If Father finds us too expensive," Louisa wrote Delia, "I'm afraid we shall have to get married. That would be a disagreeable expedient." Louisa, who had been less influenced by her mother's attitudes than Delia, soon faced that "expedient," and she discovered it to be not so very disagreeable after all.

In 1853, Louisa, then twenty-six years old, met Alphonso Taft, forty-three, while he was visiting friends in Millbury—in search of a wife. A New Englander by birth, he had emigrated to Ohio with his parents in 1838. For his education he went east to Yale and ranked third in the class of 1833. He tried teaching for a short time in Connecticut but returned to Yale to study law. Taft settled in Cincinnati, and by 1841 his law practice was well established; whereupon he married the pretty, but frail, Fanny Phelps. The marriage proved a good one—an "unbroken sea of happiness" is how Fanny described it. Alphonso's law business flourished while Fanny engaged in church and charitable work. In 1843 and 1845 two sons, Charles Phelps and Peter Rawson, were born. In 1851 Alphonso bought the substantial Mount Auburn home (where William Howard Taft was later born), but Fanny did not live to enjoy her new home. Ailing with "congestion of the lungs and of the brain," she died quietly, after kissing each member of her family good-bye, in June 1852, at the age of twenty-nine.

When Louisa met Alphonso Taft a year later, he had both a promising judicial and a potential political career in Ohio. He had liberal-minded views about women and even called for political and legal equality. Louisa's mother had always counseled her to take every advantage of opportunities, and she thought Alphonso Taft, though seventeen years her senior, presented not only an opportunity for achieving status and security but also for pursuing her own intellectual interests. Delia, bereft of her traveling companion and confidant, wrote despairingly, "Oh Louise, Louise, how can I live the rest of my life without you? I am but half a pair of scissors. She never married. And many years later, after Alphonso's death, she and Louisa took up where they had left off in 1853, traveling together from Boston and New York to Ohio and California in a happy round of sight-seeing, theater, lectures, and concerts.

Alphonso's marriage to Louisa, eighteen months after Fanny's death, was for both parties a matter of convenience. Yet their marriage was nevertheless considered very successful in "the Victorian manner." Mr. Taft, as Louisa always referred to him, was a man who kept his emotions under rigid control. In time she bore him three sons and a daughter. He did not interfere with his wife's numerous outside activities so long as she did not neglect her family. Enormously energetic, aggressively intellectual, and decidedly ambitious, Louisa helped organize a kindergarten movement and an art association and contributed time to charities. She also founded a local book club, studied German, and participated in a French club. At the same time she contributed to her husband's success in his legal practice and in local politics. When

President Grant in 1875 appointed Alphonso Taft, at sixty-five, to be secretary of war and then, in 1876, attorney general, Louisa was gratified to find herself in the midst of Washington political circles, where she was described as a lady of rare perception and of still rarer common sense. Louisa was happy to leave Ohio, for she thought none of her acquaintances there was sufficiently intellectual or cultivated. Soon she discovered to her chagrin that the ladies in Washington circles could be just as "platitudinous." In writing to her sister, Delia, she made an exception for Mrs. James G. Blaine, whom she described as "bright and smart—one of our sort of women." But she enjoyed most the company of intelligent and successful men.

Louisa's hunger for travel led her to intercede boldly with President Chester Arthur on her husband's behalf in seeking an appointment as ambassador to Austria-Hungary. President Arthur granted her request, and in 1881 they left for Vienna where, Louisa wrote Delia, "it was pleasant to find ourselves very near the throne." Because Alphonso had few official duties, the Tafts devoted most of their time to social affairs. An able student of German, Louisa easily adapted to the court. She was poised and self-assured, but Alphonso was not comfortable. Observing his dilemma, Louisa fretted, "he does not realize the embarrassment of not understanding the language." Despite Alphonso's detachment from court life—which Louisa charitably referred to as his "American self-possession"—she managed the embassy routine energetically. She refurbished their quarters, gave numerous teas, and presided over Bible readings and hymn singing on Sundays for the staff. As they traveled about Europe, Louisa reported complacently that their official rank was recognized in most regions and they were sufficiently feted.

While maintaining an active social pace in Europe, Louisa developed a surprising interest in a number of subjects normally considered the preserve of men—for example, the American stock market. Impressed by her business acumen, her son William, who by then was an undergraduate at Yale, wrote to her, "When woman's field widens, Mother, you must become President of a Railroad Co., I am sure you would be a success." It was obvious to family and friends alike that she was the most ambitious member of the family, and she pushed her children as well. She reserved praise for women who were similarly ambitious and active. Later, after President McKinley had named her son to head the civil commission in the Philippines, she took the occasion to regret not accomplishing more herself. "I find that I shine by a reflected light being a person of distinction as the mother of Judge Taft," she wrote. "I feel like asserting myself as having been *somebody* on my own account."

Louisa brought the same energy and resolution to her role as a mother. In recalling his childhood, William's younger brother Horace emphasized his mother's ambition, which she had transferred to "my father and the children." The "details of discipline in daily life were her responsibility," and she, not her husband, insisted upon a strict family regimen. She also coached the children in their studies.

Louisa's relationship with William was always special and intense. Her first baby, Sammie, died of whooping cough shortly after his first birthday. Her second, she was determined, would survive; fortunately William was a stout baby, whose good health was perhaps aided by her nourishing solicitude, though she must have been in terror when he came down with a dangerous case of dysentery. Unlike Sammie, who had been quiet and passive, William was a charming baby who laughed and played constantly. She showered more love and attention on him than her other children, and as he grew older she pressured him more to succeed. Political scientist James Barber, in a 1969 article, guessed correctly that Taft probably was spoiled as a child. In a revealing letter to Delia, Louisa wrote, "I feel as if my hands and feet were tied to this baby." The Taft family was very close, but the relationship between William and his mother was special. Once William entered school she became even more attentive, surveying every detail of his studies. Until her death, on the eve of his nomination as a candidate for president, she devotedly followed every step of his career, and though warmly affectionate, often gave him advice that was highly critical.

Alphonso Taft, in contrast, had no driving ambition to rise in the political sphere. He was contented to enjoy a successful judicial career, and even though he spent a few years in the political limelight, his goals did not extend beyond the law. Perhaps Alphonso's most notable characteristic was his self-effacing and benign personality. One historian described him as "unostentatious, kindly and gentle"; another as "learned, absent-minded, and kindly." Taft's wife, Nellie, described him as "gentle beyond anything I ever knew." The president often said that "a man never had . . . a dearer, kinder, more considerate" father, an opinion corroborated by Horace in his memoirs.

William Howard Taft, it is obvious, was very much like his father. He shared his father's lovable traits, and identified with his father's aspirations to be a lawyer and a judge, rather than a politician.

Alphonso Taft took a keen interest in the success of his children, but it was the development of their moral character that concerned him most. "He could be stern enough," Horace wrote, when the children "failed to live up to his standard of right." He inculcated in his sons the belief that the parents' accomplishments were measured largely by the honor and prosperity of their children. When he died in 1891, his estate amounted to the house and $482 in cash. Yet Alphonso believed intensely in the value of hard work, and he set a good example by devoting himself to his books and papers at home as at the office. William recalled that his father repeatedly stressed that no minor accomplishment would be satisfactory—his sons must strive only for the best that was in them. When Horace followed William to Yale, his father gave him this advice: "If you work hard for an examination and do your best in it and get fifty, you will have my sympathy, but if you get ninety-five, when you *can* get one hundred, I tell you, I am thoroughly ashamed of you." Like Louisa, Alphonso felt that William had the greater intellect. "Willie is foremost, and I am inclined to think he will always be so." Yet both boys were conscientious and excelled at their studies; each attended their father's alma mater and, like him, wanted to enter law.

William, striving to fulfill his parents' desires and, like his brothers, worrying about his ability to live up to parental expectations, manifested his anxiety by overeating. Chubby in grammar school, he had to endure the taunts of peers who called him "Lub" or "Lubber." They enjoyed describing him as a "roundish, roly-poly" boy. Yet he was not sedentary or incapable of vigorous activity; and though his friends kidded him for being fat, they did not reject him. Taft studied more than the others in order to excel; for this he was also teased.

The causes of Taft's extreme obesity may never be fully known. It might have arisen from a glandular condition, yet it was clearly aggravated by feelings of inadequacy in the face of the pressures and influences of his ambitious and demanding parents. An overweight child, medical experts generally agree, is very often the object of strong domination, particularly by a mother who holds her child in close emotional bondage. Usually the mother of an obese child is domineering, strict, and ambitious; the father, submissive. The overweight child, furthermore, often feels he is merely a possession of his parents, whose primary interest in him relates to his success. In such a home the child comes to feel that he is valued not for his intrinsic worth but mainly for what he can do for the sake of his parents, how well he fulfills the goals they conceive for him.

However well William performed, it never seemed to be enough for his parents, and he readily adopted their image of him as procrastinator. To his brother Horace he confessed years later, "one of the great and many defects of my character is my inability to do anything far in advance. I must do it under pressure." Perhaps Taft found the law so congenial because, as his son Robert suggested in 1913, "the law seems really to be the most dilatory proceeding. . . . No one is ever in a hurry and everything can be and is postponed. If you have a tendency to procrastinate, this is the place to do it." His parents openly debated the question of William's alleged laziness, since they felt the high grades he earned were primarily the result of their prodding. Characteristically, William wondered if he had a strong enough will to keep at the grindstone on his own. Under his mother's supervision he suppressed the desire to play and became a model schoolboy. One of his primary-school classmates later remembered him as a "heavyweight . . . , who buckled to it for the best there was in him." He became known for his solemn earnestness. William struggled to be, as biographer Henry Pringle observes, almost too perfect. He came to believe early that hard work and exemplary behavior were duties, but more important, he learned that the performance of those duties was the surest means of securing affection and approval. Doing his duty became a special obligation, yet he often delayed. The delays produced guilt and, in turn, anxiety. He therefore often felt that he had to work doubly hard just to catch up for his prior neglect.

Schoolwork was not easy for him despite his generally good intelligence. According to Eugene Lyle, who interviewed several people close to Taft when preparing a series of articles on his early years, Taft lacked "the competence that tempts to lazy ease." If he hoped to excel, he had to avoid idleness. Taft's high-school performance was solid, and through extra effort he achieved second place in his senior class. Upon graduation from Woodward High School in 1874, at sixteen, Taft chose for his salutatorian address the subject of woman suffrage. He had read much on the issue, he told his class, adding, moreover, that his parents were suffragists, too. While at Yale, Taft rarely tired even at the most laborious chore, and by "steady, ponderous work," he earned good grades "because he was a plodder." The impression he gave of plodding arose from his putting "the thing off until he had only two or three hours to prepare in and then he had to work like a slave." Eugene Lyle recalled that Taft did not "scatter enough 'wild oats' to feed a mustang colt." At graduation he again stood second in his class. Though excellent, Taft's record at Yale was not brilliant enough to win the coveted Woolsey Prize, which his half-brother Peter, who preceded William and Horace at Yale, had taken home.

Despite his even temperament and apparent placidity, he felt the effects of strain. Doing his duty had taken its toll, for he had repressed much. Like most obese people he had difficulty handling anger, he felt he would not be popular unless he was affable. On one occasion two fellow students came to Taft's room, hoping to tempt him away from his studies. They smoked and chatted, until Taft grew angry over their extended visit. He asked them to leave, but they continued to malinger, despite his entreaties. Suddenly he exploded and began to hurl books and anything else within reach at them until they retreated.

It was at Yale that Taft began to show the complex and ambivalent reactions of the typical obese man toward his own weight. His size made him feel stronger and more masculine; it was a means of self-assertion. One evening his brother Harry, a freshman at Yale, yelled up to his window in Farnham Hall, "Oh, Willie!" At that a dozen windows opened and a chorus of "Oh Willie's" followed. Taft later denied that his friends had had the temerity to call him Willie. They called me 'Bill'," he said, "You see, I weighed over two hundred pounds then."

Taft's brothers underwent the same parental pressures to succeed and suffered different, but no less serious, effects. His half-brother Peter had "perfect lessons" as a schoolboy and delivered the valedictory address to his graduating class. At Yale he continued his outstanding record, earning the highest marks scored there up to that time. In 1878, after graduation and marriage, he suffered a severe nervous breakdown. Obsessed with guilt, Peter felt he was not living up to his parents' expectations. His work became aimless and desultory, and his law practice declined. He suffered from headaches, eye trouble, chronic colds, and the inability to concentrate. Peter never recovered from the nervous collapse and died in 1889 in a sanatorium at the age of forty-three. Louisa consoled herself with the thought that Peter had "made his mark, and accomplished more in a few years than many others in a long lifetime."

Horace, who in contrast to William was six feet four inches tall and very thin, also exhausted himself through academic effort. Acute dyspepsia afflicted him in early manhood; he slept poorly and continually suffered severe headaches. Taft often mentioned his brother's "nervous temperament." Like his brother William, his brother Harry, and his half-brothers, Horace made every effort to succeed in a legal career in Cincinnati but gradually became more unhappy. His practice, he soon conceded, was "flat on its back." After several years of frustration, he suddenly abandoned his law office in 1886 and resettled in Kansas City. There he fulfilled his real ambition by founding a school for boys. This independent action greatly upset his father, who lamented the hardship of losing a son: "I cannot comprehend Horace's idea of founding a private school or what in the world he can hope from it," he fumed. "The law is his proper field. His plans are fanciful. . . . It seems to us a singular perversion of mind and opportunities."

Four years later Horace returned and, after an interim of tutoring in Latin at Yale, opened in 1890 the Taft School in Watertown, Connecticut. The school quickly gained a reputation for its emphasis on scholarship and character building. A sprawling white frame house with spacious tree-studded lawns, formerly an inn, became the main building of the school. By 1903 it had nine schoolmasters and eighty-six boys. Williams College named Horace the "headmaster of headmasters" when they bestowed an honorary degree on him, and in 1936, upon his retirement, Yale University called the Taft School one of the "great schools of the country."

Horace also deviated from his parents in his political views. He became interested in reform, supporting free trade and Democratic Grover Cleveland for president. He was the only Taft son to depart not only from the family's long-standing attachment to the legal profession but also from its conservative politics.

Another brother, Henry Waters, also became a lawyer after graduation from Columbia Law School. He was described as a "quiet, moody, and morbid" man, and the family often referred to his frequent "bad bilious attacks." About his wife, Julia, who cheered him out of his depressions, Henry once wrote, "I don't believe there is another girl on earth who could manage my restless worrying disposition." He eventually became a prominent attorney in New York and the author of a dozen books on various subjects, from the history of Japan to the art of conversation. In 1904 he was offered the Republican nomination for governor of New York but declined largely for financial reasons: his wife would not accept the reduction of income. At the time he was earning $55,000 per year.

William Taft was normally modest and usually the last one to be convinced that he would accomplish anything distinguished in professional life. Despite his successes on the Federal Circuit bench, Taft was incredulous when friends first talked of his elevation to the Supreme Court. "My chances of going to the moon and of donning a silk gown at the hands of President Harrison are about equal," he wrote to his father in August 1889. And a short time later, when he was named by President McKinley to head the commission to the Philippines, Taft felt sure he did not possess the proper qualifications for the job. The president "might as well have told me that he wanted me to make a flying machine," Taft exclaimed.

To the person who feels insecure, inadequate, and exceedingly vulnerable in a potentially hostile and threatening world, love and admiration appear to be the only means of securing safety. They are the emotional food that compensate for the lack of self-esteem. As a youth, William Howard Taft had repeatedly sought reassurance from his mother, who often said that love of approval was her son's besetting fault. Anxious for his parents' approbation, William wrote home from Yale, "You expect great things of me but you mustn't be disappointed if I don't come up to your expectations." Two decades later, on his forty-second birthday, his mother wrote to congratulate him on his excellent record in government service, adding that she hoped it would not be "less creditable in the future." She also took the opportunity to remind him that much happiness derived from hard work. Taft trusted that by trying to do his best he would maintain the love and approval of his parents even if he failed.

Later the same trust was evident in his feelings toward his wife, and later toward Theodore Roosevelt—even toward the American public. Yet he always feared disappointing those who expected something of him. Biographer Henry Pringle notes more than once Taft's apparent feelings of insecurity and apprehensiveness about his ability to please those who counted on his success. When, despite his best efforts, Taft ran into problems in the performance of a duty, he became bewildered and unnerved; he would, as Amos Pinchot said after Taft became president, "lose his head and thrash around with the impotent violence of a wounded whale."

As long as his parents lived, Taft continued to seek their advice in nearly every matter. Unable to sever the umbilical cord, he and they maintained the connection through constant correspondence. Even after he had moved to Washington, his mother instructed him in the pitfalls of social life as if he were still an adolescent. At Yale, friends had urged him to go out for the rowing crew, but his father forbade it, and football as well. Upon receiving a coveted invitation to join Skull and Bones, the secret society at Yale, his father expressed doubt that "such popularity is consistent with high scholarship." Alphonso, of course, had long planned that William would attend law school, for, as he proclaimed, "That is his destiny and he should be in it." The enigma of Taft's career may be traced back quite naturally to parental will and a boy's docility.

Although Taft could have attended a prestigious school he chose the Cincinnati Law School. Biographer Henry Pringle believes he was drawn by his boyhood friends and his love for Cincinnati and its social life. In the 1870's one's choice of a school did not have the importance it does today.

After he graduated from Yale and the Cincinnati Law School, Alphonso kept both eyes on all of William's affairs. "You will get a scolding when you reach home . . . for going off after pleasure instead of attending to business," Alphonso chided during his first year of legal practice. On another occasion he admonished; "I do not think that you have accomplished this past year as much as you ought. Our anxiety for your success is very great and I know that there is but one way to attain it, and that is by self-denial and enthusiastic hard work in the profession. . . . This gratifying your fondness for society is fruitless." In recognition of his dependence on his father and of his own shortage of energy and ambition, Taft wrote some years later, "I have a kind of presentiment that father has been a kind of guardian angel to me in that his wishes for my success have been so strong and intense as to bring it, and that as his life ebbs away and ends I shall cease to have the luck which has followed me thus far."

The parent who constantly directs and supervises his child with endless reminders and demands often ends with a child who has learned to rely excessively on just this sort of external direction. Children require a certain freedom to pursue their own interests and develop a personal motivating force, and that part of their development is retarded by too much parental coerciveness. Demanding perfection from the child, such parents usually withhold approval or full acceptance until superior achievement is forthcoming. Children usually respond to demanding parents by striving to meet their standards and consequently develop an overconcern for accomplishment. In addition, they learn always to demand more of themselves than most people and, also, to become dissatisfied with their achievements. William Howard Taft strove to be the "model schoolboy" that his parents desired, but at the same time he developed the life-long habit of dissatisfaction with himself and his accomplishments, hence the tendency to belittle his own abilities. Since he felt he could not drive himself enough, he sought someone to require him to "do better and be better," as he himself once put it.

A second common reaction to demanding parents is in opposition to the first, that is, the child sporadically tries to assert his independence as an individual in whatever ways he can, often by stubbornly resisting being pushed. These ways usually involve a kind of passive resistance to constant parental coercion—such as dawdling, daydreaming, and procrastinating. These tactics were, of course, precisely what young Taft adopted, causing his parents to wonder anxiously if he was a lazy boy. Because procrastination is not active resistance to parental demands, the risk of the child's losing his parents' love and approval is minimal, since he feels he can, and usually does, make up his losses before they become irretrievable.

The pattern which develops from this kind of parent-child relationship—labeled the "command-resistance" cycle by Dr. Hugh Missildine—is continued into adult life. People tend to recreate within themselves the same sort of emotional and psychological atmosphere in which they were raised. They simply feel at home in it. Adults are, in a way, "parents to themselves"; once they leave home, they internalize the parental attitudes they learned as children. Recreation of this "emotional atmosphere" includes both the pleasant and the painful attitudes that characterized their childhood relationships at home. In addition, adults often invite their spouses to treat them much as their parents had, continuing to seek their approval in the same way they once sought it from their parents. This is precisely what William Howard Taft did upon marrying Nellie Herron.

III

THE MARRIAGE GAME
1884–1886

The emotional patterns Taft had developed as a child made him an ideal mate through whom Helen Herron could pursue and realize her personal ambitions. Her personality was very much like his mother's, and William was attracted to her. Yet the period of courtship was an unhappy time for Taft. He assiduously pursued her as soon as he came of age to leave the family. But Nellie did not return his ardor, for she did not need him as much. After two years Nellie began to give him hope when she finally realized that he was an instrument through which she could fulfill her own aspirations.

After his marriage in 1886, Taft's relationship with Nellie Herron was much like that with his parents. She constantly advised him and criticized him. Her letters were written in language suggesting parental supervision. When pleased, she praised him as "the dearest sweetest boy that ever lived," or "my dear darling, lovely, beautiful, sweet precious boy." To Taft, she too was a "guardian angel." Nellie took over where his parents left off, and with an even more focused purpose.

Nellie was the daughter of John Williamson Herron, a prominent Cincinnati lawyer, influential Republican, former state senator, and personal friend of President Rutherford B. Hayes. His wife, Harriet, was the daughter of New York Congressman Eli Collins; Nellie was the fourth of their eleven children. In 1877, at the age of seventeen, she spent several weeks in the

White House with her parents as the guest of President Hayes. She was not yet "out" as a debutante, she lamented later, "so I couldn't spend my time in the White House as I would have liked, in going to brilliant parties and meeting all manner of charming people." Nonetheless, that visit was a momentous experience, for it was then, she told a *New York Times* reporter in 1912, that she fantasied becoming First Lady herself. She vowed to marry only a man "destined to be president of the United States."

Nellie Herron Taft was a fiercely independent girl and an exceptional student, who read, between household chores, such books as Carlyle's life of Schiller and his history of the French Revolution. She persuaded her parents to allow her to attend Miami University in Oxford, Ohio, where she concentrated on chemistry and German. Meanwhile she was very much attracted by the atmosphere of her father's law office and after graduation spent much of her time there reading, studying, and assisting him with his work. Throughout her life, Nellie furthered her studies in history, languages, art, and music.

She was a small, slim, but physically strong and energetic woman, who hoped to prove herself one day by entering some profession or by writing a critical book on art or music. Many people found her cold; indeed, her eyes and mouth were singularly serious and unsmiling—some said "stubborn." Strangers were often unnerved by the deliberate way she surveyed them, but her dignity and capabilities impressed her friends. An intimate girlhood friend of Nellie's recalled that she never drifted; she was always determined. According to the historian Ray Stannard Baker, Nellie Herron was "as keen as chilled steel, with that inherited instinct for self-making." Nellie defended her opinions with aggressiveness and vigor, in a manner many considered unfeminine. Taft's Aunt Delia described Nellie as self-contained and independent: "She is not a girl of many friends nor one who makes them easily." Her family referred to her "matter-of-factness" and her inclination to bossiness; but underneath her rather austere exterior, she was a high-strung, nervous, and emotional young woman.

Taft told his parents that Nellie took up teaching in a private school "without encouragement by her family . . . because she chafed under the conventionalities of society which would keep a young lady for evening entertainments. She wanted to do something in life. . . . Her eagerness for knowledge of all kinds puts me to shame. Her capacity for work is just wonderful." He readily accepted Nellie's point of view about woman's role in society, for his mother held almost identical views and expressed them in both her character and her life. Later as president, Taft told a crowd in Alabama, "I wish that every woman in the world was situated [so] that she need not think it necessary for her to marry if she did not want to." Young women, he said, haven't had "a fair chance in life to earn and carve out their own future. We have not opened all the avenues of livelihood that they are quite as well able to fill as we, and in certain respects better able than we."

In the diary Nellie began at nineteen, she revealed discontent over the constrained life of a woman. The entries began in 1879, just prior to what she called her "coming out" or "that state of young ladyhood which I have always dreaded." Her debut, she feared, would end all her plans for seriously pursuing a career. The diary also revealed her shyness and her apprehensions over the possibility of failing socially once she did enter the marriage market. Soon she could write with relief: "The season—my first season—is over and on the whole, I have enjoyed myself . . . much more than I imagined possible, for coming out has been my great bugbear ever since I have been old enough to think of it." She now could look forward to better things: "I am going to devote myself to music and next winter if possible teach." She felt that if she practiced the piano five or six hours a day "it will not leave time for much else, but it will make me happier."

Nellie loved music, but her family did not encourage this interest. "My greatest desire," she had written early in her diary, "is to take music lessons. If I only could I would be so happy." But lessons were, her parents thought, an expensive frill, though attractive dresses were not. "I would much rather give up some of the dresses I am getting," Nellie wrote, "but Mama thinks I must have them. . . . I suppose I must if I am going to brace up and try to have a good time." But the life of a debutante bored her: "I am beginning to want some steady occupation. I hate being such a good for nothing." Reading and piano playing were not sufficiently purposeful: "I should have some occupation that would require active work"; "I am anxious to be busy and accomplish something." She described one day as "useless." "Most of my life is. I am so tired of it all."

In 1880, chafing under the restrictions of living at home, Nellie wrote, "My greatest desire now is to write a book, write it, I must confess, for money . . . because I do so want to be independent." She did not begin a book, and nothing else offered her the opportunity she sought. More downcast than ever, she was sick and tired of herself: "I would rather be anyone else . . . and I am only nineteen. I feel often as if I were fifty."

Nellie shied away from the social whirl not only because she hoped for a career, but because she feared sexual relationships. When she had to confront a possible suitor directly, Nellie, ordinarily so cool and self-possessed, was completely discomfited. Three young men came to call at her house one October day in 1879, and, she recorded in her diary, "My state of nervousness was truly ridiculous even thinking of it now. Imagine sitting up trembling so that I could hardly speak, as stupid as a hitching post." She shifted the blame to the young men by dwelling upon their limitations: "I hate boys and college youths and society young men. A man is not endurable until he is twenty-eight or thirty and not always then." She got along more easily with married men ten years her senior, who were more at ease and doubtless better company.

Despite her efforts to conquer her timidity, Nellie could not learn to relax in the company of suitors. She ruminated on why her acquaintanceships did not lead to romances like other girls' and wondered about her own lack of sexual interest in men. That her feelings were deeply repressed is suggested by one of her diary entries: "This matter of fancying people is inexplicable to me." At twenty-two she wrote of the men who came into her life, "It is fortunate that I have been so utterly indifferent." She felt "blue and miserable," confessing to her diary, "I have cried myself to sleep more often than I should like to say."

One day in 1881 a quite different note appears. An offer to teach at White and Sykes, a private school in Walnut Hills, Ohio, arrived, and Nellie was elated. Over her family's protests, she took the job. She expressed in her diary her "desire for an independence . . . and a horror of the thought of waiting around, for it certainly does resemble that, to be married."

"I have been on the whole happier since I have been teaching," she exclaimed after two months, yet she was annoyed that no one seemed to understand her reasons for wanting to pursue a profession. Some friends felt she had turned to teaching because she had failed to find a beau. Although she realized that some friends admired her action because "it has spirit," most people, she observed, watch "indifferently" and merely "wonder at my queer task." She herself showed some ambivalence: "It takes a little gulp to swallow the idea of always teaching." "Of course a woman is happier who marries exactly right—but how many do? Otherwise I do think that she is much happier single and doing some congenial work." She concluded, therefore, that she was settled as a teacher for life. "I have begun now to look forward to having a school of my own as the great ambition of my life."

Nellie not only sought independence but also enjoyed defying in other ways what she considered to be outworn conventions. She and her girlfriend Sallie visited a "Bohemian" saloon opposite the Music Hall in Cincinnati, where they smoked cigarettes and drank beer. This, she gloated, seemed "rather fast."

Although she gradually began to enjoy the conversation and company of men, she continued to regret their tendency to grow sentimental and talk of love after a brief introduction. "Why is it so very rare in a man and woman to be simply intimate friends?" she wrote in her diary shortly before meeting Taft. "Such a friendship is infinitely higher than what is usually called love

51

. . . that fatal idealization which is so blind, and to me, so contemptible. From my point of view a love which is worthy of the name should always have a beginning in the other [i.e., friendship]. To have a man love you in any other way is no compliment." To Nellie it seemed that the only way she could retain her dignity, her pride, and her individuality was to repudiate the idea of being a woman who had to "come out," to be charming, to lead men on—in short, to become a sexual object. And so she decided to rely on her intellectual strengths. The only way to exist with some degree of freedom and power, she felt, was to teach, to travel, and write books. Then she met Bill Taft.

The Herrons and Tafts had been acquainted in Cincinnati when William and Nellie were children, but it was not until 1884, several years after Taft's graduation from law school that he began to court her in earnest. They had had one isolated date in 1880, but nothing came of it. Nellie and her friends took their weekly study sessions in her living room "salon" very seriously; they read and discussed novels, poetry, philosophy, and history. Taft was invited to attend and soon became, as he wrote to Nellie in March 1884, her "humble but enthusiastic disciple each Sunday afternoon." He did not summon up the courage to propose until the first of May 1885, and as he told his parents, "for nearly a month she held me in suspense and then with some hesitation consented to our engagement." She kept the decision tentative and carefully stipulated that it was to be kept a secret. Throughout their courtship he was often unhappy because of her remoteness and her frequent pleasure trips, while he was left in Cincinnati to brood, as his sister Annie said, like "a mountain of misery." Neither then nor later did she show as much interest in him as he did in her. "Oh Nellie, you must love me," he pleaded. "Any act, any expression, any look of yours, Nellie, that shows me you hold me dear . . . sets me wild with delight. Every such act, or expression or look I regard as an evidence, with however little ground, that there is dawning in your heart the love I am so hungry for." Even after their secret engagement, Nellie alternated between moods of grudging kindness and frigid distance, yet he hoped that they might marry "in less than a year, if you continue to 'think' that you are reconciled."

From the beginning she had little reason to fear him. He was kind and gentle, admired her intellectual qualities, and was impressed by her audacity. He described her in a letter to his parents as rather reserved in manner but very independent in character. With scholarly interests and a zeal for work, she possessed a "clear-cut intellect and well-informed mind." Taft later assured Nellie that his love "grew out of a friendship" and was "founded on a respect and admiration for your high character . . . and your intellectual superiority." If they married, she would be, he wrote, his "senior partner" for life. Nellie possessed the strength he felt he lacked, and he was ready to subordinate himself to her. She came to the marriage with a directional blue-print for his life. In Nellie, Taft got what he felt he most needed in his life—a whip that would drive him to achieve. For Nellie, marrying Taft was the next best thing to having a career of her own; it was the best alternative available at the time. They complemented each other, and he gave her a mandate to make of him what she could.

Nellie's correspondence indicates that when at last she accepted Taft's pro-posal of marriage it was because she finally realized that with him she would suffer few constraints and enjoy an opportunity for a kind of public career. Like Taft's mother, Louisa, she felt it was important to be free and to exer-cise some control over her future. "You know," Nellie wrote to her mother not long before the marriage day, "a lot of people think a great deal of Will. Some people even say that he may obtain some very important position in Washington."

Nellie realized she was not providing sufficient warmth and affection, and she tried to explain. Taft replied graciously: you are "afraid I shall think you too cold and you want to be forgiven for it. Why, Nellie, dear, do you think I think you are any less tender in your feeling because you do not talk about it? Ah, my dear, I know you better than you think I do. You are reserved. That is your nature." Taft appealed to her vanity by complimenting her intelligence, which always proved to be the best tack. "I send you Wallace on Russia," he wrote on a note enclosed in the book, "which I hope you can finish in time to give us a lecture on Saturday night."

Each time Nellie tested the sincerity of his respect for her opinions and judgment, Taft would assure her that he knew "no one who attaches more weight to them or who [more] admires your powers of reasoning." He sent her the novels of Henry Fielding and George Eliot and *The Geology of the State of New York* in two volumes, since geology was one of her particular interests. From the beginning he realized she needed to be put at ease, and later he reassured her that after their marriage she could freely continue to improve herself. "I wonder whether in the future you will . . . feel like writing edi-torials," he wrote. "I believe you would soon learn to write articles which in their incisiveness, force, and relevancy would astonish yourself. They wouldn't astonish me though, my dear. Your thought and speech are marked especially by direction, force, and clearness. When I grow blind or imbecile, you can support me by editing a newspaper."

Although he wrote to her continually while she was away on vacations, she rarely replied. "Well," he patiently conceded, "I shall understand silence, my darling, to mean that you are having a good time." When she wrote, her letters often proved upsetting. "I was very much hurt by your letter," he lamented on one occasion. "I read it over and over and over again. There was no word of endearment or affection from one end to the other and the tone of it sounded to me so hard and complaining." When he was able to discover even a trace of affection, it was "all the sweeter that it is unusual with you." "Oh Nellie, do say that you will try to love me. Oh, how I will work and strive to be better and do better. Oh Nellie, you must love me." He made clear his readiness to seek her guidance and direction: I expect to "draw from those dear eyes inspiration enough to keep my spirits up and my feet in the way they should go." She would have to inspire him, mold him, and direct him.

Exaggerating rationality, logic, and intellectual control eventually caused Nellie to become so rigid that she was unable to cope with stress and was often incapacitated by anxiety. Taft, on the other hand, was an emotional, sensual, passionate man. The fun-loving part of his personality led him to see the world innocently and freshly; he had intense, if childlike, feelings. But since, as a child, many of his inner desires for independent action had been denied by his parents' admonitions to work and fulfill their expectations, he remained in part an angry child, needing love. In effect, Taft retained a firm, fierce grip on the child within him, ever seeking to be an agreeable boy who merited approval from surrogate fathers, such as Theodore Roosevelt, and love from a caring surrogate mother.

Taft never felt secure enough of Nellie's love to risk testing it, nor, so the evidence in his letters suggests, to demand very much sexual satisfaction. In his letters he continually acted the role of suppliant, and an unloved one at that, fearing to cross her in even a minimal way. This posture served to reinforce the child in him. Nevertheless, in the suppliant role, afraid of rejection, the amount of his repressed rage increased. Fear of abandonment fed both the child within and the rage. Taft's successes and his assumption of increasing responsibilities would ordinarily have accelerated the process of psychological maturation, but in his case it was not fully achieved. If Nellie had not been so trapped in her aggressions and ambitions, or if Taft had been able to tap the layers of warmth and passion and affection beneath her inhibitions, she would have ceased reinforcing the hopeless, needful child in the man she married. Nellie was a powerful, and negative, counterbalance to all Taft's maturing, adult experiences. Taft was an intelligent man who normally would have expanded his adult personality, but had he made an effort to overcome the child within him, he would have had to give up every tool, every ploy, and every technique that he had cultivated for self-protection throughout his life.

A part of Nellie's repugnance to sex seems clearly to have been related to her repugnance to Taft's obesity, which she openly deplored. Apparently

Nellie never considered the possibility that he, a sensual, loving person, might have given up excessive eating, if he had had physical closeness and sexual gratification in its place, had she become an active sexual partner who did not cause him to feel like a guilty child. We know that she made only feeble gestures to control his eating and thus by implication condoned it— maintaining thereby an excuse to remain sexually isolated. Each reinforced the immaturity in the other.

The more pathetic of Taft's letters tell us that he got very little gratification as an adult. The many trivial details about his daily existence in his long letters to Nellie represent, in a way, a substitution for the physical nurturance in the contact he wanted so much.

Expressions of his importance to her and her love for him were not forthcoming. Nellie's aloofness and coldness, about which Taft complained during their courtship and indeed throughout their married life, were a part of her way of keeping him physically at a distance. Her many trips and extended vacations alone suggest that she found numerous excuses for avoiding intimacy. As he became more powerful in the world of affairs and the world of men, it became increasingly difficult for him to suppress his anger at not getting what he wanted in his intimate life.

The psychological gain for Taft in committing himself over to Nellie was the same one he sought in childhood from his parents—the promise of full acceptance and approval, which had been held out like a prize by his parents. He now sought it more fervently than ever because of the permanent internalized habits of self-doubt he had learned at home. Indeed, despite all that Taft did accomplish in the years preceding his term as president, he never developed much confidence in himself or his abilities. He had been taught in early childhood that no matter how hard he strove, he would not succeed fully, that he had never done enough to merit full acceptance and approval.

Taft unconsciously recognized very early in his career what it was that he needed—someone to take his parents' place, to take command of him, to drive him, to counsel and reassure him at each step of the way—a responsibility which Nellie Herron felt equal to. And so with their marriage Taft in effect transferred this directional control from his parents and from himself to his new wife. Without it he felt lost, as he himself testified whenever he was away from Nellie even for a day or two. He needed her, psychologically, to tell him what to do for in many respects he felt unable or at least uncomfortable in acting on his own, in assuming responsibility for his actions. There was only one arena where he did feel comfortable, relatively capable, and able to initiate action without wifely direction—the courts. But unfortunately for Taft, Nellie would soon derail his judicial career, at least for quite some time. In marrying Nellie Herron, Taft chose a wife to fill the role of coercive parent, and the security of his childhood pattern and the emotional atmosphere of his parents' home were maintained and continued for many years to come. For this, however, he traded a chance to develop in the career in which he would have matured and been happy more quickly than was possible for him even in the nation's highest political positions.

IV

SUCCESS WITHOUT TRUMPETINGS:

Solicitor General and Federal Court Judge, 1886–1900

After graduation from Cincinnati Law School in 1880, Taft, then twenty-three, went to work for his father's old law firm, and unlike his brothers Horace and Peter he got on very well in the profession. Soon he was appointed assistant prosecutor of Hamilton County, a post he held from 1881 to 1883, prior to his marriage. As prosecutor he did his work satisfactorily, but, in Henry Pringle's words, "without trumpetings." He was next appointed to the position of collector of internal revenue, "a circumstance not of his seeking," Nellie noted in her *Recollections.* Although it pleased Nellie that Taft was singled out for political posts, she would have preferred advancement to depend more on his own initiative than on the influence of his father. Yet Taft had many qualities to recommend him: he was honest, personally engaging, extremely cooperative, ready to work, and loyal. Recalling these early days, Nellie wrote that at the time she had decided on marriage, "Mr. Taft was making very satisfactory progress in his career."

The fact that Taft's first positions in Ohio came to him through offers from family friends and political acquaintances led William Allen White to observe that he was pushed from office to office with little effort on his own part. Ray Stannard Baker also felt that Taft advanced chiefly because of his loyal friendships with those in high public positions. In 1887 Taft was very pleased to be appointed to the position of judge on the Ohio Superior Court, a post his father had once held. Now thirty, Taft discovered that the court was a "pleasant harbor." The work was congenial—hearing motions, writing opinions, presiding over the court in his judicial robes. His life was orderly and undisturbed, and his conscientious efforts brought him a sense of solid accomplishment. He was happy and so successful that he and his judicial friends began to discuss the possibilities of his appointment one day to the Supreme Court.

This goal became Taft's one consuming desire. Although normally diffident about his qualifications, in 1889 he urged Ohio Governor Joseph Foraker to press his nomination with President Benjamin Harrison for a Supreme Court appointment. Harrison, not sufficiently anxious to placate Ohio Republicans, refused to appoint so young and inexperienced a judge. He did, however, offer Taft the post of United States Solicitor General, a position Taft wished to decline, but Nellie persuaded him to accept.

Although Taft was content to remain in Cincinnati, Nellie was no more satisfied there than his mother had been. Of course, he had known all along that Nellie would not be content to remain in Ohio. When they visited Washington, D.C., shortly after marriage, he jokingly inquired, "I wonder, Nellie dear, if you and I will ever be here in any official capacity? Oh yes, I forgot; of course we shall when you become secretary of the treasury." Despite Taft's inclination for the more sedate judicial life, which she considered "an awful groove," Nellie never faltered in her determination to shift him toward a national career. The effort required at times decisive action on her part, to which Taft, always anxious to please, usually submitted faithfully, as he had earlier to his parents. President Harrison's offer of the solicitor general post was for Nellie a welcome "interruption . . . in our peaceful existence." Taft was apprehensive and confided to his father just after being sworn in on 14 February 1890 that he found the prospect of such a position "rather overwhelming." Nellie admitted that Taft in farewell cast "regretful glances at his beloved bench," but she was "very glad because it gave Mr. Taft an opportunity for exactly the kind of work I wished him to do."

In her *Recollections*, Nellie evocatively—and sympathetically—described Taft's first day in Washington:

> He arrived at six o'clock on a cold, gloomy February morning at the old dirty Pennsylvania station. He wandered out on the street with a heavy bag in his hand looking for a porter, but there were no porters. Then he stood for a few moments looking up at the Capitol and feeling dismally unimportant in the midst

of what seemed to him to be very formidable surroundings. He wondered to himself why on earth he had come. He was sure he had made a fatal mistake in exchanging a good position and a pleasant circle at home, where everybody knew him, for a place in a strange and forbidding city where he knew practically nobody and where, he felt sure, nobody wanted to know him. He lugged his bag up to the old Ebbitt House and, after eating a lonesome breakfast, he went to the Department of Justice to be sworn in. After that ceremony was over and he had shaken hands with the attorney general, he went up to inspect the solicitor general's office, and there he met the most dismal sight of the whole dismal day. His "quarters" consisted of a single room, three flights up, and bearing not the slightest resemblance to his mental picture of what the solicitor general's offices would be like.

Taft soon made the acquaintance of Theodore Roosevelt, then civil service commissioner, and the two young men, who lived in the same neighborhood, began walking to work and lunching together. Their friendship, built on mutual trust and admiration, rapidly deepened. Ten years later Roosevelt turned to his friend Taft when, tired of his post as police commissioner of New York City, he decided that he wanted to become assistant secretary of the Navy. Taft had access to William McKinley, the new president from Ohio, and Roosevelt got the post.

Taft felt when he accepted the solicitor generalship that he might not like his duties and feared he might not excel in them. Arguing cases in an open courtroom was not, he knew, his forte. It was something he did not enjoy, and as a young lawyer in Cincinnati he had lost both his first jury case and a Supreme Court decision, a performance which did not please Alphonso. Henry Pringle notes that success as a lawyer at the bar required a competitive quality which Taft did not possess, and the solicitor general's main task was to present government cases before the Supreme Court. Taft said what he would say again and again throughout his career, "Well, I'm in it now and I'll do the best I can." To his parents Taft confided his problems and fears. His greatest difficulty lay, he told his father, "in holding the attention of the Supreme Court justices. They seem to think when I begin to talk that is a good chance to . . . read . . . letters, to eat lunch, and to devote their attention to correcting proof." His mother tried to reassure him: "Don't be discouraged at the indifference of the old fogies of the Supreme Court. It is a new experience which you will get used to."

Nellie, as Louisa before her, assumed the responsibility of coaching Taft in this new experience: "I . . . know how uncomfortable you felt at having to speak without more preparation when you always give so much to anything you do." She cautioned him not to overprepare, not to cite too many precedents, not to talk too long. Nellie's determination that he make a dramatic success at his new job—especially by becoming a graceful and colorful orator—was known by Alphonso, who warned his son not to be influenced by her concern over whether or not he made impressive speeches in court. This was not the way cases were won, his father advised. Taft never did become a compelling speaker, but he lost only two of his eighteen cases as solicitor general.

Nellie's idea of Taft's career lay in directions other than the judicial sphere, and she was thrilled when her husband began to associate with national political figures. Just "think of your going off on a trip with two cabinet officers," she wrote with delight during their second summer in Washington. He enjoyed telling her whenever his name was mentioned as a possibility for senator, since he knew this would please her and her approbation would follow. Although Taft did not take gossip of that kind too seriously, Nellie did. "You were right in thinking I would be interested in the remark about the senatorship," she replied on one occasion, immediately going on to advise him: "You would really have an advantage in not being identified with either faction."

Although Nellie liked Washington and delighted in planning future triumphs, she was not completely satisfied with their immediate situation. They did not have sufficient income to maintain what she considered to be a proper life style, and they had to borrow. She continually urged him to supplement his small goverment salary by taking private cases and reminded him to ask for adequate fees: "I should think three hundred dollars very low for you for trying a case"; "I am curious to hear about your case and hope there will be a good fee"; "can you not spread the impression abroad that you would be willing to take a few well paying cases?"

Nellie was also concerned about the perquisites of office. She did not, for example, know how much she had "counted on the chance of having a horse and carriage" until her disappointment when one was denied. She considered it "very mean in the Attorney General not to have it at your disposal." Modest, amiable Taft, not inclined to insist on such amenities, was instructed by Nellie to "inquire about it" immediately. She allowed no detail to escape her.

Neither was Taft completely satisfied with his job as solicitor general, and when a seat on the Sixth Federal Circuit Court of Appeals opened, which would mean returning to Cincinnati, he made inquiries. Alphonso, to whom Taft appealed, counseled his son to accept the position if offered. Taft instinctively knew what would make him happy: "I like judicial life and there is only one higher judicial position in the country than that. . . . It could be in the line of promotion to the Supreme Court. It would keep me poor all my life if I were to get it, but I don't see that people with very modest incomes don't live as happily as those who have fortunes. The salary is six thousand a year."

President Harrison promised him the post, and Taft, overjoyed, could scarcely keep quiet about it, though decorum dictated that he maintain secrecy. "I wish you would not be so expansive to reporters," Nellie admonished him. "You always think they won't tell and they always do." But talking unguardedly to reporters was a habit the affable Taft did not break until he entered the White House and became the object of their criticism. To encourage Nellie, he emphasized the great honor and prestige attached to such an appointment. He also attempted to reconcile her to the idea by pointing out that his closest competitor for the post had been perhaps the leading lawyer of the Ohio bar. Shortly after her "first pleased surprise at the honor" wore off, however, she began to reconsider. "My thinking," she recorded in her *Recollections*, "led me to decide that my husband's appointment on the bench was not a matter for such warm congratulations after all."

Nellie still found Cincinnati socially and intellectually constricted. She had warned Taft, "If you get your heart's desire . . . it will put an end to all the opportunities you now have of being thrown with the bigwigs." Nellie worried that, once cloistered in the courts, he might become "fixed in a groove for the rest of his life." "I began even then," she recollected, "to fear the narrowing effects of the bench and to prefer for him a diverse experience which would give him an all-round professional development." Her husband, she was particular to note, "did not share this feeling in any way"; the appointment on the Superior Court was "the welcome beginning of just the career he wanted." This time Taft got what he wanted. Nellie conceded that her husband had enjoyed "the work in the following eight years more than any he had ever undertaken."

Upon their return to Cincinnati in March 1892, the Tafts rented a spacious house in the best neighborhood in the city, close to both the Herron's Pike Street home and Taft's office. Taft's older half-brother Charles also lived on Pike Street in the white mansion built in 1820 by Cincinnati's first mayor, Martin Baum. The building later became the Taft museum. Charles, who had married Anna Sinton, an heiress, restored the mansion and its gardens and ornamented it with fine collections of Chinese porcelain and other objets d'art they gathered throughout Europe.

Judge Taft's salary was not large, but it nevertheless provided governesses for Robert and Helen, a nurse for Charles, and various maids and handymen. During the summers, beginning in 1892, the Tafts vacationed at Murray Bay, a small French Canadian town one hundred miles northeast of Quebec City. At first they rented cottages, but soon they bought a frame house and added to it over the years until it had fifteen bedrooms and nine baths.

Taft labored hard over his legal opinions, with the result that they tended to be thorough, however ponderous and dull. His painstaking style consisted of long, point-by-point exegeses, linking argument and fact, and he developed a specialty in judging complicated patent rights. Secure and successful as a judge, Taft soon became greatly respected for his diligence. To stem the growing voices for reform—the call for the income tax (from the farmers), for free silver, for the direct election of senators, and for workmen's compensation, minimum wage laws, factory safety regulations—conservatives looked especially to the courts to maintain the status quo. Given his conservative views and exceptional judicial record, Taft attracted the favorable attention of Republican leaders in the capital.

The judicial circuit—which included much of Ohio, Kentucky, Tennessee, and Michigan—often took Taft away from home, a circumstance which exacerbated Nellie's disaffection with life in Cincinnati, where, she said, "there were so few people who cared for conversation on the social graces in art or music." Becoming the mother of three children—Robert in 1889, Helen in 1891, and Charles in 1897—had not provided sufficient outlet for Nellie's aspirations. Unable now to attend House and Senate debates, as she had done in Washington, she turned to various community activities to relieve the monotony of her existence. Since music was one of her chief interests, she organized and managed the Cincinnati Orchestra Association. Sponsoring the orchestra, raising funds, arranging for soloists, and delivering speeches to the Association consumed only a portion of her energies. She was also actively committed, as Louisa Taft previously had been, to the kindergarten movement. In addition she found time to assist in voluntary adminstrative work at the city hospital and museum. She also attended university classes in art and current events, went to the theatre, and heard lectures on such figures as Mazzini and Cavour. Although she read extensively in Byron, Keats, Darwin, and Kipling, her favorite reading was history, especially about the reign of Louis XIV.

As always the want of money unsettled her. On one occasion Taft irritated Nellie by conscientiously returning to the government an overpayment which he had received for traveling expenses. Considering the extra money a perquisite, Nellie rebuked him: "I was dreadfully upset by your sending that money back. I don't believe it was ever intended that that money should simply cover expenses. You would not be very popular with the Supreme Court anymore than [with] your bench if your views were known and I advise you to keep them to yourself." Another source of stress lay in Taft's readiness to please friends, even mere acquaintances, by donating his time and energies to the cause of various suppliants. "Don't go and make any promises," she warned him. "Why can't you be satisfied to take your work and let other people attend to theirs?"

Nellie was, however, gratified that Taft was making good connections, in hopes of future mobility, and he continually whetted her interest by repeating all words of praise bestowed on him. He sent her a letter from the Lincoln Club telling of their intent to publish one of his addresses—"so that you may see what good work your 'hub' can do." She was very pleased and warned him to "go over the proofs carefully and correct those parts that I thought undignified." But he failed to elicit from her much interest in his law cases or judicial acquaintances, and in one instance, her boredom was so apparent, he sadly remarked, "I had hoped that the public interest in the street railway case might revive your interest in my judicial work." Yet Taft strove to discover sympathy even when it was not forthcoming. When he expressed doubt about whether he could arrive home from his court duties on schedule, she bridled, "Don't you dare to disappoint me, or I shall never hear [of] your going on the circuit again." Such threats gave him great pleasure: "it makes me feel good to think that I am a necessary part of your life, however little I really contribute to your happiness."

One of Taft's cases did attract Nellie's interest. In 1894 the Pullman Palace Car Company in Chicago cut its employees' wages and refused to arbitrate the matter. Many Pullman workers were members of Eugene V. Debs's new American Railway Union, which called for a strike. After an injunction was issued against the strikers, sporadic violence occurred. President Cleveland called in troops and crushed the strike; Debs was jailed for contempt. Meanwhile, Frank Phelan, one of the Union organizers, had come to Cincinnati and urged railroad workers to support the strikers, whereupon he was summarily arrested and brought to trial in Taft's court for inciting the workers to join an illegal strike. Taft's conservative impulses emerged in the course of the trial. He worried that management might compromise with Debs, which, he wrote to Nellie, would "mean the postponement of the fight which must be fought out to the bitter end. It is the most outrageous strike in the history of the country. . . . Demagogues and populists . . . who are continually encouraging resistance to federal authority" were much to blame, he thought. "The situation in Chicago is very alarming and distressing and until they have had much bloodletting, it will not be better." When word came that thirty men had been wounded by federal troops, he wrote coldly that "though it is bloody business, everybody hopes that it is true. . . . There are a lot of sentimentalists who ought to know better, who allow themselves to sympathize with the wild cries of socialists." In another letter Taft told Nellie: "They have killed only six of the mob as yet. This is hardly enough to make an impression." In the face of danger from numerous "lunatics," Taft insisted that he could not leave for his vacation until the strike was over "because this is the post of duty and I owe it to the country to see the trouble through." Though personally gentle, kind, and generous, Taft was a "thoroughgoing Social Darwinist," whose "enduring aim" throughout life, according to Alpheus Mason, was to safeguard private property. Taft held conservative views of society and the constitution, and in defending property—the "bulwark of civilization"—he occasionally made some rather ruthless remarks.

Nellie, on vacation at Murray Bay, followed the case in the papers: "It was so exciting I could not read fast enough. . . . I shall be so anxious to hear what you will do about Phelan." Phelan was found guilty of leading an illegal strike, and Taft sentenced him to prison. Although Taft hated "the publicity that this business brings me," Nellie loved it, realizing that her husband's reputation rose in Republican political circles as a result of his antilabor rulings. Taft issued an injunction against Debs and "all his crew," which brought approval from many influential Republicans who likewise feared the wild cries of socialists. Ironically, this publicity was later considered a serious handicap by politicians who felt Taft could never be elected president since the laboring class had begun to think of him as the "Father of Injunctions."

As Taft's reputation grew, he was invited to address legal groups and civic assemblies. He compromised with his particular bête noire—speech making—by reading verbatim from prepared texts. Sometimes he failed to gather the material necessary for an acceptable speech, and his subsequent dissatisfaction pained him. Personal failure touched him closely because it meant disappointing friends who had depended on him: "I must make every effort to speak satisfactorily because I owe it to . . . those who thought me worthy to preside." Before each speech, he would "begin to quake in my bones at the prospect and fear that I may fizzle out." Occasional poor performances augmented his already burdensome sense of inadequacy.

When he was honored with a request to speak before the American Bar Association in 1895, he anticipated the event with anxiety. Nellie and the children were at Murray Bay, and without her presence he found it difficult to write. Composing the speech was an agony: "I tremble lest I shall make a fizzle," he mourned. In the end, as on many other occasions, he appealed to Nellie, "If you have any fitting ideas, write them down for me." And she often did.

Another weakness augured ill for a political aspirant: Taft could not bear adverse criticism. This problem became especially apparent after his Bar Address received an unfavorable notice in the *Law Review*. Taft took such criticism as a personal affront. Months passed before he could tell Nellie, "I have recovered my equanimity concerning the *Law Review* and hope that I can avoid further worry about it." Nellie, knowing that no public figure could escape criticism, tried to inure him to the inevitable: "You have been remarkably free from attacks of that kind and of course you must expect your share." She realized that hostile attacks would increase many-fold once he left—as she hoped he would—the quiet security of the bench for the rough and tumble of national politics.

By 1900 it was generally known in Republican circles that President McKinley was seriously thinking of Taft for the Supreme Court. No other jurist in the country, Pringle claims, had contributed so much to judicial thought in the mid-nineties as William Howard Taft. A conservative and a Republican, Taft had much in his favor. After a trip to Washington, he reported back to Nellie, "Almost every person I met spoke of my coming there to sit on the Supreme Bench as a certainty. I wish I could think so." Yet knowing that Nellie had earlier opposed these aspirations, he could not expect encouragement about continuing in a judicial career. Her chief concern was, rather, to get Taft out of that "groove" and onto a path more likely to lead to the White House. Taft was torn in both directions; he loved judicial life but at the same time wished to please Nellie. "I depend on you," he wrote, "my life is only existence without you."

A friend on the bench, having perhaps sensed his predicament, was "very much opposed" to his leaving the bench and advised him to follow his own inclination. Ultimately, Taft turned to Nellie for guidance. He told his friend, as he explained later to Nellie, that he "should leave it to her to whom I owe everything and I shall abide by her decision." And her desires invariably prevailed. At this moment in Taft's career, however, events were to take a course which postponed the dilemma a clear choice would have created.

V

PLAYING AT ROYALTY:
Governor of the Philippines, 1900–1904

Neither Taft nor Nellie knew what was in store for them when a telegram from President McKinley arrived late in January 1900. "I would like to see you in Washington on important business within the next few days," it read. Nellie "began to conjure up visions of Supreme Court appointments." Although not her first choice, it was still preferable to staying in Cincinnati. President McKinley had begun to consider Taft for a different position, however, after an accidental encounter with Judge William Rufus Day. "I am in need of a man who is strong, tactful, and honest, for an executive in the Philippines," President McKinley remarked. "You have described Judge Taft," Day responded. When Taft was offered the post of commissioner to the Philippines, he exclaimed ingenuously, "Why I am not the man you want. To begin with, I have never approved of keeping the Philippines." McKinley replied, "You don't want them any less than I do, but we have got them and in dealing with them I think I can trust the man who didn't want them better than I can the man who did." Sensing his disappointment, McKinley claimed that he would be "a better judge for this experience," and in conclusion assured him that "if you give up this judicial office at my request you shall not suffer. If I last and the opportunity comes, I shall appoint you [to the Supreme Court]."

A public debate between the annexationists and the anti-annexationists over American involvement in the Philippines during the Spanish-American war emerged in 1899 when President McKinley began reassessing his policy for the 7,083 island archipelago. McKinley originally had no desire to annex the Philippines, only the intention to secure a strategic base in Asia, probably by taking the chief island of Luzon. But the interdependence of the Philippine Islands made this plan impracticable. Supporters of McKinley's annexation plan argued that such a large acquisition might be unfortunate but necessary if the United States were to achieve world-wide commercial hegemony, particularly with trading opportunities in China. Their arguments were couched in the language of the White Man's Burden, but strategic and economic considerations underlay their thinking. Those opposing McKinley's plan stressed the immorality of imperialism and its inconsistency with America's professed ideals.

McKinley's major problem lay in securing the cooperation of all the Filipino people, especially in face of General Emilio Aguinaldo's growing independence movement. The American strategy was to co-opt the wealthy, conservative land owners, who were willing to accept American sovereignty in the Islands and to collaborate with their conquerors. The McKinley administration got reassurances from this elite group of Filipinos, who insisted that the armed resistance involved only the Tagalog tribe seeking the balkanization of the country. The Filipino collaborators hoped to maintain their economic security and expected a large share of the political offices. But the guerillas continued to fight for complete independence, despite American military efforts to bring law and order to the islands. McKinley proposed a policy of Filipinization, once the fighting ended, for a happy, peaceful country within the American commonweal. William Howard Taft was charged with implementing that plan.

Taft was afraid to return home with the news, since he knew how much Nellie counted upon returning to Washington society. "I dreaded meeting Nellie," he recorded later. "She met me at the door and her first question was, 'Well, are we going to Washington?' " He explained the situation, and, "after a moment's hesitation, she exclaimed, 'I think you should accept!' " Taft's brothers helped Nellie allay Taft's fear that in going to the Philippines he would forfeit all chances of sitting on the Supreme Court. Louisa Taft took rather longer "getting accustomed to the idea," but she felt finally that it would be "pusillanimous" not to give her approval. Taft agreed, but Nellie later acknowledged that his resignation from the circuit court bench "was the hardest thing he ever did."

A sense of pathos surrounds these events, for Taft was greatly more suited to serve in the capacity of judge than administrator. In her *Recollections* Nellie recalled that Taft came home from Washington "with an expression so grave that I thought he must be facing impeachment. But when he broke his news to me it gave me nothing but pleasure." It meant leaving Cincinnati, and she knew instantly that she "didn't want to miss a big and novel experience. I have never shrunk before any obstacle when I had an opportunity to see a new country." And although many people warned her not to expose her children to the hazards of such a sojourn (one hundred thousand people were to die of cholera in Manila two years later), that obstacle was ignored. "It did not occur to me," she said later, "that it was a task to take them on such a long journey, or that they could be exposed to any danger." She began preparing immediately and "read with engrossing interest everything I could find on the subject of the Philippines."

They sailed in April 1900 on the army transport *Hancock*, which, carrying only forty-five passengers, seemed like a private yacht. After a four-day stop in Honolulu, they continued to Yokohama. Remote from the busy world, Taft felt calm and tranquil. He read several books on civil law and colonial problems and enjoyed walking round and round the deck. Two sailors, seeing him approach for a tenth lap, called out, "Here he comes—eighteen knots an hour." Ten-year-old Robert had taught himself chess and engaged several of the army officers on board, while Helen, eight, played happily with the younger children. Charley, though only two, was "in possession," it seemed, of everyone's attention.

Before arriving in the Philippines, the Tafts were to make an official visit to Japan, where they were received by the emperor and empress. At first sight the wooden palace in Tokyo disappointed them, being only one story and, as Taft thought, "unsubstantial" looking. But the exquisite reception chamber, with its ceiling of delicate lacquer work, awed them. Nellie was unhappy to find that ladies were received only by the empress. After bowing halfway to the throne and bowing in front of the emperor, Taft shook his hand, had a brief talk, and bowed his way out again. He assured Nellie that she had not missed a great deal, for the court was in European dress and the emperor, he felt, was "by no means a beauty." Having heard of the emperor's inordinate love of saki, Taft described him as looking like a man who had been "soaking" in it for a good many years.

At dinner with high-ranking Japanese officials, the mammoth American attempted in vain "to achieve the squatting position." Lloyd Griscom, who was present, reported that finally a Japanese politely rushed out of the room and returned with a padded stool for Taft. For the rest of the evening he "looked down majestically" on the rest of the party. During his visit, Taft discovered that the Japanese enjoyed looking at him as much as he did at them. They gathered round in crowds, openly displaying their amusement, he wrote, at "the prospect of so much flesh and size." The rickshaw men in Kyoto found a double-seater. "That suited me exactly," he confessed.

One of the few differences of opinion between the Tafts—publicly known—was over an incident stemming from their Japanese visit. The empress presented Nellie with a tapestry, but Taft, who was scrupulously honest, felt that the constitutional clause against accepting gifts from foreign governments applied. He insisted that Nellie return the piece, but she adamantly refused. Finally she appealed to President McKinley, who agreed with her rather than Taft.

En route to the Philippines, Taft stopped in Hong Kong, where he intended to acquire lightweight clothing and Chinese servants. He was unable to buy much in Hong Kong, he recorded with self-satisfaction, because "they do not deal in men's sizes." Nellie stayed some time longer in Japan, a country she found enchanting.

When Taft lumbered off the boat in Manila, he did not, apparently, make a spectacular impression on the American newsmen. One interviewer responded ironically to the qualities of innocence and trust so prominent in his character. He wired back to his paper: We ought to ship this splendid fellow back. It's a shame to spoil his illusion that folks the world over are just like the folks he knows out in Ohio. He makes me think of pies, hominy, fried chicken, big red apples . . . the little red school-house, encyclopedias on the installment plan. Taft's high-mindedness stood him always in good stead, however, and he was to enjoy a notable success during his four years in the Philippines.

Without Nellie for more than two months in the Islands, Taft grew unhappy. "I long for the time when you shall come," he wrote to Nellie, "with your knowledge of things and how to do them [you] can straighten out matters." "I cannot tell you," he lamented, referring to the problems of securing a house and servants added to his official tasks, "how helpless I feel without you." On their fourteenth wedding anniversary, Taft wrote, "It was the most fortunate day of my life"; "every year I feel more dependent on you." As her stay in Japan grew more protracted, Taft worried that maybe she would not come to Manila at all.

To induce her, Taft described all the festivities at which he was the guest of honor. The hospitality of the Filipino, he felt, "is his chief most admirable quality." He knew what she would find provocative: "There will be a good deal of interesting politics, many interesting Filipino men to cultivate and entertain, beautiful furniture and interesting curios to collect." Nellie later admitted she had been "selfish to stay away so long having a good time." At last, with her children and a Japanese maid, she set out to join him.

Nellie's first sight of Manila proved memorable. The main street, Escotta, was crowded with intriguing native vehicles—two-wheeled, box-like, pony-drawn conveyances known as *quilez*, caraboas dragging clumsy heavily-laden carts, a small tram pulled by ponies, many Victorias, barouches, and other carriages. The "gente," or common people, appeared most colorful, the men wearing freshly-ironed gauze shirts with multi-color stripes or embroidery down the front, the women dressed in red skirts and chemises, with their hair covered by blue cotton handkerchiefs and mats or baskets balanced on their heads. She saw pretty girls of Spanish descent in lace mantillas intermingled with the darker mestizas, pale-faced Americans here and there, and crowds of soldiers in tropical white uniforms with brass buttons. Manila's residential area was an interesting mixture of handsome, substantial Spanish-colonial houses with red-tiled roofs and native huts with thatched roofs. Many residences overlooked canals on whose banks laundry women, accompanied by their naked babies, labored. One street of uniformly fine homes led to the governor-general's palace, which became the Tafts' home within a year.

At the outset of his administration, Taft worried over his ability to perform the tasks at hand. To Senator Foraker of Ohio he confessed, "Good fortune has followed me with so much persistence that I tremble for the future on the principle of compensation. The work now to be undertaken is of the most perplexing and original character and I gravely fear that I am not qualified. But the die is cast—I must attempt it." His first delicate situation involved General Arthur MacArthur, father of the World War II General MacArthur who later clashed with President Truman in the Korean War. He held military charge of the Islands, which he was reluctant to relinquish, and Taft immediately encountered a struggle between the civil authority and the army. He did not shrink from confronting the problem, for he did not consider MacArthur "broad enough and big enough" (important images in Taft's mind) to cope with the political problems on the Islands. Yet MacArthur and his officers insisted that while the insurrection continued, they needed to maintain martial control. Taft disputed the premise, believing that there was no real war, but "merely a series of night attacks, and prowling by bands of robbers, whom it is very difficult to distinguish from insurrectos, and who make a pretense of political warfare if they happen to be caught." "The talk of an 'uprising' here," Taft scoffed, "is about as absurd as it would be in Cincinnati."

With the Civil Commission watching over him, Taft reported that MacArthur was "rousing himself to a little more rigor" in dealing with the remaining insurgents in the provinces. Taft hoped MacArthur would quickly defeat the terrorists and then withdraw, since he thought MacArthur did not care "to let anybody else do anything and he is not in a hurry to do it himself." "We must have civil government here and must get rid of the one-man power and that a military man."

Taft complained that MacArthur "brooks no suggestions with respect to his duties and insists in giving a great many suggestions in respect to ours." Moreover, the general kept the atmosphere tense by deporting many of the "irreconcilables" to Guam by the end of January 1901. This, Taft commented ironically, "cleared the atmosphere wonderfully." The military government also arrested all those engaged in levying contributions for the insurgents, after which numbers of guerillas surrendered every day. "The bottom of the insurrection is dropping out," and the majority of the people long for peace, Taft reported to his brother Charles. To the end, the military establishment remained utterly out of sympathy with the Civil Commission. "They resented our coming and do not enjoy our stay," Taft wrote.

As the guerillas were suppressed, the "better citizens," in Taft's view, proposed conciliation, for they were "tired and weary of this murder and assassination policy." Just as the situation was radically improving in the Islands with a definite shift of popular sympathy for Taft and the Americans, difficulties at home increased with the presidential election. The Republican convention in 1900, astutely managed by industrialist-politician Mark Hanna, had renominated the safe and respectable Ohioan William McKinley and adopted an equally safe and respectable platform, which included the party's pledge to maintain American rule over Hawaii and the Philippines. Unlike McKinley, Democratic candidate William Jennings Bryan actively campaigned against imperialism. If Bryan, whom Taft labled "the great destructive demagogue," defeated McKinley, he was certain conditions would get considerably worse in the Philippines.

"Th' convintion," Mr. Dooley announced was "wan iv th' most excitin' . . . since I attended a hankerchief drill in th' Women's Christyan Timperance Union." By way of satirizing the annexationist Republicans, Mr. Dooley quoted Mark Hanna as telling the conventioneers, "Four years ago we had only twinty millyon happy naygurs in our possession. To-day we have the Lord knows how manny, friskin' among th' palms an' sagoes an allspice threes in those island possissions that shine like jools on th' brow iv Liberty."

McKinley won a more decisive victory over Bryan in 1900 than in 1896. Taft was elated but still felt that Bryan and the anti-imperialists, "made savage by the defeat of their policy," would cause further trouble for him as governor. He took satisfaction, therefore, in the fact that in the Philippines the influence of the "federalists" was growing, and that the people reacted to it as a means of expressing their desire for peace. In January 1901 Taft wrote that Manila was "as quiet as a Sunday school." Filipinos "of the best stripe," he observed, were "coming out in the most flat-footed way" for the acceptance of American sovereignty over the Islands. The army, nonetheless, distrusted all evidence of popular feeling for the United States. Even before the capture, in April 1901, of Aguinaldo, the rebel chieftain, and Trias, the talented guerilla leader, Taft felt that the time was at hand for appointment of the civil governor to replace the military.

Taft was sworn in as governor in 1901 on the Fourth of July. The inauguration ceremonies took place in a pavilion opposite the Ayunamiento, the building that housed the Philippine Commission, where a large crowd watched MacArthur present Taft for the oath of office. Taft gave his inaugural address and then presided over MacArthur's passing the military command to Major General A.R. Chaffee. MacArthur vacated the governor-general's palace, and the Tafts moved in.

Taft initially felt that the Islands were "utterly incapable of self-government," and his chief desire was, consequently, to help the Filipinos learn how to build a stable government. Meanwhile the Filipino people were overjoyed to see a civilian government installed, and they made their happiness known. "It is . . . certain that nothing is so popular as our coming into power," he wrote home with warm satisfaction. "Everywhere we go," he wrote to Secretary of War Root, "we find arches, flowers, with lanterns and flags crossing our path and everywhere we find every evidence of real rejoicing of the people at our coming." Taft spoke kindly of the Filipino as his "little brown brother," and he openly entertained them at the palace and attended their concerts and cockfights; his friendly behavior represented quite a change from MacArthur's. By the time MacArthur left the Islands, his soldiers were singing a song which ended, the Filipino "may be a brother of William Howard Taft, but he ain't no friend of mine." Given the people's warm approbation of him personally, Taft began to think he was going to like the job after all.

Establishing a civil government was, as it turned out, quite within Taft's competence as a lawyer. His chief task, he informed Nellie, would be "the preparation of extensive legislative enactments to change cumbrous Spanish laws." Taft acted the role of "benevolent magistrate" quite at home with his duties. He was able to work well and happily, for "he was, again, a judge," as Henry Pringle aptly observes.

Taft was at work before eight-thirty every morning. From ten o'clock to one the Commission, which held the purse strings of the government and formulated required legislation, met with him to conduct its business. We "have been passing laws every two or three days," Taft informed his brother Charles with delight. He returned home for lunch but was back at work by three. At six, accompanied by General Wright, he walked the two and one half miles home. By May 1903, he had completed the "foundation work," as he called it, for the Criminal Code of Procedure, the Internal Revenue Act, a general incorporation act, regulations for the settlement and sale of land, the districting of the Islands for the Legislative Assembly, settlement of the purchase of the friars' lands from Rome, and the disbursement of three million dollars to relieve agricultural distress.

As Taft's popularity with the Filipino people grew, anti-imperialists at home spread stories of cruelties perpetrated by American soldiers, of burning, murder, and rape, in order to prove that the United States was unsuccessfully and wrongly attempting to replace Spain as colonial master of the Islands. Horace, the most reform-minded of the Taft brothers, was troubled by accounts of Filipinos allegedly subjected to the water torture or strung up by their thumbs. Taft was soon explaining to reporters and family alike that such stories were usually exaggerated. Guerilla warfare, he admitted, was by nature a warfare of "ambush, deceit and cruelty," and consequently Americans occasionally responded in kind. But, he repeatedly insisted, the American troops had shown comparative restraint. To brother Charles, he privately confided that "we have been too mild as a general policy."

One comment on Taft's explanation for the bad press the Americans were getting came in the form of Mr. Dooley's parody of the civil governor's annual report:

> It is not always necessary to kill a Filipino American right away. Me desire is to idjacate thim slowly in th' ways an' customs iv th' counthry. We ar-re givin' hundherds iv these pore benighted haythan th' well-known, ol'-fashioned American wather cure. Iv coorse, ye know how 'tis done. A Filipino, we'll say, niver heerd iv th' histhry iv this counthry. He is met be wan iv our sturdy boys in black an' blue who asts him to cheer fr Abraham Lincoln. He rayfuses. He is thin placed upon th' grass an' givin a dhrink, a baynit been fixed in his mouth so he cannot rijict th' hospitality. Undher th' infloence iv th' hose that cheers but does not inebriate, he soon warrums or perhaps I might say swells up to a ralization iv th' granjoor iv his adoptive counthry. One gallon makes him give three groans fr th' constitchoocheon. At four gallons, he will ask to be wrapped in th' flag. At th' dew point he sings Yankee Doodle. Occasionally we run acrost a stubborn an' rebellyous man who wud sthrain at th' idee iv human rights an' swallow th' Passyfic Ocean, but I mus' say mos' iv these little fellows is less hollow in their pretintions. Nachrally we have had to take a good manny customs fr'm th' Spanyard, but we have improved on thim. I was talkin' with a Spanish gintleman th' other day who had been away fr a long time an' he said he wudden't know th' counthry. Even th' faces iv th' people on th' sthreets had changed. They seemed glad to see him. Among th' mos' useful Spanish customs is reconcenthration. [In January, 1902, General Bell, in his struggle with Filipino insurgents, adopted the concentration camps, or *recontrado*, policy of the Spanish in Batangas province in Luzon.] Our reconcenthration camps is among th' mos' thickly popylated in th' wurruld. . . . ivrywhere happiness, contint, love iv th'

shtep-mother counthry, excipt in places where there ar-re people. Gintlemen, I thank ye.

At times internal conditions led to so many setbacks that Taft felt temporarily discouraged. At the same time that cholera struck the Filipinos, in 1902, rinderpest decimated the caraboa, the only draft cattle in the Islands. Because the caraboa were indispensable for the cultivation of rice and nearly as indispensable for the cultivation of sugar, this natural disaster extended the agricultural depression caused by six years of warfare. Many discontented Filipinos, Taft wrote, "naturally make the government and the Americans responsible" for all the calamities. "There is considerable agitation among the poorer and the vicious classes against the Americans," he informed his mother. Famine threatened in several areas, and Taft worried that "demagogues" at home might "seize the opportunity to raise a row." It would be easy to stir up the common people, he felt, because they were so credulous and vulnerable. The remedy lay in importing cattle and getting the people back to work in the fields as quickly as possible. Taft's inherently reactionary beliefs surfaced once more: "My own judgment is that even real suffering from famine is better than the debauching of the people by teaching them to rely on the government for food," he wrote to Horace. The economic crisis convinced Taft further of the Filipinos' "utter incapacity . . . to found and maintain a decent government" by themselves.

In January 1902, a senate committee began hearings on the Philippines, and Taft was called back to the United States to participate in the debates over the country's increasing involvement in the Islands. In the senate a bill was introduced calling for the prohibition of liquor in the territory because of newspaper accounts of Americans inspiring drunkenness in the native population. Taft was asked to testify. Secretary Root believed that "yellow journal hypocrites" had irresponsibly created the impression "among millions of good people that we have turned Manila into a veritable hell." He defended Taft, whom he represented as the only man capable of dealing with the "dissolute, lazy, gambling, tough Americans" that were responsible for these false impressions. He described them as the "offscourings of the army and camp followers, who settle in the interior towns, loaf in the American saloons, and abuse the natives."

A personal embarrassment for Taft followed the publication in 1902 of a book called *As It Is in the Philippines* by Charles Ballentine, a former AP correspondent in the Islands. Fired from his job, he decided to get revenge by damning the American presence in the Philippines and by accusing Taft of "great incapacity and great insincerity." "He makes me out a little short of a devil," Taft fumed. At home, unrewarded office seekers abused Taft and the commission. These "disappointed gentlemen," he complained, resented his insistence that the Philippine government be run primarily for the benefit of the Filipinos and only incidentally to enrich Americans. He resented the way an apparently biased press had "praise enough for MacArthur, but very little for the commission."

Despite the political turbulence, Nellie was thoroughly contented in the Philippines. There they were the "first family," with a large estate at their disposal and the luxury of a multitude of servants. She and her unmarried sister Maria, the prettiest of the Herron sisters, were together until 1901, when the latter returned to care for their mother following a paralytic stroke. They arose late for breakfast, after Taft departed, and leisurely planned their daily routine. Nellie then gave instructions for lunch and dinner and proudly drove away with Maria in a carriage drawn by two grand black horses. An inveterate shopper, Nellie patronized various stores in downtown Manila until it was time to fetch daughter Helen at the College of St. Isabel and return home for lunch. Some mornings Nellie varied her routine by attending a whist club. After lunch she took an hour-long Spanish lesson and then napped. In late afternoon Nellie and Maria returned calls, often stopping on Manila's celebrated drive, the Luneta, where a military band played every evening after six.

The Tafts soon became acquainted with a "very nice lot of young army officers," as Taft phrased it, who were happy to dine with them and would gladly squire Nellie and Maria about. It was at this time that Archie Butt joined Taft and, along with Taft's secretary, Fred Carpenter, lived in the palace. As social aide, Butt was there to assist in arranging their frequent dinners, receptions, and balls.

Nellie was immensely pleased with her residence and all the pomp and ceremony that attended her position. The thirty-five-room palace stood in a twenty-acre park laid out in Spanish style with walks running all about and shaded by big palms. It stood at a bend of the Pasig River, which, though neither deep nor wide nor clear, was picturesque. Banana trees and palms and rows of elevated bamboo huts with thatched roofs stood along the banks, broken here and there by large stone churches, some of them in ruin. Taft especially liked the beautiful view of the distant mountains from the portico overhanging the river. For her sister-in-law, Nellie described her feelings about their new way of life: "Of course the position gives us a great deal of attention which I for one would never have otherwise and of course we feel we might as well make the best of it while we have the opportunity. We are really so grand now that it will be hard to descend to common doings. We have five carriages and two smaller vehicles, and fourteen ponies, a steam launch and dear knows how many servants." In *Recollections* she noted how she "felt a sense of the utmost satisfaction the first time we stepped into the governor's carriage for a drive . . . where we were sure to see everybody we knew."

In contrast to her social discontent during the Ohio years, Nellie in Manila kept up a constant round of parties and gave dinners at least once a week for a cosmopolitan assemblage. Her own record of these years reveals clearly her ambition and love of grandeur. Many large parties were held outdoors in the moonlight under the extensive porticos fronting the beautiful grounds. The scene was made brilliant by Chinese lanterns and gay costumes of the Spanish mestizos. A sixty-piece Constabulary band usually serenaded the company. She hired an entire orchestra for her second reception, "really a lovely affair," she decided, with one hundred guests, who sampled the tea, sandwiches, ices, and cakes. With such rounds of entertainment she soon felt the need to recruit additional Chinese servants.

At Christmas Louisa Taft sent her daughter-in-law twenty-two books including *Oliver Cromwell*, *The Problem of Asia*, and *The Mississippi Valley in the Civil War*, but Nellie found that there was now little time for either volunteer work or reading. She reveled in her heavy social schedule, occasionally interrupted while she was laid up with what Taft thought was stomach or liver trouble brought on by too much activity and excessive worrying over the success of her parties.

Nellie also made the most of her opportunities to travel. She planned and executed a daring journey of several weeks on horseback into seldom-visited parts of the Philippines, where, she announced, with a satisfaction at breaking precedents, "no white woman had ever been." Taft, who felt proud of her as "a woman who can do anything," always encouraged her. Privately she observed, "I should probably have gone without [his] advice, but it was comforting to have it." She also joined Taft on many of his excursions among the Islands, and on occasion the children accompanied them as well. Though fascinating, these trips were fraught with hazard. In January 1903, they toured three provinces—Laguna, Toyabas, and Batabgas—which still harbored insurrectionists. Traveling first by boat down a river so shallow that they continually struck bottom, they then proceeded on horseback before shifting to chairs, each carried by ten men over rough trails. The entourage reached San Pablo just in time for its fiesta day. Entry into the town of Lurban, one thousand two hundred feet above sea level, was "triumphal," and a great banquet awaited them. The town of Lipa greeted them with fireworks and a *baile*. The governor of Batabgas felt the weather was "too hot" and Taft "too large" to join the others in walking to the top of the volcano of Taal, from which vantage they would be able to peer down into a crater with three burning lakes. But Taft insisted on going along.

On another trip, they were invited to dine in an elevated native hut, accessible only by means of a bamboo ladder. An official's wife traveling with them held her breath, afraid that Judge Taft in mounting the ladder would literally "bring down the house." On a trip to Antique, the celebration planned in their honor included red, white, and blue arches decorated with ribbons and mottos such as "Hurrah to the Civil Commission USA." A wooden statue representing Liberty stood on a pedestal with the lettering "Wasington, Lincon, McKinly, Taff." At each dinner Taft made a business-like speech in his straightforward manner and then leaned back to enjoy his secretary's translation of his ideas into the mellifluous Spanish tongue. The chief hazard at every dinner lay in avoiding the appearance of ingratitude by declining any of the multitudinous courses. Refusing a sweet cake from an *amigo* could very well turn him into an *enemigo*. Filipino custom dictated that the hosts serve their guests at the table, a custom which required the strictest attention to native etiquette, lest any offence be given. At a thirty-two course banquet in Cebu, the leading men of the town waited on the Tafts. A noted Filipino judge, solemn and dignified, passed out the knives and forks. After each course he could be seen wiping them on a towel behind the door; he then dispersed them, but seldom to their original possessor. They returned home exhilarated though afflicted with "tropical bowel trouble," which lasted for weeks.

By herself Nellie visited Peking, Canton, Shanghai, Hong Kong, and Nagasaki. She and Maria also took trips together, reducing the house, Taft complained, "to a deadly dullness." He was happy to have Maria with them in the Philippines, in part because she helped keep his wife occupied and contented. A comment in one of his letters betrays his knowledge that he could not fill her place: "I look forward with considerable dread to the loneliness which will come over Nellie when Maria leaves here."

The children, too, relished their new experiences on the exotic island, especially Charlie, the "bad and incorrigible" little boy, upon whom they all doted. He slept in a crib in Nellie's room, while Taft had the room next door. Taft thought Nellie a slave to Charlie's every desire. She arranged a play room in the palace for him, and a court yard in the interior was given over to the children. Charlie had numerous pets, including two lively monkeys and a deer. As Helen and Bob both had ponies, she bought "Baby," as she called him, a tiny albino pony for which a miniature saddle was fashioned in leather. Looking remarkably like a young prince on a royal progress, Charlie rode the pony surrounded by his Filipino attendants and followed by his playmates. He enjoyed his social prerogatives as much as did his mother. Once the dressmaker threatened to take Charlie to his "papa" if he did not hold still, at which Charlie exclaimed, "You must not call Mr. Taft 'papa.' You must call him 'governor.' "

The Philippine experience accustomed Nellie to high life, and after living at the palace, nothing less than the White House could hold a similar attraction for her. Everyone who attended remembered the Venetian Carnival party which Nellie gave just prior to their departure from the Philippines in 1904. She had decided, appropriately, that the hosts should be costumed as the Doge of Venice and his consort. The guests arrived by water, landing at the palace in flower-laden canoes, rafts, and launches. The Filipino women, masked, bejeweled, and elaborately gowned, were serenaded with mandolins and guitars as they strolled under the multi-color lights. It was beautiful, but poignant, Taft wrote, for most of those present seemed to feel "that an era was ended."

Although the Tafts returned home in 1904, the "Taft era" in the Philippines actually extended to 1913, as a result of Taft's continuing close connection with the Islands, first as secretary of war and then as president of the United States. Although Taft's policies drew criticism from those opposed to American involvement, he nonetheless had avoided the worst features of nineteenth-century imperialism. More coincident with classical imperialism, Taft envisioned economic development of the Islands for the sake of the natives. They would be provided with education and public services, while the United States would gain access to raw materials and native products. In addition, Taft looked forward to eventual self-government for the Philippines. During the Taft era, nonetheless, Filipinization encompassed only the lower echelons of civil service and government offices, despite McKinley's original intention that Filipinos should control island affairs at all levels. Taft reasoned, to the dismay and frustration of upper-class Filipinos, that they must first prove their efficiency and ability. Until they did that, Americans would hold the top posts. Filipino political leaders pressed Taft for complete autonomy, and after 1904 Taft expressed much bitterness over their increasingly intemperate demands, for he found that they were no longer the tractable collaborators he had known as governor. He insisted that while economic stability and material progress could be achieved, complete political independence was probably undesirable at the time. The Philippines, he had come to believe, would be best off with dominion status. Under the American aegis it was not to end until 1946.

VI

TROUBLESHOOTER FOR ROOSEVELT AND SECRETARY OF WAR

1902–1908

In Washington Taft found Theodore Roosevelt in a new role. After William McKinley's death from an assassin's bullet on 14 September 1901, Roosevelt had at forty-three become president, the youngest man ever to hold the office. Millionaire industrialist Mark Hanna, McKinley's campaign manager, exploded upon realizing the "damned cowboy" was taking over: "I told William McKinley it was a mistake to nominate that wildman in Philadelphia." To Taft, Roosevelt was "just the same as ever," though he reported to Nellie, "it is very difficult for me to realize that he is the president." Taft was even more surprised that Roosevelt "greatly enjoys being president and shows not the slightest sign of worry."

Taft suffered considerable anxiety just in returning to Washington. He feared that his role in the Philippines might make him a controversial figure. Ever since the treaty following the Spanish-American War, there had been considerable opposition to the retention of the Far Eastern and the Caribbean possessions. Even after the Filipino revolt against American intervention was put down by the military and the second Philippine Commission headed by Taft was well established, congressional debate over the Islands continued, chiefly over home rule, education, and public health. Taft told Nellie of his fears that heated attacks would come: "I doubt not that your unworthy husband will be greatly criticized and condemned. . . . I do not enjoy the prominence I have in the fight and the prospect of the abuse to which I shall be subjected." But, he added, "I . . . must go through." Senator Cuberson of Texas charged Taft with deliberately withholding information and giving evasive and misleading testimony before a senate committee conducting hearings on Philippine matters. Ohio Senator Joseph Foraker jumped to his defense, declaring that "No man who has ever known Governor Taft has ever questioned his candor or his frankness." Taft half-wished he could "get out of the country" to avoid the attacks in Congress. He tried to impress upon Nellie the fact that his aversion to controversy and his inability to withstand criticism showed his unfitness for public life. She was not listening.

Taft left the country in May 1902 when Roosevelt sent him to the Vatican to negotiate with Pope Leo the sale of church lands in the Philippines to the United States. After this it became habitual for the president to employ Taft as his personal envoy or troubleshooter whenever some entanglement or crisis developed in a foreign country where the United States had a particular interest—Japan, Cuba, Panama. Although this arrangement was very convenient for Roosevelt, it caused a good deal of anguish for Taft, who particularly disliked being involved in unfamiliar or explosive situations. Nonetheless Taft labored mightily on each assignment not to disappoint his friend. He did his work well and on most missions met with considerable success.

His first task with the Pope was not especially troublesome, although it required a good deal of tact. Delicacy was necessary because the United States did not wish to send a formal diplomatic mission to Rome; that step would have constituted recognition of the Pope as a sovereign ruler, an intolerable act to many Protestant Americans. Although Taft grew fearful before embarking on his assignment, Nellie was elated at the prospect of European travel, which she saw as "another novel experience." But just before the boat was to sail in May 1902, their eldest son, Robert, contracted scarlet fever, and for a short time she had to remain behind. When Taft informed his mother of Robert's illness she replied, "Well, Will, I don't think you ought to make such a trip alone when you are so far from strong, so I just think I'll go with you in Nellie's place." Thus she, a youthful seventy-four, joined him.

Taft's progress in Rome was steady, and he wrote Nellie that "his Pontifical Nibs and I are quite chummy." As an added incentive for her to join him soon, he promised to show her a copy of his speech to the Pope and the reply as well as copies of all his correspondence with Secretary of State Elihu Root and others. Nellie arrived to find Louisa having a grand time going places, seeing people, and enjoying the attention of every man in the party, "whether he wore ecclesiastical frock, military uniform or plain citizens' clothes." Louisa wrote relatives at home that "Nellie is not at all timid and as she speaks French we can go anywhere," a quotation Nellie later included in her *Recollections*. The highlight of the trip for Nellie was a papal audience, with Louisa and the two oldest children, Robert and Helen, accompanying her. The pope concluded the interview by giving Robert a blessing and asking about his future intentions. The future senator quickly replied that he intended to be chief justice of the United States.

After more than a month in Italy, Taft sailed back to the Philippines in July, leaving the negotiations to grind on for several years more. Eventually the friars' lands in the Islands were purchased for seven million dollars, turned into public domain, and sold to individual Filipinos. In order to travel, Nellie stayed in Europe two months after Taft departed for home.

In anticipation of his return to his post in the Philippines, Taft grew upset because he thought the American papers in Manila would show him no favor. Despite his acknowledged success as governor and his general popularity, Taft was plagued with self-doubt, as at first. He was sustained by the love of the Filipino people, however, and even looked forward to "lots of hard work" as a comfort. He could execute with ease all legal, judicial, and routine administrative matters, and he took pleasure in the appreciation shown by those for whom he did "his duty." Taft's forebodings about the kind of reception he would get were soon dissipated. Upon his arrival in Manila he discovered the whole city to be in a state of excited celebration. It seemed as if every boat in the harbor came out to greet him. As he sailed up to the mouth of the Pasig River, whistles, bells, and sirens all over the bay and the city made a tremendous din. People watched and waved and cheered everywhere, from windows, roofs, walls, and river banks. What particularly moved him was the fact that the crowd included not just the well-to-do, but thousands of barefoot Filipinos in calicoes, who came from provinces near and far to welcome him.

During his stint as governor of the Philippines, Taft had been strongly tempted to leave his post for a position on the Supreme Court. Why he failed to take advantage of these opportunities has perplexed historians. Pringle, for example, avoids discussion of Taft's motives for refusing Roosevelt's two requests that he join the Court. Despite much evidence to the contrary (often in Taft's own words), Pringle states that Taft had, in accepting the Philippine appointment, made up his mind to pursue a political career and to forego his ambitions for the bench. Taft was, Pringle writes, "to abandon, for more than twenty years, any active desire to sit in the historic room which . . . had become the abode of the Supreme Court." Actually, Taft never ceased to desire a position on the Supreme Court, and he frequently expressed, during both the Philippine period and the years he served Roosevelt, that it was his dearest wish. As Nellie herself wrote, "he wanted [it] . . . as strongly as a man can ever want anything."

Taft's motives for declining the president's invitations, proffered in October 1902 and again in January 1903, become apparent through an examination of his psychological makeup. After the first offer in 1902 he confessed to his brother Charles, "Of course I should very much have liked to go on that bench, as you know, but it seemed to me that it would be flinching just at the wrong time." His departure would adversely affect the Islands, he felt, and it would be "considered by the Filipinos as an indication that severe and unpopular measures were about to be put in force." In reply to Roosevelt's second offer, which was tendered during another trip back to the United States, Taft gives us another clue to his seemingly mystifying behavior: "It has always been my dream to be in the Supreme Court, but . . . I should go straight back to the Philippines . . . for those people expect me back and believe I will not desert them." The Filipino people's warm display of affection for Taft made him feel he could not abandon them. He needed their love as much as they, his guidance. Unlike the military administrators of the Islands, Taft had opened the governor's residence to the natives, and by his willingness to entertain without regard to the color line, he had earned their loyalty and respect. Furthermore, as Nellie pointed out, Taft's "ready laugh and the cordiality of his manners . . . always had a peculiar charm for the Filipinos." Newspaperman Mark Sullivan wrote, "From the beginning, a relation of affection and confidence existed between this jovial fat man from Cincinnati and the heterogeneous tribes of little brown men of the Archipelago. . . . He encouraged them to call on him and Mrs. Taft, he disarmed them by the openness and freedom of his talk, charmed them by his simplicity." The Filipinos honored "Santo Taft," as they called him, with a "reverence that amounted almost to adoration."

Taft had a vast capacity for inspiring affection, but of equal importance was his own hunger for love. When problems associated with labor unions and business monopoly were plaguing Roosevelt in 1902, he informed Taft that he meant to call him home and put him on the Supreme Court. Upon learning that Taft might leave them, the Filipinos prepared a nonviolent, but tumultuous, revolt. They covered Manila with placards saying *Queremos Taft* (We want Taft), and cheering crowds surrounded the Malacanan Palace. Bands played and speeches were given declaring Governor Taft a saint and comparing him to Jesus Christ. Another popular demonstration on Taft's behalf ultimately influenced the president to change his mind. Even "the most 'intransigent' of the Filipinos," Taft wrote, had joined in asking Roosevelt to let him stay. After three such protests Roosevelt cabled Taft, "All right, you shall stay where you are, and I will get another man for the Court." The "judicial life is to my taste," Taft conceded to a friend, "but the work here is of great importance." To Charles he admitted that "the matter is not free from disappointment to me," but, as he wrote Horace, "I do not like to leave a job half done." "You have done a noble thing," Horace sympathized, adding: "The spontaneous movement of the Filipinos to keep you in the Islands must have more than repaid you for all the work and anxiety."

On this matter, Pringle is misleading. After describing how the day was a proud and happy one for Taft, Pringle adds, "the elation which surged through him was not greater even on that March day, in 1909, when he swore to defend, as president, the Constitution." In actuality, no two moments in Taft's life stand out in more striking contrast. Upon his inauguration he was anything but elated; he could not have been more filled with dread and discontent.

In addition to his sense of personal commitment to the Philippines, Taft was influenced by his wife. Nellie had no inclination to leave the Islands and absolutely none to return to the life of a judge's wife, a position she felt she had successfully transcended. While Taft was debating whether to take the Court appointment, he wrote that Nellie "was quite disappointed that I should be 'shelved' on the bench at my age." Nellie's insistence that her husband stay in his present post was seconded, furthermore, by Taft's mother and two of his brothers. Although Henry felt the bench would not fully utilize Taft's many talents, he was deeply concerned about his brother's happiness. "I really cannot quite reconcile myself with your finally choosing a judicial career at your age," Henry wrote, though "I have little doubt that you yourself would find the work most congenial." He concluded, "Of course you will understand that I would not have you embitter your life by seeking to satisfy ambition in politics; we all know how you have cherished the ambition to receive this appointment."

Their stay in the Philippines was not to last much longer, however, for on 27 March 1903 an offer came which suited Nellie's tastes and ambitions even more than did their present post. Roosevelt wanted Taft to become his secretary of war. Elihu Root was retiring from his cabinet, and he needed someone with legal knowledge. The president wrote:

> You will think I am a variety of the horse leech's daughter! The worst calamity that could happen to me officially is impending, because Root tells me that he will have to leave me next fall [1903]. I wish to heaven that I did not feel as strongly as I do about two or three men in the public service, notably Root and

you. But as I do, I want to ask you whether . . . you cannot [by then] come back and take his place.

Now I want you to give this your very careful thought, and I do not want you to mention it to a soul. . . . As secretary of war you would still have the ultimate control of the Philippine situation. . . .

Remember too the aid and comfort you would be to me . . . as my counsellor and advisor in all the great questions that come up.

P.S. If only there were three of you! (for the Supreme Court, secretary of war, and governor of the Philippines).

Taft soon discovered that Nellie was as eager for him to accept this post as she was discouraging on the offers to join the Supreme Court. The cabinet was, as she later wrote, "in line with . . . the kind of career I wanted for him and expected him to have." Despite her insistence, Taft was hesitant because the appointment was likely to involve him in the 1904 presidential campaign, which, experience had taught him, "would be most distasteful to me, for I have no love for American politics." Politics were to Nellie's taste however, which determined the issue. Bewildered, Taft later confided to a friend, "It seems strange that with an effort to keep out of politics and with my real dislike for it, I should thus be pitched into the middle of it."

Taft wondered whether Roosevelt was, in effect, demoting him. Upon becoming aware of Taft's self-doubts, the president took pains to reassure him that he was "the best man in the entire country" to govern the Philippines. "Good heavens, old man," Roosevelt expostulated, "it simply never occurred to me that you could dream I wanted to change you, except for the reason that I wanted to put you in what I regarded as an even bigger post near me."

Taft also worried—with humility—whether he possessed the abilities required for such a position: "I am seized with doubt as to my capacity to take up the enormous problems which [Root] has handled with such signal success, the contrast will prove, I fear, humiliating." "I do not know how much executive ability I have," he confessed to Nellie, and "I very much doubt my having a great deal." Although executive tasks later proved difficult for Taft during his presidency, he was not severely tested in the War Department where administration was an insignificant part of his work. Taft was aware, however, that he had "no particular aptitude for managing an army" and did not "know anything about it." Taft may have had nightmares about standing in front of a million men totally wanting any Napoleonic inspiration or inclination. He was happy to find that Roosevelt intended to manage the army himself. Taft instead became Roosevelt's jack-of-all-trades, confidant, and troubleshooter, now doing full time what he had done occasionally while serving as governor of the Philippines.

Taft was persuaded to accept the cabinet post, after twice rejecting Supreme Court appointments as we have seen, not least because Nellie encouraged him, because Roosevelt called upon him as a friend for help, and because as secretary of war he would not be deserting the Filipinos. To his mother he confided, "I am not sure but that I have made a mistake in accepting the president's invitation to enter his cabinet." Louisa Taft replied, "It is not strange that you wish to avoid the whirlwind of politics. . . . The chief justiceship is the place I covet for you." She consoled him, nevertheless, with the thought that a cabinet office would be "a stepping stone" to the Court.

Before him loomed the 1904 campaign. In contrast to his dismay, Nellie was jubilant and confident. She anticipated only one possible impediment to happiness: in Washington they could not live in the princely fashion they had enjoyed in the Philippines. The "expenses of living on a limited salary will make life rather hard for Nellie," Taft wrote to his mother. "You should see Nellie's lip curl," he told a friend, "at the suggestion of Sunday high teas and dinner parties without champagne." He expressed his financial concerns to Roosevelt, who replied that the Tafts should try to live modestly in Washington as he and his wife had done before he became president. Even now when they went to Oyster Bay, Roosevelt insisted, "we have two maids and live as any family of gentle-folk of small means should live. . . . Mrs. Roosevelt . . . never minded our not having champagne at our dinners."

Nellie was soon relieved from fears of penury by Taft's older brother Charles, who had married one of Ohio's richest heiresses. Always greatly interested in his half-brother's career, Charles began the generous outlays that not only enabled them to maintain a reasonably high standard of living but later helped finance Taft's campaign for the presidency. When they returned to Washington in 1904, Charles presented his brother with one thousand shares of Cleveland Gas Company stock which added eight thousand pretax and preinflationary dollars a year to their income.

Before leaving the Islands Nellie further enhanced their cash reserves with some horse trading which matches Thackeray's Becky Sharp's in shrewdness. Taft reported that she took considerable pride in having sold the Australian horses and carriage for $1100 and had plans for raising $800 more, in gold, for the black horses and the second carriage. Upon her return to Washington, as Nellie related in her memoirs, she met a woman who said to her, "Why, out there you were really a queen, and you come back here and are *just nobody!*" Nellie did not smile. She soon missed the luxuries of her Philippine life, complaining in particular that her cook and her Negro butler and maid were greatly inferior to her Chinese servants.

From the beginning of his tenure as secretary of war, Taft's relationship with Theodore Roosevelt was very friendly. The two men enjoyed such deep personal affection for one another that, as Archie Butt observed, it was "beautiful to see them together." There was so much harmony and camaraderie among Roosevelt, Taft, and the president's favorite assistant, Elihu Root, that they were nicknamed The Three Musketeers. Roosevelt had all the worries and responsibilities, and Taft was content just to work for him. Because he was kept so busy executing Roosevelt's commissions, Taft scarcely had time to give more than a passing thought to the affairs of the department. "I have had so much outside work to do," Taft admitted, "that I was entirely willing to turn the control all over to the chief of staff." He left the details of the department to subordinates, whereupon a dozen different men began to compete for control, a situation which eventually led to confusion and strife. In becoming secretary of war, Taft replaced an extremely dynamic and efficient leader and he suffered by comparison. Within a week after Elihu Root's departure, C.W. Thompson recalled, "persons having regular business at the War Department began to wear a look of missing something. The atmosphere was a little flat and tame after those pungent years."

Roosevelt's warm appreciation of Taft's assistance was immensely gratifying nevertheless, and the president sensed how important that reassurance was to him. "The president seems really to take much comfort that I am in his cabinet," Taft wrote proudly to Nellie. "He tells me so and then he tells people who tell me." As he grew more devoted to Roosevelt, Taft found it almost impossible to differ with him. Oscar King Davis of the *New York Times* recorded: "Taft was an open, and sometimes almost extreme supporter of the Roosevelt policies, and it was not unknown among Washington correspondents who were on terms of confidence at the White House that the President sometimes wished the Secretary of War were not quite so unrestrained in his utterances." Although Pringle notes Taft's obsessive insistence on being in complete agreement with Roosevelt, he fails to speculate about its causes or its significance. "One searches in vain," Pringle simply states, "for a major issue on which Taft took a stand, even in private, against Roosevelt." Donald Anderson, a more recent biographer, finds disagreement over at least three minor incidents, but nevertheless concludes that Taft "found little difficulty in subordinating his personal views to those of the President." Anderson is bewildered by Taft's wholehearted support of Roosevelt, doubting that any man—especially a conservative—could have served Roosevelt for five years without having second thoughts about many of the president's actions. Second thoughts, about substantive matters, never seem to have occurred to Taft. Eager for affection and approval, he agreed with Roosevelt even when it meant revising his own earlier views.

Roosevelt, whom friends often described as the most competitive man alive, clearly enjoyed Taft's faithful friendship and was intrigued by his obvious lack of political ambition. Ray Stannard Baker commented sardonically that Taft's amiability might explain why Roosevelt thought so highly of his war secretary's intelligence. But much more was involved—for example, genuine respect and warm admiration. Taft's booming laugh, his sunny, sweet nature, and his personal integrity quickly made him the greatest imaginable comfort to Roosevelt. "I know of no man in public life," Roosevelt personally complimented Taft, "who would be prompter than you to follow his own conscience . . . whether it hurt his future or not." Taft had strength, courage, clear insight, and practical common sense, as well as a very noble character, Roosevelt with complete sincerity personally informed historian Sir George Otto Trevelyan.

As a reward for doing the president's bidding, Taft asked only for Roosevelt's appreciation. Yet Roosevelt soon realized he had to express it continually, for Taft reacted with alarm and hurt even to mild criticism. Wounded, for example, by Roosevelt's mere suggestion that he delete proposals about cutting the tariff from his speeches, Taft felt their relationship might be at an end. In consternation and surprise, Roosevelt replied, "Fiddledeedee. I shall never send you another letter of complaint if it produces such awful results. As for your retiring from the cabinet, upon my word, Will, I think you have the nerves, or something." Even though this crisis was quickly resolved, Taft continued to consider complete agreement on every issue the necessary proof of friendship, a trait which later caused him many disasters as president.

Given their wide divergence in personal style and political outlook, Taft accommodated himself remarkably well to Roosevelt's views. Roosevelt, whose fierce and independent character was laced with a spirit of self-righteousness, became the symbol of progressive reform. Yet the Republican party, which had generally held power since the Civil War, stood for the gold standard, a high protective tariff, and government support for big business. At the top, the industrial elite amassed great fortunes, and thousands of smaller businessmen made good livings, but the masses of people worked long hours and sometimes earned barely subsistence wages. The spirit of materialism reigned triumphant; politics, the handmaiden of industry, was equally moved by it. Big businessmen desired and secured presidents who opposed progressive taxes and favored curbs on labor unions, as well as a foreign policy tied to expanding commercial and investment opportunities for American business overseas. Then Theodore Roosevelt burst onto the scene, and by the end of his seven years in office, the Republican forces were in disarray, divided in their views on the merits of reform.

Distinguishing between good and bad trusts, Roosevelt called for governmental regulation of businesses which restrained trade. He asked for a permanent Department of Commerce and Labor with the power to investigate the practices of corporations and to protect the rights of workers. Shock waves reverberated in business circles when the administration brought suit against the Northern Securities Company, for with that move Roosevelt was at once taking on J.P. Morgan, James J. Hill, and Edward H. Harriman, three of America's most powerful magnates. Upon Roosevelt's successfully wielding the heretofore ineffective Sherman Antitrust Act, the public and press saw him as "the trust buster." Roosevelt sought and secured several statutes intended to help small businessmen compete with big firms, including the Elkins Anti-Rebate Act empowering the federal courts to issue injunctions to prevent rebates to big-volume shippers. Always sensitive to public reaction, Roosevelt interpreted his growing popularity as a mandate to proceed with progressive reform, and after his great victory in the 1904 election, he moved securely ahead.

Unlike preceding presidents, all of whom had favored industry, Roosevelt sometimes sought to arbitrate between management and labor, especially demonstrating his sympathy for the latter during the Pennsylvania anthracite coal strike in 1902. Seeking an equitable resolution, Roosevelt became disenchanted with the mine owners because of their unresponsiveness to his personal efforts. In the coal dispute he took a pro-union stance, shocking the business community by breaking the precedent of federal intervention on behalf of the employers.

The Hepburn Act expanded the Interstate Commerce Commission and extended its authority to jurisdiction over railroad rates. The Pure Food and Drug Act and the Meat Inspection Act of 1906 met the public demand for legislation correcting abuses in those industries. Roosevelt also urged an investigation into child labor, warned that the use of injunctions in labor disputes could injure the workers' rights, and proposed a workmen's compensation measure for federal employees, though very few of these proposals resulted immediately in legislative action.

In the field of conservation Roosevelt achieved further legislative success. The Newlands Act of 1902 directed the proceeds from western land sales into dam construction and irrigation projects. Working with his friend Gifford Pinchot, chief of the Forestry Service in the Department of Agriculture, Roosevelt withdrew from public sale 150 million acres of forest lands, millions of acres of coal and phosphate lands, and several water power sites. In 1903 he vetoed a bill awarding to private interests dam construction privileges at Muscle Shoals. He oversaw a conservation conference in Washington in 1908 and appointed a National Conservation Commission with Pinchot as chairman.

Although the sum of Roosevelt's legislative achievements was not by modern standards lengthy or startling, his presidential record marks the beginning of a more complex attitude toward issues affecting powerful economic groups, and consequently the public welfare. It was chiefly Roosevelt's vigorous action, his enormous energy, his gift for rhetoric, his moralistic and patriotic pronouncements, his disdain for purely material ends, and his devotion to the national state which captured people's hearts and made businessmen uneasy about the future direction of Republican policy. Taft followed his friend's lead, happily acquiescing in Roosevelt's every action, including his expansion of executive power.

Roosevelt, increasingly confident of Taft's ability to manage special assignments, placed more burdens on him. Taft was absent from Washington more than any other member of the cabinet, with over two hundred and fifty-five days of his four-year tenure spent on special missions. At one point the War Department auditor received a complaint stating, "As a tax payer and citizen I beg to ask the following question: How many days, or if not days, hours, has Secretary of War William Taft spent at his desk in Washington?" Roosevelt finally suggested that Taft's brother Charles back his trips to quell the din about the government spending large sums of money for his travel expenses.

As Arthur Wallace Dunn later recalled, Taft had been a "veritable pack-horse" for the administration: "Roosevelt loaded tons of work upon his secretary of war and the harder he was pushed the better work he did." "I rather think I am to do more work than any other member of the cabinet," Taft told Nellie proudly, "but I don't object to that." Roosevelt initiated and Taft assisted. From personally observing their relationship, Mark Sullivan concluded that its conditions were ideal for both men. Taft—always "jovial, never excited, considerate and smiling"—exclaimed, "I love my chief and . . . I admire him from top to toe." Sullivan aptly concluded that Taft was "a comfortable receiver of place, and equally an able bearer of responsibility . . . a dutiful payer of the loyalty that the gift to him called for." Feeling secure in his relationship with Roosevelt, who expressed gratitude often for his "strength and comfort and help," Taft managed to reduce his weight from over 300 to 250 pounds. For Taft the progress toward true adulthood was impaired by his attachment to this second parent-substitute. Instead of learning to de-idealize his parents so that his own sense of confidence and self-esteem could develop from within, Taft idealized not only his wife, but also Roosevelt. Roosevelt was both mentor and father-leader in one.

VII

THE RELUCTANT
CANDIDATE
1905–1908

Before the national elections in 1908, Theodore Roosevelt, forty-eight years old and at the height of his national popularity, began to regret his declaration that after serving the remaining three years of McKinley's term and one elected term of his own, he would not run again. On election night, 1904, after he defeated the Democratic candidate Alton B. Parker, Roosevelt announced, "under no circumstances will I be a candidate for or accept another nomination." His attorney general, Frank Kellogg, later tried, unsuccessfully, to explain that Roosevelt made the statement because he was determined to do battle against the corporations and especially the railroads, along with all the other evils he thought needed throttling. He would be greatly hampered in his work, Roosevelt felt, if he planned to try for a third consecutive term. Later, in 1911, when Roosevelt prepared to contest the Republican nomination with Taft, his friend H.H. Kohlsaat suggested that his 1904 victory statement had been a mistake. Roosevelt looked intently at Kohlsaat, screwed up his mouth, and exclaimed, "I would cut that hand off there [indicating his wrist] if I could have recalled that statement."

In anticipation of the 1908 election Roosevelt was obliged to search for another candidate, preferably one who would carry on his policies. Although some people doubted if it was proper for Roosevelt to handpick his successor, the president felt no reservations. Secretary of State Elihu Root was Roosevelt's first choice, moving Taft to declare, "I should be personally delighted with this arrangement." Root, however, was "not willing to pay the price" of the nomination. "I would rather see Elihu Root in the White House," Roosevelt finally decided, "than any other man and would walk on my hands and knees from the White House to the Capitol to see Root made president. But I know it cannot be done. Wild horses couldn't drag him into making a public campaign." Referring to his disinclination for the job and to similar protests emanating from Taft, Root quipped that the ambition not to become president was one of the easiest goals in the world to gratify. Little could he imagine just how difficult a time Taft would have avoiding it. "Root would make the best president," Roosevelt concluded, "but Taft the best candidate." Root too thought Taft would be the best candidate, for Taft had a personality which made friends on contact, and in addition, he came from Ohio, the birthplace of presidents: Harrison, Hayes, Garfield, McKinley.

Charles Evans Hughes was another likely candidate, and many people expected Roosevelt to select him. Taft also felt Roosevelt might end up having to support Hughes for the presidency: "If you do you may be sure that you will awaken no feeling of disappointment on my part . . . it will leave not the slightest trace of disappointment." Roosevelt might have turned to Hughes were it not for a misunderstanding which had occurred when Hughes ran for governor of New York in 1906. Roosevelt vented his anger in a letter to Taft, calling Hughes "a thoroly selfish and cold-blooded creature. . . . When I strove to help him, he started the entire mugwump press cackling with glee about the way in which he had repudiated my help . . . and relied purely on the people." As his biographer Merle Pusey writes, after Hughes had rejected Roosevelt's aid, he was eliminated as a possible successor. "He was not a Roosevelt man in the sense of subordinating his judgment or his individuality to that of the famous Rough Rider," Pusey notes. Nonetheless many people respected Hughes's conscientiousness, his pure motives, his courage, and his desire for good, clean government.

Roosevelt finally turned to Taft, who had publicly endorsed his policies many times—"too fervently at times for the entire satisfaction of the President," said Oscar King Davis, reporter for the *New York Times*. Roosevelt also considered his loyal subordinate "the most loveable personality [he had] ever come in contact with." Furthermore, as Roosevelt told Davis, he had great regard for Taft's "stability and serenity." No matter what the issue, Roosevelt knew he could count on Taft's unqualified support. According to Davis, "in Cabinet meetings, or at gatherings of friends to say 'Isn't that so, Will?' was Roosevelt's way of getting what he regarded as . . . buttressing of his own opinions—an attitude never modified by the fact that at evening gatherings in the White House study, the question would sometimes wake Taft from a nap." Taft's lack of enthusiasm and drive—qualities with which

Theodore Roosevelt was, some thought, overendowed—had the effect of raising Roosevelt's estimation of the soundness of Taft's judgment.

Mr. Dooley, had his own observations to offer, of course, with respect to Roosevelt's selection process.

> It looks to me as though Tiddy was thryin' in a bunch iv green motormen to see whether they could run th' car th' way he wants it run. . . . An' now he's thryin' out Taft. Look at thim comin' up th' sthreet. Taft knows th' brakes well but he ain't very familyar with th' power. "Go ahead," says Rosenfelt. "Don't stop here. Pass that banker by. He's on'y wan fare. There's a crowd iv people at th' nex' corner. Stop f'r thim an' give thim time to get aboard. Now start th' car with a jump so they'll know something is goin' on. Go fast by Wall Sthreet an' ring th' gong, but stop an' let thim get aboord whin they're out iv breath. Who's that ol' lady standin' in th' middle iv th' sthreet wavin' an unbrelly? Oh, be Hivens, 'tis th' Constitution. Give her a good bump. No, she got out iv th' way. Ye'd iv nailed her if ye hadn't twisted th' brake. What ailed ye? Well, niver mind: we may get her comin' back."

In March 1907, the *Kansas City Times* printed this satirical poem suggesting Roosevelt's high-handedness.

> Says Roosevelt: "I announce no choice,
> To no man will I lend my voice,
> I have no private candidate,
> I care not whom you nominate—
> Just so it's Taft.
>
> The people are untrammeled, free,
> To pick out their own nominee,
> Far be it from me to dictate
> Who shall direct affairs of state—
> Just so it's Taft.

One evening in May 1906, Taft told Nellie, "I went to the White House for a long talk with the president. . . . He thinks I am the one to take his mantle." Though elated, Nellie began to harbor a deep distrust of Roosevelt's motives. She thought that he was using Taft as a stalking horse and planned ultimately to support either Root or Charles Evans Hughes or to capture the nomination for himself. Nellie could scarcely believe that Roosevelt would really relinquish such a position of unchallenged power and status, an act inconceivable to her. Mark Sullivan observed that she also distrusted Roosevelt because she mistakenly interpreted his eagerness to appoint her husband to the Supreme Court as a clear sign that he was hesitant to see Taft "make any progress toward the presidency." Nellie kept him busy reporting all that Roosevelt said and did. But whenever Taft told the president anything she had said, she became furious. He admitted to Roosevelt, for example, that Nellie had formed the impression that his first choice for the presidency was Charles Evans Hughes. "Mrs. Taft could not have told you that I said I might probably have to support Hughes for the presidency," Roosevelt replied, because he had never said it. "What I said," Roosevelt insisted, "was that you must not be too entirely aloof." Hughes, he reassured Taft, "is an honest and able man, but neither in intellect nor character is he for one moment to be compared to you."

Nellie reprimanded Taft for being so indiscreet. She knew Roosevelt had become somewhat annoyed by her persistent interference on her husband's behalf, and she well-remembered the day he had told her plainly that she was too ambitious. "He seems to think," she later fumed, "that I am consumed with an inordinate ambition [for you] to be president and that he must constantly warn me that you may never get there." Nellie now considered Roosevelt her chief competition, and she increasingly viewed him with distrust and hostility. Furthermore, she angrily reported, "he now says that while you are his first choice, that in case you are not persona grata to the powers that be, it may become necessary for him to support someone else." Regarding this word play as more Rooseveltian perfidy, Nellie said she felt like retorting, "D——you, support whom you want, for all I care."

Nellie's hostility to Roosevelt came naturally; she understood his ambition because she herself was equally charged with it. What she could not understand was Roosevelt's willingness to relinquish the presidency to her husband. That she would never have done had she been a man. But she did have a canny understanding of the nature of his ambition, and so was not at all surprised when he later turned against her husband. She had expected it as the most probable thing in the world—in 1909. As time told, she had been right in the essential thing. Nevertheless, when the split finally came, it angered her, angered her doubly because Roosevelt, campaigning in 1912 against Taft, demonstrated with every speech how much more talented he was and with every public appearance how greatly more beloved he was by the people.

Nellie began her own campaign as early as 1906 while Taft was engaged in another of those political speaking tours for Roosevelt that were so repugnant to him, this time for the congressional elections. Because she feared his performance in this endeavor might determine Roosevelt's decision later for or against him, Nellie was especially anxious that he do well. She followed the press accounts of his speechmaking, continually advising him. One of his dull speeches, she berated him, read like a judicial opinion and lacked snap and point. He acknowledged the merit of her criticisms and promised to revise it. Angry over his mentioning the politically sensitive tariff issue, she wrote, "I shouldn't wonder if your dragging the tariff into that Maine speech would cost you the nomination." The Washington papers, she fumed, gave his references to the tariff so much prominence that it appeared to be the principal subject of the speech.

Taft meanwhile complained about the campaign grind in letters home. "Politics when I am in it makes me sick," he wrote. "I hope it won't give you the blues to think about it, because you must put aside any hope in the direction of politics." The president had sent him on a "wild goose chase." "I do not think I make any votes with my speeches." When he complained to Roosevelt that his speeches would draw criticism, the president replied, "Now you beloved individual . . . you ludicrously exaggerate the weight of the attack that will be made upon you, [and] ascribe to yourself a culpability that is wholly nonexistent."

While Taft was away, Nellie, closely watching Washington politics, became upset by the clamor Republican Senator Joseph Foraker of Ohio was raising over the riot in Brownsville, Texas. Foraker felt little friendship for either Roosevelt or Taft, especially after Taft had rejected his offer of support in the presidential race in return for assistance in securing the Ohio governorship. The Brownsville episode arose when Roosevelt had, in a fit of rage, ordered the dishonorable discharge of several units of Negro troops whom he mistakenly believed were guilty of concealing the suspected murderer of a bartender in this notoriously anti-Negro town. Since Taft as secretary of war had issued the order dismissing the three companies, he had to suffer a share of Foraker's indignant criticism, even though Roosevelt issued a statement declaring that he bore the entire responsibility, that "no credit or blame" rested with Judge Taft. "The papers are still full of the Foraker row and I am glad you are not here to be wounded by it," Nellie wrote to her husband. "I fear it will be very injurious to your chances." Though not responsible for the manifestly racist Brownsville decision, Taft was even more apathetic about black rights than was Roosevelt, and he consistently and openly declared that the dismissals were entirely justified. Roosevelt told Taft not to let people think Foraker was getting the best of the argument or that he was afraid of standing up to the senator. "If possible," he urged, "you should give Foraker a mauling." But Taft had no stomach for a fracas.

Even as Taft's chances for the nomination steadily improved, Nellie's anxieties nevertheless mounted, for he would do nothing on his own behalf. He resisted being called an "avowed presidential candidate," though everyone considered him in the running. To Horace he complained that he would just have to face these misinterpretations of his actions. And misunderstood he was. "Secretary Taft is playing masterfully silent politics," one newspaper began its lead article. Actually Taft was in a state of terror. He wrote one brother that he hoped his early judicial decisions on labor cases in the 1890s had made him suitably undesirable as a candidate. And he hoped Roosevelt would save him by running again after all.

Knowing that his speeches were uninspiring, and smarting from occasional press criticism that he was too long-winded, he grew discouraged. Yet by alternating affectionate encouragement and gentle reprimand, Nellie kept him moving over a relatively smooth course. "Never mind if you cannot get off fireworks," she counseled soothingly. "It must be known by this time that that is not your style and there is no use trying to force it." Taft replied, "I need you to scold me." And scold she did, especially whenever Taft insisted in public that he should not be considered a serious candidate.

Right up to the day of the Republican convention, Taft "wiggled and squirmed," according to Nellie, and suggested other men for the job. "I very much enjoy being in the cabinet," he told Edward Lowry, "and shall be quite content if the nomination goes elsewhere." To another friend he confided, "Don't sit up nights thinking about making me president. . . . Any party which would nominate me would make a great mistake." Earlier Taft had said to his brother Charles, "The horrors of a modern presidential campaign and the political troubles of the successful candidate, rob the office of the slightest attraction for me." Taft truly believed in his father's statement that "To be chief justice is more than to be president."

Although he made known again and again his lack of interest in the presidency, at no time did he move decisively to crush Nellie's and Roosevelt's hopes. As a consequence he was bound to appear at least ambivalent. "Few . . . will credit me with anything but a desire, unconscious perhaps, to run for the presidency," he said; "I must face and bear this misconstruction." To Nellie he wrote that Roosevelt "evidently thinks that I am not sincere in my statement that I don't take any interest." "I think what the president is anxious to do is stir you up to stir me up to take more interest in the presidential campaign."

Indeed, Roosevelt did turn to Nellie to prod him. Roosevelt confided to her that he was getting complaints from politicians that her husband had turned them down "by saying coldly" that he was "not a candidate." In turn Nellie warned Taft, "You must be more encouraging." Desperately Taft turned to the one source of comfort left—his mother. Louisa had opposed from the beginning any talk of his candidacy. She cautioned him, "Roosevelt is a good fighter and enjoys it, but the malice of politics would make you miserable." "I do not want my son to be president, he is not my candidate," Louisa insisted publicly just before his nomination. "A place on the Supreme

Bench, where my boy would administer justice, is my ambition for him. His is a judicial mind, and he loves the law. . . . He has not sought to be a candidate for it; it has been thrust upon him. I know that he does not want it, and that his views are the same as mine."

To enhance Taft's stature as the prospective nominee, in late 1907 Roosevelt sent him on a trip around the world. Taft's knowledge of foreign affairs, especially the Far East, was a strong asset, and Roosevelt intended to capitalize on it. Ostensibly Taft was going abroad to attend the opening of the first Philippine Assembly, but publicity was the chief goal. Roosevelt also wanted him to placate the Japanese, who were outraged at the discriminatory treatment of Japanese immigrants in California and other western states. He charged Taft with the delicate task of negotiating substantial decreases in Japanese emigration and simultaneously of soothing Japanese sensibilities. "There is a good deal of fun connected with the trip," Taft wrote Horace, but also "a good deal of work, a good deal of nervous strain." "'Tis all a gamble [in the presidential race] and I shall not be disappointed if I come back to find the whole thing is 'busted'."

Although Taft's mother was ill, she would not hear of him postponing his plans. "No Taft to my knowledge," Louisa wrote in her last letter to him, "has ever yet neglected a public duty for the sake of gratifying a private desire. You promised the Filipinos that you would be present at the opening of their first Assembly, and if you should break that promise and neglect your plain duty on my account, it would give me no pleasure."

On their way to the West Coast for embarkation on the *Rainbow*, the Tafts took a three-day excursion to Yellowstone National Park. After dinner at Old Faithful Inn, they joined a whist game in the lobby. The next morning, Taft recalled, Nellie came to him "frightened to death," saying that "she had just realized that they were playing cards on Sunday instead of Saturday, and that somebody would report that." Taft's Unitarian affiliation had already offended many potential voters, but the incident of the card game was kept secret. Nellie overlooked no detail that might affect his chances for nomination.

Taft and Nellie covered twenty-four thousand miles and visited eight countries. For their warm reception in Japan, Taft was grateful and later reported to Roosevelt that the Japanese government indicated no desire for war, a declaration which had rather startled him when it was made. In Shanghai, after the Chinese merchants entertained them at a lavish garden party, Taft delivered a speech on the subject of American attitudes toward the development of China. In a letter to Roosevelt, Taft ascribed the friendliness of their reception to Chinese fears of Japan, Russia, and England: "They know that we do not want to take any of their territory and that we don't ask any exclusive privileges."

Their next stop was the Philippines, where their reception proved "flattering and cordial." He revived many old friendships and took satisfaction in the improved business and agricultural conditions in the Islands. The *Rainbow* then took them to Vladivostock in early November, where they were entertained splendidly by Prince and Princess Bariatinski. Roosevelt was annoyed by public criticism over Taft's "going about to visit Kings," and Elihu Root was resentful that he was "getting into the foreign relations business." The Tafts set off for Moscow on a twelve-day railroad trip across Siberia in a private car. There they were "royally entertained" by the governor-general and permitted to see the Kremlin's treasures. After three days in St. Petersburg, they left for Berlin and Hamburg, sailing home in December on the *General Grant*. By then Roosevelt thought it politically unwise for Taft to visit any more European courts.

On board ship Taft received a message from Harry reporting their mother's death. Deeply saddened he felt even sadder for Louisa's sister Delia, whose heart was almost broken by the loss of so beloved a sister and companion. Louisa Taft died at a time when her son's career was about to take a critical turn. Arriving back in the United States in December 1907, Taft soon learned that Roosevelt had publicly recognized him as his successor.

VIII

"THE AWFUL AGONY":
Campaign and Inauguration
1908–1909

Theodore Roosevelt chose to support William Howard Taft for the Republican nomination in 1908 chiefly because, in his words, "I believe with all my soul that Taft . . . represents the principles for which I stand. His policies, . . . purposes, and ideals are the same as mine." Taft's fervent endorsements of Roosevelt's policies were, however, a source of irritation to Nellie, who suspected that the president was actually seeking his own renomination. Therefore Nellie wanted her husband to assume a far more independent stance in preparation for a convention battle which she conceived was imminent. In exasperation she wrote, "I do hope . . . that you are not going to make any more speeches on the 'Roosevelt policies' as I think they need to be let alone for the present." Her fears of political machinations increased, and she became agitated as the date of the Republican convention grew nearer. Could Roosevelt smash all her hopes at the last moment, just when her chief desire in life was about to be fulfilled? Nellie knew the vulnerability of her position. She was well aware of the large, enthusiastic following Roosevelt commanded and of the minimal degree of political support Taft inspired on his own. If Roosevelt decided on another term after all or switched to another candidate, she knew her husband would not have the faintest hope for the nomination.

Actually Roosevelt was sincere in his support. His energies were devoted to convincing his most ardent followers to assist in Taft's nomination. There was opposition even among Roosevelt's closest friends, Ike Hoover noted, but he "rode over them all rough shod. It was a pleasure to see him take up the gauntlet. He had never been so fierce when fighting his own battle four years previously."

Sensitive to labor hostility, Roosevelt tactfully told Taft, who was a friend of many large industrialists, to avoid staying at private homes in the future: "Go to a hotel," he advised, "and give everybody a fair show at you." Aware of Taft's propensity to talk unguardedly to reporters, Roosevelt coached and advised, "Don't talk on delicate subjects where there is a chance of twisting your words." The president's concern extended to anything Taft prepared for press release as well as what he said informally. Taft was to say nothing for publication until they had talked it over. Planning and strategy were precisely Roosevelt's strengths, and he proceeded, while keeping Taft under close surveillance, to lay the ground for Taft's conquest at the June convention. Ironically, Nellie's staunchest ally was the man she had fancied would be her greatest potential enemy.

Some time prior to the convention Roosevelt charged a few of his closest associates, Arthur Vorys, Myron Herrick, Nick Longworth, and Frank Hitchcock, with the task of securing pledges for Taft. In early June he explained to Henry Cabot Lodge, "Of course everything I can do for Taft's success will be done, but after all, most of what I can thus do has already been done, and I do not wish to become officious or a busybody." Disturbed by the speculation in some quarters that he might be coveting another term, Roosevelt assured his friend Lyman Abbott, "I doubt if Taft himself could be more anxious than I am that [he] be nominated, and that any stampede to me be prevented." In correspondence with Taft, he disavowed the charges of the Democratic press that he was "trying to force you down the throats of a reluctant people" or "merely using you as a stalking horse to gratify my own ambition." Although Roosevelt would have had difficulty understanding Taft's sentiments, his handpicked candidate was in fact hoping that the suspicions about Roosevelt's intentions proved true.

With more sincerity than reporters could surmise, Taft told them just before the convention, "I'd rather not say what I think of happenings in Chicago. Besides I am the man least interested." Roosevelt made a public virtue of Taft's private reluctance to help himself by ascribing it to his "utter disinterestedness." However, he took all precautions against an uncontrollable movement at the convention to renominate him and prepared a letter which was "to be shown quietly to any of the Taft delegates who show the slightest symptoms of going for me." Mark Sullivan observed that Roosevelt "devoted all his political resourcefulness" to forcing Taft upon the convention. Roosevelt was like a father who delighted in his political potency by "promoting the fortunes of a particularly beloved son." Such a description aptly applies not only to Roosevelt, but to the recipient of his paternal concern as well, for Taft, though a year older, consistently related to the president much as a son might act toward a revered and powerful father.

Several days before the opening of the Republican National Convention in Chicago on 16 June, the usual multitude of visitors rushed into town, but reporters noted that the crowd was not as large as they had anticipated and the enthusiasm was less feverish than on past occasions. The party had seen to it, however, that the streets were ablaze with lights, the tallest buildings festooned with flags and bunting, and Taft posters were everywhere.

The headquarters of the candidates sounded with glee clubs and the streets with marching bands. Cries of "Taft, Taft" "Knox, Knox" rang out in the city. Political pundits reckoned that Taft would probably be able to win the nomination on the first ballot. Frank Hitchcock and Roosevelt's private secretary, William Loeb, excelled in lining up delegates. Of 194 Southern delegates, they had secured 128; of 125 delegates who were federal officeholders, 97 declared for Taft. Before the convention opened, 563 delegates were committed to Taft—72 more than he needed for the nomination. According to the *Washington Post*, nothing short of a "sudden and hysterical upheaval" at the convention could prevent Taft's nomination.

Yet an undercurrent of feeling that Roosevelt might be persuaded to run persisted. It seemed to grow stronger as opening day neared, and some believed the conventioneers would peremptorily refuse to allow the president to retire. The anti-Taft group, known as the Allies, included such men as Governor Charles Evans Hughes of New York, Senator Philander Knox of Pennsylvania, Vice-President Charles Fairbanks, and Senator Robert LaFollette, the former governor of Wisconsin. They had, however, no consensus on an alternate if Roosevelt could not be renominated, for Old Guard Allies like Cannon and Senator Murray Crane of Massachusetts vowed never to accept a progressive like Hughes or Knox. A *Washington Post* editorial pointed out that with the exception of Rutherford B. Hayes, Taft was less known to the public than any other Republican ever seriously considered for the presidency. If Taft came to the convention he could not only enliven what promised to be a "tame affair," the editorial suggested, but he could "remove in ten minutes the reproach that he is merely another man's selection." But Taft had no intention at all of attending the convention.

When the convention assembled in the huge stone Gothic pile known as the Chicago Coliseum, reporters immediately noted with disappointment that it was likely to prove a colorless affair. The delegates sat stolidly in their seats "like mourners at a funeral," determined to nominate whomever the man in Washington with the big stick decreed. Roosevelt wanted the convention to choose the historian and Senator from Indiana, Albert Beveridge, as temporary chairman, but the conservative majority chose instead Senator Julius Burrows of Michigan. Burrow's keynote address was long and dull. The only lively moments came when Burrows reluctantly managed to choke out Roosevelt's name. Whenever he did so, a great shout went up from every side, drowning out his voice: the delegates sprang to their feet, waved their hats, echoing back the tumult of the galleries, where fluttering handkerchiefs, fans, and parasols broke into moving color. Thereafter, every mention of the president's name brought a similar wave of enthusiastic tribute, which broke the monotony of the otherwise lackluster convention. Burrows never once mentioned William Howard Taft. Nothing could have prevented Roosevelt's nomination had he withdrawn his promise not to run.

After Chairman New swung the huge gavel at noon to open the proceedings, Claude Watts of Columbus, Ohio, unfurled a large painting of Taft which he held aloft and carried up to the platform. The idea was, of course, to set off a vigorous Taft demonstration, but the plan fell flat. Although a few delegates from California stood up and cheered, and a few others applauded, the thousands of delegates and visitors packed into the convention hall remained portentously silent.

The next day the convention crowd put on a spontaneous and frenzied demonstration—but not for Taft. The torrent of cheers and applause again erupted solely at the mention of Roosevelt's name. The convention had been plodding along lifelessly when the permanent chairman, Senator Henry Cabot Lodge remarked, "The president is the most abused and [yet] the most popular man in the United States today." That statement touched off a forty-nine minute stampede for Roosevelt. The floodgates were opened and swept everything before it, the *Post* reported. The *Herald Tribune* reporters described the demonstration as a volley of cheers, yells, and whistles that threatened to blow the roof off. The convention approached "the verge of a good-natured riot." Teddy bears bobbed up and down while the audience of ten thousand men and women shouted itself hoarse with the slogan, "Four, four, four years more!" Meanwhile, Chairman Lodge, who earlier had strolled along the platform and blown a kiss to Alice Roosevelt in the gallery, now began to strike the table with his black-beribboned gavel and to call for order, but in vain. He finally in desperation ordered a roll-call. When the tumult quieted down, the convention once more became listless.

To forestall any plans based on the hope that Roosevelt might change his mind and run, Lodge quickly announced that "no man is a friend to Theodore Roosevelt who, from any motive, seeks to urge him as a candidate for the great office which he has finally declined." Fearing disbelief, Lodge reiterated, "He says what he means and he means what he says." "So do we," was the response from the gallery. But with that, the delegates accepted Lodge's statement as coming from Roosevelt himself.

Seven candidates were placed in nomination—Speaker Cannon, Vice-President Fairbanks, Governor Hughes, Senator Foraker of Ohio, Senator Knox, Senator LaFollette, and Taft. Hisses and catcalls came from the galleries as Arkansas, California, Colorado, and Connecticut cast their votes for Taft. "Pay no attention to the crowd," Senator Lodge told the clerks, "I shall not have the president nominated by a Chicago mob." The chairmen of the various delegations, unable to make their voices heard above the din, had to go up to the platform and yell the votes of their states into the secretary's ear. By the time the secretary called for Kentucky's vote the crowd had quieted down. But when Pennsylvania cast 64 votes for Knox, 1 for Taft, and 3 for Roosevelt, the galleries greeted the announcement with a resounding cheer. The final count gave to Taft 702 votes, Knox 68, Hughes 67, Cannon 58, Fairbanks 40, LaFollette 25, Foraker 16, and Roosevelt 3.

The only remaining question was the selection of a vice-presidential nominee. Most interested parties looked to Roosevelt for the decision, although the *Evening Star*, which had been dismayed at the extent of Roosevelt's influence over the proceedings, supposed that Taft would probably be consulted before the candidate was named. When the Iowa delegation sent to the president a telegram requesting that he not insist upon naming their own Senator Dolliver for the vice-presidential slot, the *Star* expressed outrage: "Mark you, the message was sent not to the nominee, the man who might rightfully be consulted about the choice, but to the President." Difficulties arose when in quick succession several nominees refused the offer—Senator Jonathan Dolliver of Iowa, Senator Long of Kansas, incumbent Vice-President Fairbanks, Charles Evans Hughes, and Albert Beveridge. Speaker Cannon then rounded up support for "Sunny Jim" Sherman, a rotund, ruddy-faced congressman from New York. The delegates followed Cannon's lead and Sherman was chosen to run with Taft.

The *London Times* called the convention "the greatest and most striking of all Roosevelt's many victories."

As the balloting in Chicago was taking place, Taft, in Washington, seemed uninterested; Nellie, however, was tense and nervous, ever distrustful of what Roosevelt might do. As bulletins on developments at the convention arrived over the special teletype machine set up in an adjacent room, Charlie Taft, their youngest son, rushed them into Taft's office. He presented the bulletins to his mother, not his father. Charlie then listened while Nellie read the information to Taft and their guests. Finally Charlie came in with the bulletin announcing his father's nomination. Nellie's face turned pale, sitting "white as marble and motionless," she read the announcement with visible effort. She had triumphed.

Almost immediately Nellie was bubbling over with happiness, and all the evidence of the nervous strain which had shown on her face during the afternoon disappeared. She was "aglow with excitement." As news of his nomination was re-confirmed by a later telegraphic message, Taft turned first to his wife: "Oh Will!" Nellie cried, while kissing him. At that Taft beamed and seemed "as happy as a big boy."

Henry L. Stoddard, who was present in the war secretary's office when the news of Taft's nomination arrived, later wrote: "Mrs. Taft sat in her husband's chair at his desk in the center of the room, while he sat at one side. [Taft] sat calm and composed during this time, but Mrs. Taft was obviously in great agitation. 'I only want it to last more than forty-nine minutes,' she exclaimed, 'I want to get even for the scare that Roosevelt's cheer of forty-nine minutes gave me yesterday.' Mr. Taft merely smiled and said, 'Oh, my dear, my dear!' "

On that same day President Roosevelt sat at his desk in the White House alone, enjoying each bulletin confirming his power over the convention. He refused, however, despite his interest in the proceedings, to give up his tennis game, and he was on the court when news of Taft's nomination arrived. Later, Roosevelt dictated a victory announcement for release to the press. He expressed his delight over the result to friends and reporters: "Don't waste any sympathy on me," he said briskly and cheerily. "I have enjoyed every minute of my stay here. . . . I have had a perfectly corking time."

With the nomination secured, Taft left his office for an inspection of the Army War College, and returned home in the early evening. Meanwhile telegrams and messages were pouring in—including one from Horace at the Taft School which said, "We are jubilant. Discipline gone to smash." But Taft read none of them for he was late to dinner and very hungry. Mrs. Taft and her daughter stood at the door receiving callers while Taft calmly ate his dinner.

A group of men from the University Club assembled outside to serenade the victor and his wife. Later Taft joined her on the porch, happy to see the revelers but apprehensive lest they expected anything of him in return. "My fellow members of the University Club," he addressed them, and after expressing his thanks he pleaded with them, "You don't expect me to make a speech tonight—much less a political speech." Then he turned toward his wife and exclaimed, "I thank you on behalf of the real ruler of the family, the lady who . . . is near by looking on and listening." Taft slept soundly that night and was uncharacteristically late for breakfast the next morning.

Regarding Taft's nomination, the president wrote to the English historian George Otto Trevelyan that it was a "curious contest . . . for I have had to fight tooth and nail against being nominated myself. I could not have prevented it at all unless I had thrown myself heart and soul into the business of nominating Taft and had shown to the country that he stood for exactly the same principles and policies that I did." And to Sidney Brooks he wrote, "I wisht to see Taft elected as my successor so that my policies could be continued. I fought hard and openly for him." Among those who did not find this interference a matter for complacency was Henry Stoddard, who angrily declared that Roosevelt's nomination of Taft "represented an unfortunate, unpardonable exercise of presidential power over a party convention."

With the excitement over, the nominee had to face the dreadful task, as he saw it, of writing an acceptance speech. When Taft communicated his anxiety, Roosevelt replied soothingly, "Of course your speech hangs over you like a nightmare," but it is destined to be one of the "great utterances of the campaign." Afraid nevertheless that Taft might put it off too long, he hastened to add, "You cannot work too carefully over it." Taft sought and received suggestions and ideas from family and friends. The speech grew to a length of seven thousand words—and covered the tariff, trusts, railroad legislation, labor injunctions. Roosevelt tactfully criticized Taft's legal style, advising him to cut such possibly self-damning passages as, 'there are new propositions not considered by the Republican party, and upon which, without further consideration, you do not feel justified in expressing an opinion.' He also objected to particular phrases "which would not please the Negro and would displease the white," to several pages about the injunction, and to the sections expressing Taft's views on the identity of interest of labor and management. Finally, in agreement with Nellie, Roosevelt suggested that the number of direct references to the president ought to be reduced. Oscar King Davis of the New York *Times* saw a draft of the address and suggested that much of the material might be saved for future speeches: "Mr. Taft heard me, all through, good-naturedly. Then he got up from the sofa and came over to the chair where I was sitting. 'That's a long, hard work,' he said." The speech was left untouched.

The address, lavish in its praise of Roosevelt, pleased the president, but not Nellie. Taft announced that after the Republicans won, "the essence of the next administration is to complete and perfect the machinery by which [Roosevelt's policies] . . . may be maintained." On the next day the *New York Times* dryly commented, "We had hoped that Mr. Taft would put more of himself and something less of Mr. Roosevelt into his speech of acceptance." And the *New York World* queried, "The speech leaves one question unresolved—will Taft be a President or a proxy?"

The Democrats nominated William Jennings Bryan to oppose Taft, in what was to be his third presidential race. From the start, the Democratic national convention at Denver belonged to Bryan. Alton B. Parker's resounding defeat by Roosevelt in 1904 left him with little chance for a second nomination, and weak candidates such as Judge Gray of Delaware and Governor John A. Johnston of Minnesota had little hope of succeeding. As the *Wall Street Journal* marveled, Bryan had "built up a personal following unparallelled for one with a record of nothing but defeat, and with no patronage to strengthen his control." Denver welcomed the Democrats with free shows featuring cowboys and Indians, but there was no more excitement inside the hall than in the Chicago arena. Bryan stayed at home in Lincoln, Nebraska, having already outlined the platform on which he wished to run. He won the nomination by an overwhelming majority and as his choice for vice-president, he nominated his friend, the Indiana lawyer John W. Kern. George Harvey, an anti-Bryan, conservative Democrat, thereupon remarked bitterly, "The Democrats will now resume their accustomed occupation of electing a Republican president."

Taft immediately began to worry that Bryan might mention him in his acceptance speech. "I find myself a bit nervous over what he may say for I am unused to occupying a personal position in a campaign," he told Roosevelt. The president responded buoyantly, "Don't be in the least nervous. Whatever he does, we will beat him all right." Still happily in control, Roosevelt was already preparing an attack which would "riddle" the Democratic platform.

Nellie was overjoyed at the prospect of confronting Bryan, but her husband remained fearful and apathetic. "The next four months are going to be a kind of nightmare for me," he wanly remarked. In response to questions about his plans for the summer, Taft told the press he had not even decided where to spend the next few months. "I just haven't got as far as that yet." Before the drudgery began, however, Taft savored some of the rewards of victory. Returning to Ohio and Cincinnati for a brief visit, he was deeply touched by the enthusiastic receptions a presidential candidate enjoyed in his home state.

Taft's first desire was for some recreation to take his mind off the campaign ahead. The location he chose, with its pleasant, hilly golf links, was the Homestead, a resort in Hot Springs, Virginia. There Taft took up the game which later became his major indulgence when he sought to escape the demands of the presidency and its duties. He at the same time devised his alibi for spending so much time at golf: he required the exercise in order to reduce. To the press he announced that 297 pounds was too much to carry through a campaign, and he hoped to drop 25 or 30 of them before he started. While in the White House, he went on to gain an additional 55. Taft also began the regular horseback riding which he was to enjoy so much when he became president. Roosevelt had discouraged his secretary of war from riding because he felt it was "dangerous for him and cruelty to the horse." One day his horse collapsed beneath him, and the search for a sturdier horse was publicized. "I have got one so big," one humorous citizen wrote to the White House, "that I had to build a special stall to keep him in. He's twenty-five hands high (8′4″) and weighs three thousand five hundred pounds. I am sending him on free by freight."

After his nomination, Stoddard recalled, Taft was a listless candidate—but what he lacked in the political arena he made up for on the golf links, where he played ever more persistently and keenly. Roosevelt had assumed, of course, that Taft would have few opportunities to play golf until after the election: "Whether you have the chance or not, I hope you won't. I have received literally hundreds of letters . . . protesting about it." Although Roosevelt had regularly played tennis while president, his partners kept quiet about it. And unlike Taft, he never allowed photographs. Roosevelt's admonitions embarrassed Taft, and he explained that newsmen had "magnified the golf and other things because there was so very little other news for them at Hot Springs." Yet in August he told reporters that "golf precludes, for the time being, all thought of business cares and worries." He complained to his Aunt Delia that his summer was interrupted only by "the notification ceremonies and the speech of acceptance." By September, several months after the convention, he was still golfing as much as possible and avoiding all political activity. Luckily several newspaper correspondents assigned to cover him during the campaign were golfers also.

Anxious to hide from the public the truth of Taft's reluctance to enter the fray, his campaign managers often wrote press announcements for him. Senator Joseph Dixon of Montana told the press that "it is not true that Mr. Taft is dodging Mr. Bryan . . . I want the people to know that Judge Taft is pulling at the bit and anxious to get to them. His only regret is that he has not been able to start the campaign earlier."

Taft succeeded in delaying his first tour until the end of September. His managers had mapped out an itinerary, he wrote to Roosevelt defensively, that would show sufficient activity "to remove any doubt that I am in the campaign." To Nellie he reported how greatly cheered he was to find that the people were receiving his speeches enthusiastically. At first his fear was that he would not be able to hold an audience; now, he informed her, he worried that his voice was growing hoarse and might not hold out. Alarmed, she quickly replied that she was dreadfully concerned. The idea of his not being able to speak, she later wrote, had "frightened me from the beginning." She was "so jubilant" until she learned that.

Nellie's excitement during the campaign was, on the whole, immense. "I can hardly wait for the evening paper," she wrote him, "to see how you got through the day." Her counsel was continually forthcoming. "Your answer to Foraker was quite right," she wrote when he successfully withstood one attack. But she grew exasperated because he would not assail Foraker again when the newspapers charged him with having a compromising alliance with Standard Oil. Instead, the genial candidate announced publicly, "I won't hit a man when he is down for all the votes in the United States." When she saw occasional reports in the newspapers of potentially damaging utterances which he had inadvertently made, she was frantic. "I lay awake three hours last night and worried," she reproved him. "I hope that they [his managers] will continue to wire me as I am frightfully nervous."

Once Taft had been nominated, Roosevelt initially planned to avoid further involvement in the campaign, since there would be little for him to do. His secretary, William Loeb, speaking for the president, told the press that "under no conditions or circumstances" would Roosevelt take to the stump for Taft. "It's quite out of the question." But Roosevelt soon saw the danger in leaving everything up to Taft. Not only was Taft an indifferent campaigner, but he seemed unable to cope with political details. Roosevelt had, as Charles Thompson expressed it, "to watch over Taft like a hen over her chickens." A friend, accompanying Taft when he made his first speech in Brook, Indiana, afterwards told interested parties why it had been such a dud. Taft, he said, read to these landbound midwesterners "his views on the Philippines and an adequate coast defense system." Speaking to a crowd at the Cumberland station in Maryland, Taft, unaware precisely of where he was, expressed thanks for the solid vote which West Virginia had given him at the convention.

When he was "tricked" into agreeing to speak in Chicago at the same time that Bryan was scheduled to visit the city, Taft wrote to Roosevelt for help. No second invitation was necessary. The president jubilantly entered the campaign, craving for a good battle and a little excitement. "Painstakingly, and also joyously," Mark Sullivan observed, "Roosevelt took the role of trainer." Taft, happily relieved to have Roosevelt actively interceding, appealed almost daily to him for guidance, especially in handling the various suppliants who approached him.

Each time Taft spoke too freely to reporters, Roosevelt hurriedly would admonish him, "Great Heavens, Will, I hope that the next time you will let me know privately and in advance if there is anything like this on foot"; "You will have to act with great caution in every . . . matter"; "Be careful what you commit yourself to"; "I believe you will be elected *if we can keep things as they are;* so be *very* careful to say nothing, not one sentence, that can be misconstrued and that can give a handle for effective attack."

Taft also turned to Roosevelt for assistance in speechmaking. He preferred subjects he knew well—America's involvement in the Philippines or matters of judicial import—and was disinclined to talk about most other subjects. Roosevelt particularly warned him off the prohibition controversy. "I think you will have to speak on the government guaranty of deposit business," Roosevelt wrote, adding, "Of course, it is very difficult for one man to advise another just how to go at a thing. . . . I should go hard at Bryan and the Bryanites, on this as on other matters. . . . Point out that your chief care is for the small depositer." Then, to alarm no one, "say that . . . you are delighted to consider any plan for protecting the large depositors." Or he would make suggestions, such as the need to "challenge Bryan on his record." Archie Butt, Roosevelt's aide and companion at this time, wrote his mother that the president was "too funny when he described the making of Taft into a popular campaigner." Roosevelt told Taft that he simply had to stop citing his previous court decisions since people at once cease to understand and promptly begin to nod. "I think Mr. Taft thought I was a barbarian and a mountebank at first," Roosevelt chuckled with glee.

Mr. Dooley offered the following dialogue for the instruction of his readers:

> Says Willum: 'I've wrote an answer to Bryan's letter,' says he,
>
> 'Read it to me,' says Tiddy.
>
> 'This is th' way it starts,' says Willum. 'Dear Mr. Bryan, ye ar-re doubtless unaware that undher th' rulins' iv th' Probate Court f'r th' First Disthrict iv Utah—'
>
> 'Hold on there, Willum,' says Tiddy. 'That's no kind iv a letter to write to a polthroon an' thraitor like Bill Bryan.'

Roosevelt also took care that Taft did not publicly admit his ignorance on any issue, something, given his forthrightness, he was only too apt to do. When Bryan discusses unwanted subjects, "do not refer to them at all," counselled Roosevelt. On the delicate issue of labor rights, he pointed out that he had already "outlined loosely the policies that I believed you were going to stand for." Taft's instincts were for defense and explanation, Roosevelt's for attack. The president frequently drew analogies between politics and sports: "Prize fights are won by knocking out the other man when he is groggy." No chances were to be taken, and a "fighting attitude [should be held] throughout." "Above all," he emphasized, "it is a mistake for you to seem to be explaining your position." The "hardest and most aggressive hitting" was wanted. "Don't be in the least nervous about what Bryan says," Roosevelt urged; "do not *answer* Bryan; attack him! Don't let *him* make the issues."

When Taft submitted his speeches for comment, Roosevelt often referred to speeches he had previously made, tactfully pointing out that they were "comparatively short" but "as aggressive as possible." On one occasion when Roosevelt was unable to edit an upcoming speech, he advised by letter, "Go over every word of it . . . and if possible submit it to that ever present help in time of trouble—the beloved Root." Arthur Wallace Dunn noticed that Roosevelt made no secret of his constant supervision of Taft. Once when visiting the White House, Dunn overheard Roosevelt detain his secretary of war: "Will, just a moment. I guess you had better let me see that speech. I understand that you are going to discuss southern questions, and I would like to see what you have to say." Then turning to Dunn, the president commented dryly, "I have to revise Taft's speeches."

Taft's political talks failed to arouse much admiration or enthusiasm. When his brother Charles expressed alarm over his forensic failures, Taft asked him not to be "so sensitive" or he would have a lot to suffer over. A year later Archie Butt described his speeches as "dry and full of statistics, and we cannot get him away from figures. As I see him sometimes laboring to interest an audience and failing to do so, I feel so sorry for him I could almost cry."

Roosevelt's patience and good humor were sustained by the flattery of Taft's continued deference. "For the past ten years," Taft said in a typical speech, "he and I have on every essential point stood in heartiest agreement, shoulder to shoulder. We have the same views." Nellie continued to deplore Taft's subservience, and even the president sometimes thought he overdid it. Once in exasperation Roosevelt said, "you are now the leader, and there must be nothing that looks like self-depreciation or undue subordination of yourself. . . . My name should be used only enough to convince people of the identity and continuity of our policies." To Taft it was a matter of feeling, to Roosevelt simply strategy. Later he insisted, "I think it essential that your personality should be put with all possible force into the campaign." "Let the audience see you smile *always*, because I feel that your nature shines out so transparently when you do smile—you big, generous, high-minded fellow." Taft's smiling was perhaps his most energetic contribution to his campaign.

The following joke was commonly circulated:

> That's a splendid phonograph, old man. It reproduces the sound of Roosevelt's voice better than I ever thought possible. What make?
> We call it the Taft.

Another explained that T.A.F.T. stood for "Take Advice From Theodore."

Since Taft had no desire to tangle with William Jennings Bryan, Roosevelt took every opportunity to shake his fist in Bryan's direction. He even did some stumping. "Cheap and shallow," was Roosevelt's private assessment of Bryan, whose theories he thought to be "almost as preposterous as those of Jefferson himself." By contrast, Roosevelt considered himself a sane "radical on the conservative side." In his initial attack, Roosevelt blasted Bryan for trying to ally himself with Samuel Gompers in order to secure the labor vote. Roosevelt assured the country that Taft was not in truth the father of injunctions, but the true friend of labor. (Taft's main labor statement had sounded very judicial: "I believe that there ought to be no favored class in litigation at all, that a man who has property and a man who has labor to sell shall stand on equality in court.") Roosevelt's friend Henry Cabot Lodge warned that speaking for Taft was not a wise course: "You cannot put Taft into your place with the American people." And the *New York Times* suggested that while the president's assistance was very gallant, "would it not help Mr. Taft more . . . if such things were done not for him, but by him? . . . if he spoke for himself instead of having Mr. Roosevelt continually speak for him?"

Enraged by Roosevelt's tactics, Bryan complained about having two opponents to battle: "I say to the president that he should stand aside and let his man and me fight it out before the people." "The president's endorsement is of no value," Bryan countered, "unless the president will agree to stay in Washington and see that Mr. Taft makes good." "As Mr. Taft is alive and able to speak for himself," he snapped, "it is hardly necessary for Mr. Roosevelt to tell us what Mr. Taft will do." But Roosevelt cheerfully continued the same refrain: "There is only one way to preserve and perpetuate the great reform . . . [of] the past seven years, and that is by electing Mr. Taft." Roosevelt's friend and political supporter, Oscar Straus, who had campaigned with him four years earlier, noted with incredulity that Roosevelt had thrown even greater energy into Taft's campaign than his own.

Roosevelt's vigorous attempt to elect Taft simultaneously pleased and humiliated Nellie. She did not want to be beholden to Roosevelt once they arrived in the White House, and of course she would have liked to see her husband show up well on his own. Nellie had to agree with the sentiments expressed by the editor of *The Nation*, who wrote that in allowing Roosevelt to thrust him into the presidency, Taft "was putting himself under a greater personal obligation than any man ought to assume, and that the fruits of it could not fail to be bitter." But neither she nor Roosevelt could elevate Taft into an active candidate, and he remained, as Pringle remarked, "relatively forgotten in the campaign."

Roosevelt tried increasingly to discuss with Nellie her husband's problems. On more than one occasion he called her to the White House to confer about the campaign. He knew they had one great interest in common. Roosevelt, she recalled later, grew ever more impatient over Taft's apathy and continually "urged him to take a more active interest in the situation." Although Nellie agreed with Roosevelt's prognosis, she nonetheless was resentful of the role he played. She did not like to admit even to herself just how apathetic her husband was, since it reflected her share of the responsibility for his emergence as a presidential candidate, so much against his will, in the first place.

"Politics when I am in it makes me sick," Taft had complained in 1906, and the campaign he anticipated proved an "awful agony." Impolitic though it was, Taft frequently confessed in public his distaste for the whole affair. In Topeka, Kansas, he told an audience, "I didn't think I was going to be foolish enough to run for the presidency when I was on the bench." In Chattanooga he said, "I was engaged in the respectable business of trying to administer justice. I have fallen from that state now, and am engaged in running for the presidency." Many newspapers reported Taft's many expressions of regret for having left the peaceful security of the bench. His ambivalence was satirized by a press Gridiron Club skit:

Is Secretary Taft a candidate for the Presidency?

Yes.

Does he want to be Chief Justice?

Yes.

Does he want to remain . . . Secretary of War?

Yes.

Has he a longing to return to private life?

Yes.

How do you know all these things?

I read the statement he put out a few days ago.

Taft became more active after Republican advisers appealed to his deep-seated sense of responsibility. They told him it was "his duty to begin the canvass because of the obligation he owed to his friends who had nominated him." Oscar Davis and others informed Taft that in accepting the nomination he had implicitly pledged to make a fight "whether he wanted to do so on his own account or not."

Out on the campaign trail, however, the guileless Taft could not conceal his feelings: "The truth is," he said at Athens, Ohio, "I am not much of a politician. I feel very deeply the responsibility that I have upon me now as the candidate of a great party, . . . and I am from time to time oppressed with the sense that I am not the man who ought to have been selected, and yet, my friends, I am not going to decline." Under stress, Taft often expressed his fear of being unable to "fill the measure." Perhaps to compensate, he ate more and soon had to order clothes in ever larger sizes. "It's not easy to be a presidential candidate," he said, "not much easier than it is to keep down one's flesh."

Taft's reservations about his own capacity to fulfill the duties of the presidency were noticed by the press. Wondering why Taft's campaign efforts were so listless despite the many pep talks he received from associates, Oscar King of the *Times* guessed that the secretary of war doubted "his own success in case he should be elected President." Taft was far more realistic about his capacities than either Nellie or Roosevelt cared to be, and his unenthusiastic campaigning revealed a half-recognized hope that he would lose and never have to assume the "weighty burdens" of the White House.

Taft actually felt the Republican ticket might lose. He told Roosevelt that he declined to consider anything after November, "save the necessity for hunting a law office in which to supply bread for the mouths of those dependent on me." On one such occasion, Roosevelt replied, "Of course you are having a hard time, but you old trump, surely you know by this time how rare it is to find men who will give you both disinterested and efficient service. There are a number of such entirely disinterested men under me . . . [but] you are the chief of them." When Taft continued to complain, Roosevelt wrote, "Poor old boy! Of course you are not enjoying the campaign. I wish you had some of my bad temper. It is at times a real aid to enjoyment." Taft's close friend Edward Lowry recalled that he was "blue and depressed" throughout those months. "I never get up now and look at the headlines," he complained, "that I do not do so with a fear that there is to be found something . . . calling for denial or explanation."

Roosevelt, although rather baffled by the degree of Taft's passiveness, was sophisticated enough to turn his nominee's aloofness to political advantage. "Taft has pitched this campaign on a higher plane than any campaign in the history of this country," he said to the press. "He has not made one demagogic appeal." He excused Taft's reluctance to tangle with Bryan by saying that "he hates to fight unless it is necessary. . . . There isn't a mean streak in the man's make-up." Following Roosevelt's lead, the newspapers began to find that indeed Taft truly was a novel politician. "Never do we find in his speeches," the *Herald Tribune* suddenly marveled, any "bursts of vindictive denunciation of his opponent."

When Taft exhibited the extreme propriety so natural to him in soliciting political contributions, Roosevelt praised him warmly: "It is characteristic of you in every way. It shows the qualities of entire fearlessness and entire disinterestedness." On the other hand, the president could not wholly conceal his growing impatience. When Taft rejected forthwith a proposed $50,000 campaign gift from William Nelson Cromwell, a Wall Street lawyer he had known for years, Roosevelt tried to edge in. "You blessed old trump," Roosevelt wrote a month later. "I have always said you would be the greatest president, bar only Washington and Lincoln, and I feel mightily inclined to strike out the exceptions. My affection and respect for you are increased by your attitudes about contributions. But really I think you are altogether oversensitive."

When Taft initiated independent action in the campaign, he usually flopped. Scheduled to address a group of Union Army veterans at the Grant Monument, Taft told a story that did not help him with the military voters. After praising the Union commander, he continued with a true story from Grant's early history: "In 1854 he resigned from the army because he had to. He had yielded to the weakness for strong drink, and rather than be court-martialed, he left the army." Among the outraged veterans, one wrote directly to Taft: "I trust you will have the grace to go and hang yourself."

Taft heard from Nellie that the president was dissatisfied with the campaign and unhappy because he had avoided cooperation with the Republican political organizations. "I have decided," Roosevelt privately announced on 21 September 1908, "to put a little vim into the campaign." Soon he was talking to Taft as though they were both on the ticket: "I want us to choose our ground and make the fight aggressively." "Of course, we have got to make up our minds to fight hard but we are going to win." Within a short time the line was clearly drawn between the president and Bryan. Except for Roosevelt's interference, Henry West noted, there would not have been "a ripple upon the smooth sea of political events." The newspapers, which had been complaining that "no election struggle of recent years has been so colorless, so marked by apathy," now began to take heart.

Despite Taft's passivity most pundits expected from the start that the Republicans would be victorious. As Charles Hilles, Taft's secretary in the White House, later put it: Taft "had the finest press agent ever a man had in Teddy." The public was quite ready to believe that if Roosevelt thought Taft his proper successor, then he must be acceptable. The *New York Times* objected to the want of a close inquiry into Taft's specific qualifications for the job, but most newspapers helped to create a favorable image by portraying him, according to James Pollard in *The Presidents and the Press*, as "capable, experienced, liberal but safe . . . in short 'Big Bill' Taft, affable, competent and promising." Many newspapers, including the *New York Times*, supported Taft because he represented the popular Roosevelt policies and yet, as *The Nation* asserted, he promised "the serene atmosphere of a Federal Circuit Court."

Of course, progressive and liberal Republicans, to whom Taft owed his nomination, supported him because he was Roosevelt's candidate. One exception was Ray Stannard Baker, who had his doubts about Taft from the beginning. Baker thought that of all the possible candidates Roosevelt could have chosen, Taft was the weakest. Even in Ohio, Senator Foraker could certainly have blocked Taft had he stood forth on his own. But with Roosevelt on his side, he was invincible.

The election came and Taft's victory was overwhelming. He carried all but three states outside the Solid South and won 321 electoral votes to Bryan's 162. Roosevelt was "simply radiant" after Taft's victory, for he saw in it an endorsement of his own presidency. "We have beaten them to a frazzle," Roosevelt exulted. In his public statement, the president said, "The nomination of Mr. Taft was a triumph over reactionary conservatism, and his election was a triumph over unwise and improper radicalism."

"I was never so happy in my life," was Nellie's simple response.

Nellie was proud of Taft, but even more proud of what she began henceforth to refer to more frequently as her own "very active participation in [her] husband's career." She openly declared to reporters that she had "always had the satisfaction of knowing almost as much as he did about the politics and intricacies of any situation in which he found himself." Yet Nellie also had some unsettling premonitions: "Mr. Taft calls me the politician of the family," she had explained to a New York reporter in June. "His own ambitions always have been toward the judiciary. But I have persuaded him to remain in politics. Perhaps I may regret it."

After the election Taft was consumed by an urge to get back to the golf links. Pursued by the press to the rambling cottage he rented in Hot Springs, Virginia, he appeared on the porch the next morning for an interview: "I really did some great work at sleeping last night," he announced to the assembled reporters. And that was about all. He had little to add concerning political matters. A month later he told a group of persistent reporters, "there is nothing to be said at this time on current politics. I am feeling first rate. I have had eighteen holes of golf nearly everyday for the last week or two, and enjoyed it all." Eager to assume the privileges and position of first lady, Nellie complained that in isolated Hot Springs they could not find out "what's doing." She wanted to get on to Washington, unwilling as she was to forego a moment of the glory she had so long anticipated.

Newspaper reporters, intent upon bringing news from the president-elect to the rest of the country, continued to chase Taft around the golf course. In particular, they hoped to discover whom he was considering for the cabinet, but Taft disappointed them: "I haven't given the subject of my cabinet any consideration at all." He intended, he said, to relax now and defer all decisions "until some time in February. I suppose I must do it then." When the reporters returned to the subject in late February, Taft was still tired and "did not want to talk politics." There were a few things, he admitted to *Washington Post* newsmen, that he had intended to do in preparation for assuming office, but he had just not gotten around to them.

Despite President-elect Taft's inability to provide any news beyond his golf scores, the press continued to support him generously. Eager to praise, the *Washington Post*, which had earlier lauded his bearing and his tact, now found eloquence in his "flashes of silence." The country could rejoice, said the *New York Times*, that such a "brave, modest, well-balanced, clean-cut citizen" had been elected President.

Since Taft despaired of selecting a cabinet, John Hays Hammond recalled that he privately hoped Roosevelt's cabinet members would stay on to assist him "in the new job the president has picked for me." "The people I would select," Taft complained, "don't wish the places and those who would like the places don't commend themselves to me."

Eventually the cabinet took shape. After Elihu Root, and Henry Cabot Lodge had declined the post of secretary of state, he chose the conservative Philander Knox. An able corporation lawyer from Pennsylvania, Knox had been counsel for Carnegie Steel during the bloody 1892 Homestead Strike. Carnegie's manager at the Homestead plant, Henry Frick (later personal friend of Taft) had imported three hundred Pinkerton detectives to break the strike, but when they arrived on barges, the workmen resisted. In the gun fight which ensued, three detectives and ten strikers had been killed, and a few dozen wounded. Although the Pinkertons were ignominiously compelled to surrender, the strike failed, and unionism in the steel industry was set back for many years. As Roosevelt's attorney general, Knox had prosecuted several cases, including the Northern Securities Company, under the Sherman Antitrust Act. Elected senator from Pennsylvania in 1908, he succeeded in winning back the esteem of businessmen. The diminutive Knox, whom Roosevelt referred to as "Little Phil" or the "sawed off cherub," was rather cold and remote in manner. Yet, as Elihu Root said, he was "peppery" and quick to argue. Knox soon became Taft's one confidant in the inner circle.

New York corporation lawyer George Wickersham, a member of brother Henry Taft's law firm, was the choice for attorney general. Taft appointed another lawyer, Charles Nagel, a congressman from Missouri, as secretary of commerce and labor. The appointment of Richard A. Ballinger, an attorney and former chief of the land office in the Department of the Interior as secretary of the interior, had fateful consequences. Ballinger soon became the center of a struggle between conservationists and anti-conservationists that seriously disrupted the administration and brought Taft into disfavor with Roosevelt. Jacob Dickinson, the new secretary of war, was a former railroad attorney who had been counsel for the United States in the Alaska boundary case. Although a Democrat, Dickinson had voted for Taft in 1908. Taft greatly enjoyed Dickinson's gift for telling droll stories, but as he explained to reporters, the most "important factor" in choosing Dickinson was the man's bravery and courage. While visiting Detroit in 1895 on his judicial rounds, Taft told newsmen, he had seen Dickinson rescue a drowning man. Taft picked another Democrat for secretary of the treasury, Franklin MacVeagh, a lawyer, wholesale grocer, and Chicago banker. The forty-two-year-old Frank Hitchcock, a fellow Ohioan who had been chairman of the Republican National Committee during the election, was appointed postmaster general. The only two hold-overs from Roosevelt's cabinet were secretary of agriculture James Wilson, a Scottish emigré who had served under both McKinley and Roosevelt, and George von L. Meyer, a former Boston businessman who moved from postmaster general to secretary of the navy.

With the cabinet finally assembled, Taft did not find the relief he had expected, for progressive Republicans immediately found fault, since none of them was tapped, whatever may have been their contribution to the campaign. Widely criticized at the time, Taft's cabinet selections are still unfavorably assessed by many historians. MacVeagh accomplished little of note in the Treasury Department; Nagel as secretary of commerce and labor put his department entirely at the disposal of business; Secretary of Agriculture Wilson hurt his department with the Wiley affair; Wickersham antagonized big business with his zealous antitrust crusade; and Secretary of the Interior Ballinger involved his department in one of the biggest imbroglios of the administration through his feud with chief forester Gifford Pinchot. Dickinson's leadership in the War Department proved equally weak, and Secretary of State Knox's policies angered Latin America, Japan, and Russia. Accolades today generally go only to George Meyer, who reformed and streamlined the Department of the Navy.

In *Recollections* Nellie discloses that once in the White House she ceased to advise Taft in political matters. With her husband "safely elected," she wrote, "I considered all important affairs satisfactorily settled." She found "little time or inclination at the moment to worry about who should have the high offices in the new President's gift, or what policies should be pursued during his administration." Of course her interest in such matters shortly revived. But for a time, she was busy with plans for the many changes and improvements to be made in her new home.

While vacationing, Taft at first openly spoke his mind. Addressing a crowd which had applauded him heartily, Taft, with remarkable prescience declared, "The first thought that comes to me after hearing what I am quite free to admit is very sweet music to me, is a sort of trembling fear that, after four years, such a meeting as this and such expressions of good will may be impossible—that I shall be like the man who went into office with a majority and went out with unanimity." He returned to this fear many times thereafter. In Augusta, Georgia, he related to a crowd an anecdote about the man who was the most popular person in the United States every day but election day. "Well," he concluded, "I would a good deal rather be the most popular person in the United States for three-hundred sixty-four days in the year than on the three hundred and sixty-fifth."

As inauguration day drew nearer, Taft's apprehensions became more public. The *Washington Post* reported his having declared that Elihu Root "ought to be the President-Elect." "And I," he added, "ought to be a prospective member of his Cabinet, because I [would] know how to serve under him." On the evening before his inauguration Taft attended a Yale Club dinner in New York. "I am now facing the greatest responsibilities that come to any American citizen," Taft said, "and it is better to leave office with the plaudits of your countrymen than to enter it with them alone. . . . The opportunity for mistakes, failure, or the dead level of doing nothing are so many I look forward with hesitation to the next four years." Then in an attempt to boost himself up he added, "A man ought not to put himself in the attitude of fearing these difficulties, but have the courage to meet them as they come. That is my hope." The worse consequence of failure, Taft told his fellow clubmen, was the attending criticism. Gifford Pinchot, Roosevelt's chief forester, observed with amazement that Taft's speech was "curiously full of hesitation and foreboding," with scarcely a confident note in it. He found it "shocking that Taft was approaching his new task with doubt and dread." The presidency, Pinchot thought, seemed to have "got him down even before he tackled it."

"It is a very different office from that of governor of the Philippines," Taft complained on another occasion, "and I don't know that I shall arise to the occasion or not." Even his personality began to change. Roosevelt noticed Taft's altered manner and mused, "something has come over Will, he is not the same man." To photographers assigned to cover the inaugural events, Taft snarled, "Don't you think six exposures of me in my most ungainly postures ought to suffice?" Uncertain of Taft's behavior, both Nellie and his brother Charles kept a watchful eye on him, so Henry Cabot Lodge reported to Roosevelt. Inauguration day, the fourth of March, was close at hand, and Nellie did not intend to allow any unforeseen developments to spoil it.

By the second of March, Washington had been readied with great festoons of electric lights stretched across Pennsylvania Avenue from the Capitol past the Treasury and to the War Department. In front of the White House, the path to the Court of Honor was ablaze with thousands of colored glass globes. American flags made of red, white, and blue lights and shields with Taft's face in the midst of bright lights hung on many buildings along the parade route. The weather was ideal and large crowds, estimated early at one hundred thousand persons, poured into the warm and sunny city. Hotels and boarding houses were soon filled. Street vendors prospered with Taft badges and knick-knacks. Since a broadly smiling face had already become synonymous with Big Bill Taft, thousands of people wore badges which read "Smile, Smile, Smile." A well-known organization of cavalry, Troop A of Cleveland, arrived to escort Taft during the parade, and crowds of Ohioans, already in the capital, went to the station to meet them. Bleachers sufficient to hold fifty thousand people were erected along Pennsylvania Avenue leading up to the Capitol.

In the midst of all these lavish preparations, Taft, it seemed, was the least interested person in Washington. *Herald Tribune* reporters described him as "holding aloof from all details of the inauguration." He spent his last two days of freedom on the Chevy Chase links, appearing to be more concerned, the *Washington Post* protested, about his golf game than "in matters of state." When reporters tried to engage him in discussion about the next day's events, Taft rebuffed them by turning the subject to golf.

At the White House, meanwhile, President Roosevelt was nearly deluged with visitors coming to bid him farewell. Mrs. Roosevelt held a late afternoon reception for their best friends. Archie Butt felt that he had never seen so much emotion, "Nearly every woman wept a little and the eyes of the men were oftentimes dimmed." On the day before inauguration, the French ambassador broke down in the middle of his speech while presenting a silver bowl from Roosevelt's informal or "tennis" cabinet. And at the reception, old political hands were able to contain their emotion only by uttering no more than perfunctory goodbyes. A Supreme Court Justice from New York offered him a solid gold hunting knife for his upcoming African hunting trip; on the hilt Teddy bears were represented and on the crown, an American eagle's head with ruby eyes. Roosevelt himself wept a little when he discovered that the Townsends, close friends of the family, had left a platinum necklace inlaid with diamonds for Mrs. Roosevelt. As a last gesture of goodwill, the Roosevelts invited the Tafts to stay overnight at the White House following a farewell dinner party.

Already there were rumors that a breach between Roosevelt and the president-elect was in the offing. Taft tried to put such talk to rest in his note accepting the invitation: "People have attempted to represent that you and I were in some way at odds during the last three months, whereas you and I know that there has not been the slightest difference between us, and I welcome the opportunity to stay the last night of your administration under the White House roof to make as emphatic as possible the refutation of any such suggestion." Many felt the situation would become awkward and embarassing. Archie Butt remarked, "I think we all dreaded this dinner, the last one in the White House for the Roosevelts and the first one for the Tafts." Archie was relieved when it went off "without a hitch." Mrs. Taft, he believed, had never seemed more gracious than she did that evening. Mrs. Roosevelt, he proudly noted, was a perfect hostess. Relations between the two women had always been a little strained, and by now they were only formally polite to each other. Years later, Taft recalled that "dreadful dinner the Roosevelts gave us with Lodge and Root trying to make things bright and Mrs. Roosevelt teary and distraught."

After dinner, Taft went to a Yale Club smoker at the Willard Hotel. Other guests departed until only President Roosevelt, his wife, Nellie Taft, and Archie Butt remained. Mrs. Roosevelt finally rose, said that she was going to retire, and kindly advised Nellie to do the same. She took Nellie's hand and "expressed the earnest hope that her first night in the White House would be one of sweet sleep." Instead, Nellie worried into the early morning hours over every detail of the whole inaugural program. She awoke with a start, feeling less than refreshed, to loud, crackling noises which seemed to be in the immediate vicinity of the windows. Arising, she looked out the window and saw a stormy, ice-bound world. The tree limbs which had awakened her hung encased with ice, breaking and banging against the windows.

Despite the weathermen's favorable predictions, late on the eve of the inauguration dark clouds descended on Washington. A furious snow and sleet storm shredded the bunting and flags set out for the ceremonies. The Court of Honor and all the elaborate decorations along the parade route were reduced to a monochromatic sludge. The marchers in the parade ploughed through six inches of snow and slush; two spectators died from exposure, and the hospitals were crowded with casualties. Because of the howling blizzard, some of the inauguration plans had to be changed. For the first time since Andrew Jackson took the oath of office in 1833, the ceremony was held in the Senate Chamber.

Despite the weather, Roosevelt was cheerful and hearty. "I have had a bully time and enjoyed every hour of my presidency," he told friends and reporters. Taft, in contrast, was in a somber mood. Ike Hoover, who began his White House service in 1891 and was now chief usher, observed that Taft was "cross and uncomfortable." "It is my storm," Taft said to friends. "I always said it would be a cold day when I got to be president of the United States."

The Senate galleries were filled, and the ladies' colorful gowns supplied the color lost on the streets in the storm. President-elect Taft took a position facing his family, grouped in the gallery above. Although other presidents had used family Bibles, Taft chose to take his oath of office with his hand on the Supreme Court's century-old Bible. When he later returned it to the Court archives, he wistfully remarked that if he was ever sworn in as a Supreme Court justice he would take the oath on this same book. As Chief Justice Melville Fuller administered the presidential oath, Taft, breaking all decorum, smiled up at Nellie and the children in the gallery.

After the swearing in, President Taft gave his inaugural address. He did not read all he had written on that occasion, but later released the whole text to the press. The opening sentence revealed his sense of apprehension: "Anyone who had taken the oath I have just taken must feel *a heavy weight* of responsibility." Then he went on to affirm his intention of upholding Roosevelt's policies. He would keep the trusts under control, revise the tariff, maintain the army and navy, conserve natural resources, and supervise the building of the Panama Canal. The *Washington Post*, catching Taft's mood, said his speech was the "plain, unvarnished delivery of a plain, simple-hearted man, confronted with the gravest of responsibilities, which he appreciates." When the new president had finished his speech, Roosevelt advanced to the rostrum and warmly shook his hands, exclaiming, "God bless you, old man. It is a great state document." With their hands on each other's shoulders, they stood talking earnestly for a few moments—while everyone around watched with great interest. Roosevelt then hurriedly bid his adieus and left for Union Station and the train to Oyster Bay.

The new president's dull reserve in the midst of celebrating well-wishers contrasted with the vitality of his triumphantly smiling wife. "The day," she exulted, "was a glorious one for me." She later told a *Washington Post* reporter that "it always has been my ambition to see Mr. Taft President of the United States, and naturally when the ceremonies of inauguration were in progress I was inexpressibly happy." The *Post* echoed the current gossip about Mrs. Taft's role in directing her husband's steps toward the presidency: "There is every reason why she should feel satisfaction in her husband's success, for had it not been for her determination to keep him from becoming a Supreme Court Justice he would not have been able to accept the nomination."

Breaking precedent, Nellie joined Taft in the drive from the Capitol to the reviewing stand. To do that she had to leave the Senate chamber before he finished his address in order to reach in time the rotunda where the presidential carriage was waiting. The awkwardness of the situation did not trouble her. "I see no reason," she later remarked, "why the president's wife may not now come into some rights on that day also." Although there was opposition to establishing such a precedent, Nellie, who was always delighted to break what she considered outworn conventions regarding women's behavior and rights, proudly recalled, "I had my way and in spite of protests took my place at my husband's side. For me that drive was the proudest and happiest event of Inauguration Day. Perhaps I had a little secret elation in thinking that I was doing something which no woman had ever done before. I forgot the anxieties of the preceding night; the consternation caused by the fearful weather; and every trouble seemed swept aside." Archie remembered that the weather had cleared sufficiently for the top of the carriage to be lowered during the journey, which permitted Mrs. Taft to see and be seen by everyone. Ike Hoover remarked in retrospect that custom was thrown to the winds that day, but it was only "a shadow of events that were to come."

In notable contrast to Nellie's joyful countenance during that drive from the Capitol, Taft's face was grave and downcast. Not once on the entire trip did he look from the carriage, nor did he once bow or wave his hat. As Ike Hoover described it, the new president, upon his return to the White House from the reviewing stand, threw himself into a large comfortable chair, stretched out to his full length and prefaced his first command with the remark, "I am president now, and tired of being kicked around."

Nellie glowed that evening at the Inaugural Ball. Ten thousand guests attended the event, which was held in the ballroom of the Pension Building. The lavish decorations cost twenty thousand dollars. There were yellow and gold curtains, tall cedars, and vases of rambler roses everywhere. Mrs. Taft, with a diamond aigrette in her hair, was dressed in a gown of heavy white satin, draped with white chiffon and embroidered with goldenrod. She stood in the scarlet presidential box, which she unquestionably adorned, looking at what she described as an almost kaleidoscopic scene. Sitting in the presidential box with them was Taft's eighty-three-year-old Aunt Delia, visibly enjoying the scene. She was dressed in a rich black velvet gown ornamented lavishly with old lace she had for years been saving for just such an occasion. "It was a wonderful glittering throng, more magnificent than any I have ever seen," Nellie wrote, and as she looked down, she fondly recalled, "I saw a great semi-circle of faces—thousands, it seemed to me—smilingly upturned toward us."

After leaving the Ball and taking possession of the White House, she suddenly burst into tears of joy.

IX

THE MALICE OF
POLITICS

Except for Roosevelt in 1904, Taft received the largest plurality in the popular vote of any president up to that time. The American people, Democrats and Republicans alike, extended their esteem and good-will and wished him success. Taft was the recipient, the *Washington Post* asserted, of more "universal gratulation and good will" than any other incoming president. Americans in 1909, said the *Post*, were a prosperous, united, and happy people, and being so, had taken the large, good-natured president to their hearts. After seven years of the Roosevelt administration, many people were ready for a period of less storm and stress. The former president's hunting trip to Africa was generally felt to be well timed. The country was "tired of the din" Roosevelt made, Ellen Slayden remarked, and the jungle was "yawning" for him. No one was likely to dispute Roosevelt's claim that while in office he had been president most "emphatically." As one admirer said, "You had to hate the colonel a great deal to keep from loving him." At least one group of congressmen may have hated him just enough, for prior to his embarkation they raised a toast "To the lions!" The country said farewell to Roosevelt and settled back to enjoy a period of progressive government by quieter means.

Taft did not think of sending Roosevelt a present and farewell message until Archie Butt suggested it. He selected a gold ruler with a pencil and inscribed it "To Theodore Roosevelt from William Howard Taft," followed by Roosevelt's customary phrase "Good-bye—Good Luck. And a safe return." In his letter Taft began, "If I followed my impulse, I should still say 'My dear Mr. President.' I cannot overcome the habit. When I am addressed as 'Mr. President,' I turn to see whether you are not at my elbow." Taft chose Archie as his emissary, for he knew Roosevelt was always glad to see him. Roosevelt quizzed Butt about people on the White House staff and whether Taft was retaining them. He told him to convey love and thanks to the new president, and then he sent a telegram: "Am deeply touched by your gift and even more by your letter. Greatly appreciated it. Everything will turn out all right, old man." Roosevelt's departure was intended to be unpublicized, but New York was as excited, Butt thought, as if it were holding an inauguration. A tremendous demonstration developed spontaneously. Frenzied throngs tried to catch glimpses of the ex-president.

Roosevelt explained to William Allen White the reasons behind the timing of his trip: "Down at bottom, my main reason for wishing to go to Africa for a year or so is that I can get where no one can accuse me of running [for office] nor do Taft the injustice of accusing him of permitting me to run the job." Perhaps Taft would have felt such charges to have been small cost in return for Roosevelt's helpful advice to head off the provocations for harsh criticism which lay immediately in his path.

Every president enjoys a honeymoon period with the press and with the opposition party, a time allowing him to become accustomed to new duties, to create a cabinet, and to learn to work with his staff. Most contemporaries anticipated that Taft's honeymoon would be a long one. For Taft, Mark Sullivan commented, the usual sentimental interlude was "exceptionally sugary." The press confidently predicted peace and prosperity under a capable leader and an intelligent administration. Taft was hailed as a fearless executive, an unexampled administrator, a far-seeing lawmaker. In short, Ray Stannard Baker wrote, "He was this, he was that, he was everything wonderful."

Despite such "paens of praise," the new president was not sanguine. This "sweet music" will not last, he soberly calculated. It did not, indeed, but no one expected the change to come quite so quickly as happened. Harsh criticism began within a few weeks of the inauguration. Attempting later to account for the brevity of Taft's term of grace, Baker acutely perceived that the country's disillusionment arose because the people had known very little about their new chief executive before electing him. Taft was just a "large, dim, charming personality hovering somewhere" in the background. The country had expected Rooseveltian aggressiveness and expertise from Taft and was subsequently shocked when he did not measure up. The general feeling was, as Taft himself noted, that his "coming into office was exactly as if Roosevelt had succeeded himself." Baker had almost alone taken a skeptical view and felt that any person who had observed closely the differences in training and character between the two men should have known that Taft at heart differed greatly from Roosevelt. Because that difference had not been sufficiently noted, Taft soon appeared an enigma. James Hornaday of *The Indianapolis News* pointed out that the captains of industry confidently thought they could control Taft's administration; at the same time the progressive Republicans in the West were equally confident that their cause would not suffer. Surely somebody was being fooled, Hornaday mused, or perhaps Taft had fooled everybody. Most people thought, along with Senator Dolliver, that "the one thing about Judge Taft that has endeared him to the American people is that for the last ten years he has been connected with the great achievements of the administration of Theodore Roosevelt." When the country found the connection to be in actuality tenuous, disenchantment followed.

On the eve of his departure for Africa, Roosevelt betrayed some foreboding. Asked by Mark Sullivan about Taft's probable chances of success, Roosevelt replied, "He means well and he'll do his best. But he's weak. They'll get him. They'll lean against him." Sullivan observed the new president early showing the strain of decision making. He became irritable and on occasion snarled in the presence of newspapermen. Without Roosevelt, he felt lost and unhappy. Not only did he look around, expecting to see Roosevelt whenever he heard someone say Mr. President, but to Nellie's great annoyance, he himself continually referred to his predecessor as "President Roosevelt." "Ex-President Will!" was the inevitable remonstrance.

Archie Butt, who remained in the White House, now as personal aide to Taft, said after observing Taft during his first month in the White House, "President Taft is one of the finest human engines I ever knew, but like every other engine, is not very effective without a fire under the boiler. Roosevelt used to be constantly building the fire." Taft possessed a distinctive and strong personality of his own, but in this situation it could not emerge from Roosevelt's shadow. To the ex-president in Africa, he wrote, "I want you to know that I do nothing in my work in the Executive office without considering what you would do [first] . . . and without having . . . a mental talk with you." Taft confided to Butt that when he read of a conference between the president and the Speaker of the House, he wondered what the subject of the meeting had been, not realizing immediately that it was he who was the president. On one occasion Butt started to apologize after calling Roosevelt the "president," but Taft quickly replied: "Well, never mind, he is *my* president, and *we* will have him as *our* president, you and I, even if he is nobody else's president." Taft at first wished to reject the very idea of himself in the role of final arbiter. As time went on, however, assumption of the most powerful political office in the country began to work its magic, and when it did, the dependent child gave place, as we shall see, to the man.

The uninterrupted success of Taft's career and his obvious talents for various kinds of public service had for the most part blinded even Roosevelt to the fact that whereas Taft had been an excellent agent, a fine subordinate, the "loyal errand boy" of his administration, he could never make a good chief executive. "Taft is a well-meaning, good-natured man," Roosevelt at last conceded (in November 1910), "but not a leader." "He is evidently a man who takes color from his surroundings. He was an excellent man under me," he recalled ruefully. Reassessing Taft after two years in office, various friends and observers concluded that executive ability was foreign to him. Other qualities were his in abundance, and it is a sad irony that he succeeded to an office that showed him at his worst rather than to one allowing him to fulfill during his mature years his great potential as a jurist.

Taft confused most everyone because his principal talent lay in seeing both sides of a question, in proceeding with caution, in applying the rules of reason and precedent, in making careful, deliberate decisions based as firmly as possible on principle and not expediency. Unlike Roosevelt, Taft was no starter, no pusher; he saw no grand visions and disliked pioneering. He was instinctively conservative. Roosevelt thrived on stress and discontent, whereas Taft could not deal with tumultuous political discord and was not excited by the idea of change. When conditions demanded swift, bold action, Taft reacted hesitantly and slowly. His conservative views—which quickly surfaced in Roosevelt's absence—and his presidential style were suitable for a late nineteenth-century administration, but seemed outmoded in the twentieth century.

While he worked for Roosevelt, Ike Hoover relates, Taft always had a pleasant smile and a word of welcome for everyone whenever he visited the White House. He could not comprehend what had come over Taft once he became president. The careful considerateness disappeared; curt orders replaced the smiles. Several members of the staff who suppressed their rebelliousness soon became infected with ire, according to Hoover. It continued that way throughout Taft's term, which Hoover characterized as a most "unnatural" condition.

Eating was one of president Taft's very few solaces, and the presidency offered him unlimited opportunities to indulge. His face was wreathed in smiles, newsmen noticed, when on his first Thanksgiving day in office he received a giant turkey from Rhode Island poultrymen, a fifty-pound mincemeat pie from New York bankers, and a twenty-six pound possum from Georgia, reputed to be the largest ever shot in the state. Guests present at the feast recounted that Taft sat back after his prodigious meal, smiled broadly, and said, "Thank goodness, I've had a dinner at which I haven't been compelled to make speeches. I've enjoyed food—real food—and I haven't had to work to get it."

Like many obese men, Taft erroneously believed in "the magic of exercise," and he determinedly rode horseback, played golf, and walked long walks regularly. He liked in this way to break the White House political routine, yet, as Butt observed, Taft had no aversion to routine in his recreational activities. Butt would occasionally suggest their taking a different trail in the park, for Taft left to himself would ride in the same place every day and never alter his path in the least. Once he became accustomed to his route, to lead him elsewhere was "like changing the course of Niagara." "Let us take the old road, Archie," Taft would always insist. By riding on ahead of Taft and leading the way, Butt discovered how to introduce variety in their daily excursions: nine times out of ten, Taft docilely followed.

"I never had to do anything of this kind with President Roosevelt," Butt complained. "He did the thinking, the planning, the scheming for all his playmates." Roosevelt "swept one off one's feet in a sort of whirlwind motion and . . . left one exhausted" after a game of tennis or whatever. Boxing, wrestling, fencing, and running were Roosevelt's favorite diversions. He invited boxing champion Mike Donovan to the White House to spar with him. Joe Grant, the District champion wrestler, came for two- to three-hour matches with the president. And General Wood engaged in broadsword battles with him. With his friends Garfield and Pinchot, Roosevelt enjoyed hard hitting bouts with the medicine ball. Not content with his usual pastimes, Roosevelt also spent two seasons learning the art of jujitsu.

Whereas Roosevelt took regular exercise to stay trim and keep up his fighting style, Taft turned to sport for pastime and escape. As we have seen, when on the job, he often had difficulty staying awake. Either Nellie or Archie stood guard to keep Taft awake during those moments when a nodding president could be particularly disagreeable. Sleep may suddenly overcome an obese person while he is sitting up or even engaged in conversation because large abdominal girth leads to shallow respiration which induces drowsiness, a condition medical experts have labeled the "Pickwickian Syndrome." But Taft's unexpected sleeping bouts can be explained psychologically as well as physiologically, for in sleep he often escaped his anxieties. Once while attending a funeral with Taft, the vice-president, the Speaker, and other notables, Butt made the mistake of giving up his usual place next to the president to Justice Edward White. From a distance he watched nervously as Taft fell asleep and then was horrified when he heard "an incipient snore." On another occasion when Taft fell asleep in church and emitted an "audible snore," Archie simply punched him, but he "woke with such a start as to attract the attention of everybody around him." After that Butt resorted to signaling with a spell of coughing, which served as a warning.

Historians have noted that Taft's weight normally decreased when he was really content, that is, when he was least troubled by problems like those he faced in the White House. Henry Pringle mistakenly attributes the loss to the extra time Taft had out of office to attend to diet and regular exercise. After his presidential term Taft reduced his weight well below three hundred pounds, because he was happier, situated in a position more suited to his own tastes and abilities, first as a Yale professor of law and then as Supreme Court justice. But before those contented years arrived, Taft had to navigate four trying years in the White House. By 1911 it seemed almost a lifetime. To Butt he wailed, "it seems to me I will never catch up with my work . . . there is so much to be done . . . that I feel discouraged. I would give anything in the world if I had the ability to clear away work as Roosevelt did. Roosevelt could always keep ahead of his work but I cannot do it, and I know it is a grievous fault."

No one knew where the administration was going, Henry Stoddard said, not even the president himself: "It was drift, drift, drift—little attempted, nothing done." Ray Stannard Baker complained that "nothing clear, nothing sure, nothing strong" came from President Taft. His administration was irresolutely "tossing about aimlessly . . . drifting toward a crisis." Gifford Pinchot, upon returning to Washington from a trip in the West not much more than a month after Taft had assumed office, described the capital as "scarcely recognizable . . . a dead town." It was, he quipped, as if a "sharp sword had been succeeded by a roll of paper, legal size." Taft's close friends said, "Wait, wait," but each time with a fainter and fainter voice. Taft, William Allen White wrote, battled "futilely, desperately, stupidly, an unhappy, ill-fated figure."

Learning of the rapidly growing dissatisfaction with his successor at home, Roosevelt conceded in November 1910 that he *might* have made a mistake in choosing Taft. His summary of the problem was that Taft lacked "the gift of leadership," was "too easily influenced by the men around him," and did "not really grasp progressive principles." Taft had been "a good lieutenant, but is a poor captain." Though thousands of miles away, Roosevelt continued to dominate the headlines. There was a "fanatical interest" in everything the Rough Rider did, and as before the papers overflowed with scraps of news about him. "Theodore Roosevelt Attacked by Two Dozen Hippopotamuses," the headlines read on one occasion. The two natives on the rowboat with him were tremendously frightened, but not the colonel, who calmly shot the finest bull and the largest cow. Another headline article described

Roosevelt's hunting party being charged by an angry rhinoceros. A native porter was gored, but Roosevelt came to his rescue. A third told of Roosevelt's narrow escape when, charged by a bull elephant, he fired at him and missed—but he got him with the second shot. There were weekly news stories about the various big game he shot, most of whose carcasses found a final resting place in the Smithsonian Institution. The ex-president's safari terminated in the Belgian Congo with a final climactic hunt for the rare white rhinoceros. During the eleven-month expedition Roosevelt bagged 296 animals including 6 buffalos, 7 hippos, 8 elephants, 9 lions, 18 rhinoceroses, 15 zebras, and 28 gazelles.

Coming home from a Gridiron dinner Taft rather pathetically remarked to Archie Butt, "Nothing shows what a hold Theodore has on the public mind more than the dinner this evening. Even when he is away and in no way interfering in politics, such is the personality of the man that almost the entire evening was wit and humor devoted to him, while the president with most of the cabinet present . . . were hardly mentioned."

Everyone agreed, it seemed, that Taft was an "uninspiring figure, ponderous and honest, but tame and unmagnetic." Students at Harvard Law School held a straw vote on whether to recall President Taft. Senator Joseph Bailey of Texas spoke the thoughts of many when he declared that Taft was less fitted to the presidency than any other man who had ever held the office. Taft took refuge in the idea that he was only an interim standby: "I don't know much about politics; but I am trying to do the best I can with this administration until the time [comes] . . . to turn it over to somebody else." He looked forward to leaving office. He willingly admitted what everybody already knew—that the presidency was first and foremost a political office and that good presidents were good politicians. But for himself, he cared not to learn the game. "Political considerations," he candidly admitted, "have never weighed heavily with me."

Donald Anderson, another of Taft's biographers, finds this view "difficult to accept"; he remains convinced by Roosevelt's campaign fiction that Taft's high-minded disinterestedness was what kept him from pursuing public acclaim, concluding that "Taft's indifference toward his public image was the prime cause of his failure as president."

On the contrary, Taft was very concerned about his public image. In fact, Taft desperately desired everyone's approval and hoped that he might somehow manage to gain it before his term ended. Just by "sitting on the lid," as Roosevelt so often had told him, he might do four years successfully, but never, he feared, eight. Anderson supposes that Taft became "resigned" and "unconcerned about his personal image"; although "not completely blind to criticism of his administration," he chose to ignore it. Actually, Taft, deeply concerned, trying to please everyone, contributed to the irresolution and inconsistencies so characteristic of his administration. When friends told him to answer his critics, Taft forlornly replied, "Oh, what's the use. Whatever I do or say is sure to be misconstrued or twisted around in such a manner that even I will not be able to recognize my own motives."

Upon taking office Taft had hoped to be the president of all the people and to maintain friendly relations with all groups, no matter what their political philosophy or affiliations. He abhorred argument and dissension, especially when they could not be controlled by rules of procedure and precedent. And differences were resolved usually by Taft's conforming his opinions to those around him. Even as chief justice, years later, Taft avoided making dissenting judgments. Moreover, he assessed the merits of potential jurists by whether or not, if placed on the bench, he thought they would agree with their fellow judges.

Archie Butt, normally a sympathetic observer of his boss, noted that he had "never known a man to dislike discord as much as the president." He "hates to be at odds with people, and a row of any kind is repugnant to him." This trait, in fact, is not uncommon among obese men, who find it difficult to express negative or angry feelings or to become assertive. But the angry feelings are usually there in abundance nevertheless. Taft often showed them, Ike Hoover claimed, more by his red face than by his expression. Rage and hostility would at times master him, but only his intimates were aware of these feelings. Soon after the inauguration Butt noticed this discrepancy in Taft: he might appear "all warmth, all fervor, all humanity," yet he could "deal out the cards which make one shiver at the touch." "When he takes a dislike to anyone it is for some reason known [only] to himself, and he does not easily forgive." "He is persistent in his antipathies. Mr. Roosevelt once said that Mr. Taft was one of the best haters he had ever known. . . . He does not show his dislike."

Taft sometimes unburdened himself to his brothers. He called Connecticut Senator Frank Brandegee an "infernal ass," and Herbert Bigelow of Ohio an "infernal liar and fool," and to Butt, he called Indiana Senator Albert Beveridge a "selfish pig." On rare occasions Taft lost his temper in public, as when he excoriated Justice Strafford at a Board of Trade dinner one evening in May 1909. Strafford gave an after-dinner speech advocating that citizens of the District of Columbia be given the right to vote. Taft considered those views demagogic and irresponsible. In rebuttal, he not only declared against the franchise, but astonished the diners by ridiculing Strafford, belittling his judgment, and denouncing his entire theory of local government. Archie had never seen Taft so aroused. Afterwards, Senator Tillman remarked to Taft, "Mr. President, I did not believe it was in you. I sat there astonished."

Because as party leader Taft disliked saying no to any Republican, he made ineffective and even disruptive use of patronage. Just by agonizing too long over which of half a dozen candidates should get a given job, Taft postponed filling the offices which needed filling as soon as possible. He admitted to the National Press Club that he had spent three to four hours a day discussing candidates' qualifications for offices. But "that's not real work," he added with a broad smile. Being "too goodnatured," Taft disgruntled many politicians by holding out hopes that were doomed to disappointment. As president he also made the serious mistake of trying to placate his political opponents at the cost of seeming to slight his friends. Frank Kellogg, the great trust-busting prosecutor in the Standard Oil case and later a successful candidate for the Senate from Minnesota, tried to advise Taft that patronage should be used to cement his own political strength. Yet Taft insisted that merit was the only ground for appointment, and he sometimes proved it by putting one of his former political opponents in office. Perhaps he hoped in that way to win them over. Kellogg remonstrated with the president and got assurances that he would not appoint any more men unalterably opposed to him. Taft's dinner parties also suffered as a result of his indiscriminate invitations to guests holding significant political differences. He made it a rule to pay little attention to personal squabbles and so invited guests regardless of their personal antagonisms or ideologies. And he often invited more Democrats than Republicans—"queerly assorted" parties were the inevitable result.

Favor seekers came to consider Taft an easy mark. The White House was soon infiltrated by political enemies because, as biographer Edward Cotton observes, Taft "could hardly keep anyone out of the circle of his friendship who wished to come in. Mr. Taft was too friendly." Taft promised more than he could deliver. Even when he remembered a promise, he often did not know how, according to his friend James Watson, "to implement the machinery of the presidency to bring it about." Inevitably, the result was just the opposite of what the president had aimed for. The White House under Taft, William Allen White maintained, was an unprecedented scene of "pulling and hauling, intriguing, contention, bickering, and strife."

Archie Butt was constantly annoyed at Taft's "fool engagements"; almost anyone could arrange an audience with the president, for Taft would not turn people away. He made some appointments about which no one, not even his personal secretary, had any knowledge. He always liked to have someone with him whenever he read or studied, for he imagined he worked better when there was company in the room. Taft made "engagement after engagement" which he could not keep and then left Butt to make excuses. Once Butt had to secure his release from attending the commencement exercises of the Blind Asylum, and on another occasion, his promise to present himself at the unveiling of a Longfellow statue had to be withdrawn. "He makes more enemies," Archie remarked, "than if he declined in the first place."

Butt despaired over Taft's habit of sitting and discussing some matter for fifteen minutes with a visitor who did not deserve five seconds. President Roosevelt, in contrast, "seized his visitor by the hand, wrung it hard, and sent him flying out of the nearest door." Yet the visitor generally thought that he had left of his own accord. Not only did Taft agree to meet all those who approached him, he accepted requests of every sort to attend colleges, social clubs, civic organizations. To one and all, Taft responded, "If I can find time I will be glad to come." And he kept a surprising number of his promises. In replying to his critics, Taft revealed his basic motivation: he accepted so many engagements because the White House was a lonesome place.

Taft particularly delighted in going to Yale University for graduations, alumni meetings, and various other events. He did so because he could always depend on a warm reception. "I am here because I could not help coming," Taft explained during a New Haven trip at the end of June 1909. "You may think before the end of the presidential term that I shall be as inevitably present at alumni dances as the ham and chicken we're all so fond of." Taft and his Yale alumni friends frolicked together like schoolboys out on holiday, Butt observed. The president enjoyed being with these men, they neither importuned him for favors and offices nor offered him advice and suggestions. Instead they rallied round and gave him their support and loyalty, proud that at last a Yale man had become president.

Taft made more of his college connections than any other president, and for good reason. A man with few close personal friends, he found an easy, nonthreatening sense of belonging and ready-made fellowship with his former Yale classmates. His behavior parallels that of compulsive neurotic personalities who are generally loners. Like Taft, they seem gregarious, desirous of approval, and sometimes even desperate to be liked. But when a friend comes close to them, touches them physically, or wants to know them intimately, they are suddenly uncomfortable and retreat. A gregarious exterior is not inconsistent with painful insecurity. He saw these Yale men only on occasion and parted from them as suddenly as they came together.

Taft's cabinet members found him pliable. Senator Dolliver, the progressive Republican from Iowa, described President Taft in the memorable metaphor—a "large amiable island, surrounded entirely by persons who knew exactly what they wanted." Gifford Pinchot complained that Taft had a fatal tendency to be swayed by the last man who talked to him. Aware of this kind of criticism, Taft attempted to defend himself: "Every man is entitled to his day in court, and I should feel a coward if I hesitated to say that . . . I consult every interest, and when an interest presents an argument that I think fair, I yield to it." The methods of the court, however, did not transfer so easily to the White House. Taft's older half-brother Charles, greatly disturbed by Taft's weakness in the hands of cabinet members, exclaimed, "It makes me sick, Archie, the way the president lets his cabinet run riot with him. All he would have to do is fire one of them, and the others would . . . toe the line. . . . That man Hitchcock simply defies the president." Since Taft had directed members of Congress to bypass him and go straight to the cabinet officers, this state of affairs was not surprising. "Knox does not even stay in Washington," Charles Taft raged. "Meyer is holding on until he sees what Roosevelt is going to do. . . . Fisher is seeking reputation for Fisher. Wickersham has done nothing but embarrass the president since he entered the cabinet. . . . MacVeagh means well, but he ought to be given a bottle of milk and allowed to crawl on the lap of Mrs. MacVeagh and sleep. I can't say much to the president, but I am going home tonight, and I propose to write him a letter that will open his eyes."

As a consequence of allowing cabinet heads great leeway, each department grew into an independent fiefdom, which aggravated the political turmoil. When cabinet appointees harassed and bullied him, as they frequently did, Taft was discomfited, but he failed to do anything about it. Even Vice-President Sherman, a rather insignificant figure, often attacked Taft. "Sherman's indictments," the president complained, "are as abrupt and severe as a school master's." When Taft suggested that Sherman stay in touch with the Speaker of the House, he haughtily replied, "I am the vice-president, and acting as a messenger boy is not part of the duties of the vice-president."

Taft had few intimates. Within the cabinet, the only other member besides Knox whom he truly liked was Secretary of War Dickinson of Tennessee. Even though he got a little impatient with some of his long-winded stories, Taft declared he would rather hear a poor story from Dickinson than a good one from anybody else. Dickinson talked interminably, but Taft never took his eyes off him and kept a warm smile throughout. They sat for hours discussing various matters, Butt wrote, and hammered at each other like two boys in a debating society. They invariably ended by reminiscing about the old days when they were friends in Tennessee and Chicago. It was this kind of relationship which mattered most to Taft.

Taft's need for amity with the people around him proved to be a political liability of some magnitude. His explanation of his philosophy about the role of the party leader partially explains a major source of the trouble: "If you have to say no, say it in such a way as to indicate to the person to whom you say it that you would like to say yes." Thus *no* not infrequently ended up sounding like *yes*. Petitioners sometimes came away convinced of their success, only to discover later that Taft had given their rivals the same impression. Mr. Taft, Lloyd Griscom observed, "was for party unity at any price." As his friend Edward Lowry wrote in *Washington Close-Ups*, "Mr. Taft couldn't please anybody, [because] he tried so hard to please everybody." Pringle, a very sympathetic biographer, gently admits that Taft "made gestures of amity and good-will—perhaps too many gestures." He consistently strove to make friends, hoping thereby to remove some of the unpleasantness of his situation.

Like presidents Woodrow Wilson, Lyndon Johnson, and Richard Nixon in more recent times, Taft came to view political dissent as a sign of personal disloyalty. Loyalty to friends and the Republican party had, of course, been an important factor in the series of promotions from a junior law partner in his father's law firm to president of the United States. Almost everyone recognized that Taft's immense capacity for both personal loyalty and strenuous work were largely responsible for his rising political fortunes. Being the son of an eminent Ohio Republican helped also, as Taft once acknowledged: "I got my political pull through my father's prominence." And now, as head of the Republican party, Taft expected the same kind of unquestioning obedience that he had previously granted superiors. He interpreted any deviation from Republican policy as a personal affront to the party chief. The president, Archie Butt observed, "does not like those who differ from him and will not permit criticism." Most who challenged him became his enemies. Predictably, the numbers grew, and many people were soon alarmed. Ray Stannard Baker observed that the heretofore genial Taft could now on occasion be seen to be furiously angry: "he storms and swears. He makes it a personal matter with every man who opposes his measures."

This overriding wish to avoid acrimonious confrontations was the main reason, in Baker's estimation, for Taft's meager success in obtaining effective legislation, for nearly all schemes resulted in "futile compromises." His inordinate need for ideological solidarity worked to his detriment, as concessions led to ineffectual measures.

Previously Taft had strongly supported the income tax sponsored by the progressives, but once he became the chief executive he began to waver. By 1911 he had abandoned the measure altogether. He told his brother Horace that he was "afraid of the discussion" and the "criticism" which would follow if there was a division over the constitutionality of the tax in the Supreme Court. Yet when questions arose over the policies or actions of some administration official, Taft, heedless of the issue at hand, loyally rushed to the defense. When Secretary of State Knox was criticized in the Senate for his "dollar diplomacy" in Nicaragua, Taft not only defended him, but in his zeal to quell the debate insisted upon a whitewash. Although such action was held to be "generous, kindly, and well-meant," it also stands as another example of how Taft suffered from the defects of his virtues.

On one issue, however, Taft refused to give in to his critics. Even though the cabinet members made plain their disapproval of his constant traveling, especially to such insignificant events as some school's commencement exercises, Taft only laughed, remarking that he was "somewhat of a tramp by nature." Even his brother Charles, who was rarely critical, suggested that it might be a good rule to make no more than one or two speeches a month. As for his excessive railroad travel, "I just wish you would cut it out," Charles wrote with exasperation. But nothing could dampen Taft's wanderlust or persuade him not to indulge it.

The preparation of messages to Congress, Taft soon discovered, was his hardest task. And so he often arranged to flee the capital just prior to their coming due. He generally delayed preparing state papers until it was too late to mail them to newspaper editors throughout the country, and as a consequence, many smaller papers carried only telegraphic summaries of his addresses. Before he left for his 1909 crosscountry trip, he charged the cabinet members to begin work on his annual State of the Union message and warned the press in advance not to expect a long one. Finding it hard to get back to work upon his return, Taft confessed to reporters just a week before the due date that he had not yet written a line.

Since he had never sought the office, Taft did not look upon it as an opportunity for personal leadership or achievement. Instead, he continually played down the office. After eight months in the White House, he told reporters: "The president has far less power than you think. . . . He is sort of [a] figurehead for the nation for four years. He is a kind of man that they blame everything for if it goes wrong, and if it goes right he does not get any credit for it." Then he announced, "In four years I shall step down and out." After becoming president, Taft felt that he had earned the right to relax and enjoy himself, as Arthur Wallace Dunn perceptively saw: "Something very strange happened in the life of William Howard Taft almost immediately after election; he was free, and he began to feel his freedom." This was the first time that he "was responsible to no one." To Butt Taft said, "I give you warning that the day is near when I will do just as I please and will not be bullied." Taft played golf daily, rode horseback, and took more and more to excursions by automobile. He indulged himself, taking his ease exchanging stories with friends with his feet extended on the lower drawer of his desk. With the single exception of the Philippines, there was no subject, newsmen complained, which the president liked to discuss more than golf. Unlike Roosevelt, who was an "indefatigable and omnivorous reader, often devouring three or four volumes in an evening," Taft never spent an evening with his books. The White House had echoed with Mrs. Roosevelt's voice calling "Theo-o-dore!", for after promising to come to bed each evening, he invariably picked up one more book, or magazine, or report before retiring. If Taft were left alone, he promptly went to sleep to escape loneliness and depression. Most of all he dearly loved to get away from the White House.

Many close associates with a first-hand knowledge felt that Taft did not care to be a success. Whenever an unavoidable decision arose, he spent such an inordinate amount of time deliberating—or seeming to deliberate—that when he finally decided on a course of action the immediate crisis had usually already passed. And when his mind was made up, he seldom stayed firmly on course. Ray Stannard Baker has charged that Taft often was moved by those around him from one stand "which he had taken apparently with firmness to quite the opposite position." At other times Taft made up his mind to end the matter, after which he wished to be left alone. Several individuals who tried later to induce him to reconsider some matter met with his wrath.

Nevertheless, as Taft's attorney general, George Wickersham, concluded, Taft was just "too judicially minded . . . indisposed to act swiftly, as an executive often must," and he soon became known in Washington as a "do nothing" president. Most of the newspapers coming to the White House contained editorials branding the president as a weakling and devoid of character. "He is weak," Butt agreed, "but it is a weakness which comes from openhearted trustfulness of those about him."

There are clearly turning points in every person's psychosocial development, crucial periods during which he will either grow and progress or, instead, shrink from the increased opportunities available to him and go no where at all or, worse yet, regress. Such a period occurred for William Howard Taft during the presidential years. Most people, watching Taft in the White House at the time or evaluating his performance in later years, have been chiefly concerned with viewing the facts and events of the administration externally, interpreting his presidency according to political philosophy or political and institutional pressure. These are important instruments for assessing the man and his administration, but there are equally important happenings—inner changes in the man—which ought not to be overlooked. In these interior realms, where vital psychological forces exist, one may discover meanings which cannot be touched except by considering the man personally, prior to the public roles he assumed. From this perspective, explanations will be found for many puzzles which elude those who employ the usual historical approaches. In seeking an intimate understanding of

Taft's sense of himself, one must examine how his own values, goals, and aspirations were either met and satisfied or instead frustrated during his four years in office. In some ways, as we shall see, the presidency served to invigorate Taft, to confirm him in his personal values and goals, which led later, almost a decade after he left office, to his actively seeking and achieving his "heart's desire," a place on the Supreme Court. But in many other ways the political office of the presidency clashed with those same values and feelings, causing Taft untold misery during his years in the White House. Yet the unhappiness he experienced in the presidency, which made him feel uncomfortably exposed and vulnerable, also pushed him ahead toward another stage of growth. He underwent subtle changes in his relations to Nellie and others, in his perceptions of the time remaining to him to achieve his own ambitions, and in the disequilibrium he experienced between his sense of personal well-being and safety and his feelings of threat and danger from those who harassed and criticized him and his policies.

Taft's entrance to the White House, despite the problems, was also a liberation; it would be only a matter of time before he realized he had finally succeeded in answering everyone's desires for themselves and expectations of him. After that he could look to himself. His becoming the most powerful man in the country led to his adjusting his ideas about how much he would be pushed and coerced by others and how much he might do to fulfill himself. Like other men, he could not ever be entirely his own man, but four years as president were nonetheless crucial in Taft's psychosocial history as he found ever greater maturity and self-motivation.

X

FROM HARMONY TO SNARLING

Soon after Taft took office, the *Washington Post* observed that "harmony sounds the keynote of the Taft administration." It was to be an administration in which neither political conniving nor expediency was expected to figure. But despite his efforts to maintain friendly relations with the conservative and progressive factions of the Republican party, Taft conciliated neither group. By 1912, the groups split into warring parties, and most people laid the blame directly on Taft. By 1912 progressivism had largely run its course.

Progressivism was, according to Ray Stannard Baker, a "deep-rooted, far-determined, slow-growing movement of the whole people." This movement for reform, beginning around the turn of the century, encompassed many groups with many different objectives. The adherents tended to be members of the urban middle-class who desired to see government take an active role in confronting the problems of an industrialized, urbanized America. Some progressives stressed the need to control predatory big businesses, some to clean up boss-dominated city governments, and some to achieve equal rights for women. Most agreed that government should be more responsive to the people, hoping to achieve the ends of reform through a variety of political procedures: initiative, referendum, and recall, the direct election of senators by the people rather than by business-controlled state legislatures, and the people's voice in the selection of presidential candidates through direct primary elections. At city, state, and national levels, progressives, spurred on by the revelatory articles of the "muckrakers," the investigative reporters of an earlier era, sought to remedy a variety of abuses from unsafe working conditions in the factories and child labor to unclean and adulterated food and drugs. Their achievements included employer liability acts, workman's compensation acts, minimum wages for women, widow's pensions, and mother's assistance acts. Progressive ideas for more efficient city government, like the commission and city-manager plans, were quickly implemented, and new progressive mayors such as Tom Johnson of Cleveland and Brand Whitlock of Toledo cleaned up their cities by eradicating, however temporarily, machine politics. Progressive governors Charles Evans Hughes of New York, Hiram Johnson of California, Joseph Folk of Missouri, Robert LaFollette of Wisconsin, Albert Cummins of Iowa succeeded in bringing a myriad of overdue reforms to their states.

Theodore Roosevelt, who fancied himself a "progressive conservative," described the increasingly independent, vocal, and insurgent Republican congressmen as progressives who are "exceeding the speed limit." In the House there were perhaps forty insurgent Republicans, led by George Norris, until he entered the Senate in 1913. Originally a lawyer from Ohio, Norris had moved to Beaver City, Nebraska, in 1885 where he served three terms as prosecuting attorney of Furnas County and then as district judge until 1902 when he sought and won election to Congress. When the 1912 split came, Norris went with Roosevelt and the "Bull Moosers." Later, as senator, Norris's most notable service was his battle for federal water power regulation and public ownership of hydroelectric plants, culminating in the TVA system under Franklin Delano Roosevelt. He was, in addition, sponsor of the Norris-LaGuardia Anti-injunction Act of 1932 and the Twentieth (Lame Duck) Amendment to the Constitution (1933).

The Senate insurgents were a dedicated group of eleven led by Robert LaFollette of Wisconsin. His colleague Joseph Bristow called LaFollette "the best informed" and "the ablest of all the progressives." After receiving his law degree from the University of Wisconsin, young LaFollette had opposed the political bosses of Dane County and succeeded in his bid for district attorney in 1880 and for election to Congress in 1885. In Washington he broke with the conservative leadership of Wisconsin Senator Philitus Sawyer and began the long fight for causes that were later labeled as progressive. Believing he could accomplish more at home, he sought the governorship unsuccessfully in 1896 and in 1898, before his energetic campaign to bring the issues directly to the people won him the office in 1900. His "Wisconsin Idea," which included railroad control, tax reform, direct primary elections, workman's compensation, and the conservation of forests and water power, served as a model for all progressive governors. After three terms as governor, LaFollette took his seat in the Senate where he continued to battle "standpatters" of every political stripe. LaFollette's single-minded dedication to the fight derived from his belief that "half a loaf is fatal whenever it is accepted at the sacrifice of the basic principle. Half a loaf, as a rule dulls the appetite." Believing that big industry and finance had captured and corrupted the federal government, he declared "unceasing warfare" against these special interests. The leading conservative spokesmen, Nelson Aldrich and his friends in the Senate, intensely disliked LaFollette. They handicapped him in every imaginable way, including personal discourtesies and brutal snubs, which were keenly felt. As a reward for his long years of service, culminating in the drafting of the program for the National Progressive Republican League, LaFollette justifiably expected the Progressives to support him for president in 1912. But he had not reckoned with Theodore Roosevelt's decision to regain power.

The progressive or reform wing of the party had, at Theodore Roosevelt's command, nominated Taft, whereas the conservative or Old Guard Republicans had nominated him because they thought he was preferable to the unpredictable incumbent. This was certainly no secret to Roosevelt, who explained conservative reasoning in this way: "We won't have Taft; but if we don't take Taft we will get Roosevelt; so we will take Taft." The insurgent progressive leaders had expected Taft's active support of their policies. But President Taft, they soon discovered, had no intention of becoming continually embroiled in the dispute between progressives and conservatives.

During the campaign Taft led many progressives to believe that he would aid their attempt to topple powerful Joe Cannon, who had been Speaker of the House for many years. A congressman for twenty-eight years before he was elected Speaker in 1903, Cannon, at the age of sixty-seven, was a coarse, uncultured, but witty man, who well deserved the epithets attached to him: "despot" and "tyrant." The "Hayseed from Illinois," as he was sometimes called, had tremendous power under existing congressional rules. His arbitrary and partisan control of the House was soon dubbed "Cannonism." He selected most of the members of the Rules Committee, which held the power to decide what legislation would be considered. Because Cannon also made appointments to other House committees, he naturally resisted all attempts to change the House rules and curtail his powers. "I am goddamned tired of listening to all this babble for reform. America is a hell of a success," was typical of his public statements. He arrogantly challenged and freely insulted the progressives in Congress and out. "The insurgents would have competed with Judas over the thirty pieces of silver," he snarled on one occasion. "The insurgents should be hanged," on another.

During the campaign Taft had expressed his distaste for Cannon in letters to friends and political supporters. "I do not hesitate to say to you confidentially," he wrote Colonel W.R. Nelson in August 1908, "that the great weight I have to carry in this campaign is Cannonism, which is the synonym for reactionaryism." He expressed similar sentiments to Elihu Root just before the election: "I have not said anything for publication, but I am willing to have it understood that my attitude is one of hostility to Cannon and the whole crowd. . . . Just because he has a nest of standpatters in his House and is so ensconced there that we may not be able to move him is no reason why I should pursue a policy of harmony." It was not long after the inauguration, however, that Taft assumed a neutral pose. After testing anti-Cannon sentiments in Congress, he found that ousting him would be a near impossible task and began to backtrack. To a reform congressman who had counted on the president's help, he pleaded a constitutional defense: "I would be very severely criticized if I should attempt to use executive power to control the election in the House." Thus he rationalized his motives for avoiding a confrontation over the issue. On constitutional grounds he smiled impartially at insurgent and regular alike.

To the progressives' dismay, Taft went so far as to seek a reconciliation with "Uncle Joe" and his conservative supporters. Although Cannon had no respect for Taft as a politician (he once joked that "if Taft were pope he'd want to appoint some Protestants to the College of Cardinals"), he was glad to have the president's friendship. The progressives, who had reasonably assumed that Taft was their ally, were initially hopeful about defeating Cannon. But they suddenly had to reassess their strategy upon finding Taft actively courting Cannon and other Old Guard leaders like Senator Nelson Aldrich, the high tariff apostle from Rhode Island.

Aldrich, the master spirit of the Senate, placed the men in the Senate "like puppets on a chess board." Barely a month after Taft had received the Republican nomination, Aldrich began making overtures. Taft replied warmly to the congratulatory note: "I am anxious to see you and talk with the levelest-headed man in the country. I am very grateful to you for your assistance and good-will." After the election, Washington was surprised to learn that Taft had invited Aldrich and other conservative Republicans to dinner, sat with them on the White House porch, and taken automobile rides with them around the countryside. Some who had opposed Taft's nomination, now crowded round him, and Taft's "easy-going temperament responded" to their friendly overtures.

Even before Taft's inauguration, Butt felt that "the old crowd," typified by rich, conservative Senators such as Aldrich, George Wetmore, Chauncey Depew, are already " 'licking their chops.' They are looking forward to seven

Roosevelt's Secretary of War (1905)

Taft with his brother Charles (1907)

Taft the Candidate (1908)

Helen (Nellie) Herron Taft (1908)

President Taft (1909)

Helen, Charlie, the President, Robert, and Nellie (1909)

The First Lady (1909)

Taft at play (1909)

The President with his Aide, Archie Butt (1911)

Professor of Law, Yale University (1913)

Nellie with the Chief Justice (1924)

fat years after the seven lean years which are just now drawing to a close." It was feared that Taft would unintentionally turn the government over to these men. As progressives became furious, observers noted a "tremendous relief in and about the headquarters of Speaker Cannon." In Kansas, William Allen White, progressive Republican journalist, suggested at the time that Taft detached himself from the Progressives because he desired to avoid "disagreeable encounters" with the opposition. When newspaperman Oscar King Davis tried to advise Taft on his unpopularity with a large portion of the Republican party because of his change in course, Taft looked at him "as if that were the very first time any such idea had occurred to him." "There's something in that, Oscar," the president replied, "I don't know but you are right." Yet there followed no effort to moderate his overtures to Old Guard leaders.

Shortly after Taft signed the Payne-Aldrich Tariff Act in August 1909, he was persuaded to go to Massachusetts, where he made a speech which Champ Clark called "a gorgeous eulogy" on Nelson W. Aldrich, chief of the standpatters. Previously critical of Aldrich, Taft could now be heard describing the Rhode Islander as "one of the ablest statesmen in financial matters in either House," "the real leader of the Senate," and a legislator who had "an earnest desire to aid the people." Taft later confided to Butt, "I may have made a political mistake in doing it, but I have the satisfaction of knowing that I said what I believed." The president added, "the muckrakers think Aldrich has captured me, and I think I have captured Aldrich." "The results will show which is right," Taft concluded, and they did.

As a result of his peace efforts, Taft was rapidly alienating the insurgent Republicans and falling ever more completely into the hands of their enemies. Ray Stannard Baker thought that Taft had "played like the child . . . [who] pulled daisies for friends in both armies." Moderate and liberal newspapers ran a cartoon depicting a huge Taft with a crouching Uncle Joe Cannon behind him. Taft was shown protecting Cannon from flying bricks while the Speaker shouted in glee, "May your shadow never grow less, Bill." The *New York Times* claimed Taft had "foolishly and needlessly [linked] his fortunes with a band of men who are losing and ought to lose the power they have so long and so ruthlessly abused."

When the progressives called at the White House seeking support for the fight against Cannon, they got little encouragement. To the president they proposed to abolish the Speaker's arbitrary power to recognize members on the floor of the House, and to elect a committee on rules to reduce the speakership considerably. "I do not think it is a good time to meddle," Taft explained to Democratic Congressman Bourke Cockran after the meeting. "I may have to use the very machinery they are denouncing to pass a tariff bill. And a tariff bill must be passed." He also tried to joke about it, calling the insurgents' action against Cannon "revolutionary." How could he, as the head of an orderly state, be expected to join in a revolution? He still insisted, however, that he had much sympathy for the insurgents in their battle against Cannonism; he wished them well, but refused to become involved.

When the progressives failed in their attempt to recapture the House from Cannon's iron-fisted control in March 1909, Taft uneasily justified his about-face to the insurgent leader Joseph Bristow by appealing to the need for party harmony. Perhaps his assistance in the fight against Cannon might have brought success, he wrote Bristow, if he had "gone in hammer and tongs," but that would have set an "ugly precedent." "Had I beaten Cannon, I should have had a factious and ugly Republican minority, willing and anxious to defeat all progressive measures, and with the power to defeat them," he said. Party unity was most important to the president whenever, by invoking it, he could escape an unpleasant confrontation. Uncle Joe had agreed to help Taft with his legislation, and Taft was quickly convinced that Cannon and his House machinery were indispensable. Aldrich too pledged help, so "I would be a fool," Taft wrote to Horace, to join the "yelping and snarling" reformers, who "do not look beyond their noses." To critic Lucius Swift Taft explained, "I am trying to do the best I can with Congress as it is, and I am not to be driven by any set of circumstances into an attack upon those who are standing faithfully with me in attempting to redeem the pledges of the party." Champ Clark, the progressive Democrat who succeeded Cannon as Speaker in April 1911, recalled that after their defeat in the rules fight, his colleagues were "astounded and angered" at Taft's desertion. "We got a bloody licking," Clark wrote of the Democratic-insurgent debacle, and we "never forgave" him.

XI

HOLDING COURT IN THE RED ROOM:
Nellie in the White House

Contemporaries described Nellie Taft as "immensely capable," a woman with a "quality of managing energy," and a lady "of exceptional learning, intelligence, and ambition." She not only stirred Taft to his "best endeavors," but also functioned effectively as housekeeper, mother, and community servant. Although modern biographers describe her as a forbidding woman, Nellie enjoyed, at least in the beginning, a favorable press in Washington circles. "In the matter of mental attainments," said the *Washington Post*, "she is probably the best fitted woman who ever graced the position she now holds and enjoys." She is a "splendid, intelligent woman, an accomplished singer and pianist, and a linguist who speaks French with particular proficiency. Furthermore, she loves literature and fine art. She has been a student all her life and takes an interest in every public event." The *New York Times* proclaimed that Mrs. Taft "has brains and uses them." Archie Butt, who personally preferred Mrs. Roosevelt to Mrs. Taft, admitted that Nellie was "an intellectual woman and a woman of wonderful executive ability."

Nellie enjoyed the conversation of men but not of women. Like her mother-in-law in Cincinnati, Nellie avoided the society of women in Washington. "Mrs. Taft," Butt commented, saw very little of the cabinet wives because "she would not take the trouble to do so." And Nellie did not enjoy accompanying Mr. Taft on his numerous out-of-town trips, because "He is taken in charge by committees and escorted everywhere with honor, while I am usually sent with a lot of uninteresting women." After she became first lady (as she at the age of seventeen had fantasized she would), Nellie reveled in the political excitement of Washington. Whatever William Howard Taft lacked in the way of strength, energy, ambition, and political curiosity, was made up twofold by his wife. Together they would succeed—and fail.

Nellie Taft, after Roosevelt the chief architect of Taft's political career, played a somewhat different role, however, once she was in the White House, ceasing to prod her husband so much and concentrating on entertainment and White House management instead. Nellie had long planned for the day when she would become first lady of the land, and as Alice Roosevelt Longworth remarked, she had "her own ideas of how the White House should be run. They were rather grander than ours." To Irwin Hood Hoover, chief usher in the White House, it seemed that shortly after her arrival Mrs. Taft was planning "to revolutionize the place." The details of management were to be radically changed, and she wanted many of these changes implemented before she and Taft moved in. What particularly bothered Hoover was that Mrs. Taft's aggressive methods for changing White House routine made it seem "as if there were no possibility that anything had been conducted properly before this time." Naturally he resented the implication. Nellie gave some clue to her motivation in declaring, "I could not feel that I was mistress . . . if I did not take an active interest in all the details of running it."

Butt helped prevent some ill feeling by arranging work transfers to the executive office for those White House staff members Mrs. Taft had summarily dismissed. Although somewhat uneasy about her manner, Butt felt that Mrs. Taft's honesty and directness deserved admiration. To Clara, he confided, "I am beginning to believe that I am going to get along with her simply by adapting myself to her straight-forward method and direct mode of thought." Others were not so readily brought round. Nellie began her reign by gratuitously insulting Alice Roosevelt Longworth, who possessed no little spirit of her own. Alice had explained to Mrs. Taft that she might be late for the inaugural luncheon as she had to see her father off at the station, upon which Nellie offered her a ticket to permit her re-entrance into the White House. Furious, Alice went away "shouting to friends and relatives with the news that I was going to be allowed to have a ticket to permit me to enter the White House. I—a very capital I—who had wandered in and out for eight happy winters!" Right then it was, Alice wrote in *Crowded Hours,* that "I gave myself over to a pretty fair imitation of mischief making."

Eager to direct personally the social life of the White House, Nellie planned to dispense with the social secretary that most first ladies, including her predecessor, Mrs. Roosevelt, had employed. In *Secrets of the White House*

Elizabeth Jaffray described how Mrs. Taft, who had decided upon hiring a new housekeeper, called her to the White House for an interview. Even though Mrs. Jaffray had retired, Nellie insisted upon having her for the job. Mrs. Jaffray recalled that she was rather overwhelmed by the first lady at their meeting. "Sit down," Mrs. Taft commanded sharply, and after a short conversation Mrs. Jaffray found herself agreeing to join the staff. "I simply found myself swept into the position, by this rather outspoken, determined lady," she wrote.

Although Nellie's enthusiasm for readjusting White House routine caused considerable consternation among the permanent staff, under her management the presidential mansion was running quietly and orderly, in sharp contrast to the way it operated under the Roosevelts. During the Roosevelt years, Ike Hoover conceded, a nervous person came around the White House at his own risk. The Roosevelt children held nothing sacred and made the Executive Mansion their playhouse. Rooms that had been in mothballs for years came alive with their howls and laughter. They took delight in roller skating and bicycle riding all over the house, especially on the polished hardwood floors. Giving the pony a ride in the elevator was another of their famous stunts. Under the Tafts, one heard little noise; even the servants learned to whisper.

Immediately after moving into the White House, Nellie began redecorating the living quarters in oriental style, a style she had grown so fond of during her travels in the East and their sojourn in the Philippines. She brought in great quantities of oriental furniture, tapestries, floormats, or *petates*, and decorated Japanese screens. In addition, she created something of the verdant look of the Philippine palace they had once inhabited by crowding the White House with plants of every description. Disgruntled servants began to refer to the mansion as the "Malacanan Palace." Parts of the White House formerly open to the public were now closed off for the Taft family's private use. Nellie, who disliked being confined only to the traditional living quarters, made as much use of the downstairs rooms—especially the Red Room—as of the upstairs area. Other rearrangements included the installation of a vault in which, for the first time, the White House silver was cleaned by electricity. Nellie also required daily an abundance of cut orchids and roses, for she insisted that the living quarters be always redolent with the odor of flowers. Taft was very proud of the way Nellie had "taken hold" of affairs.

Nor did Nellie stop with strictly private arrangements. She decided that what Washington needed most was some of the lovely cherry trees she had seen in Japan. When the mayor of Tokyo heard that she planned to purchase some of these beautifully flowering trees, he decided to make a gift of them to the United States. Consequently, in December 1909, three railroad cars, loaded with two thousand Japanese cherry trees and accompanied by a special agent, were on their way to Washington from the West Coast. As millions of visitors to Washington have seen each spring, they were successfully planted around the tidal basin of the Capitol. The following spring the Tafts rode along the Potomac Drive Way to view the trees, all of which were covered with delicate pink flowers, causing Mrs. Taft to clap her hands in delight.

Nellie Taft had always relished pomp and pageantry, and the Red Room became her favorite place to "hold court," like a queen. One of her first decrees was that the entire staff dress in fancy uniforms. "I decided," she wrote, "to have, at all hours, footmen in livery at the White House door." In addition, she insisted that all male employees in the White House be clean-shaven, a decree which provoked a temporary revolt, since many of them had either mustaches or beards and were loath to lose them. Archie Butt realized Mrs. Taft's fondness for having aides about her in full regalia, and he asked the president about how much gold braid he ought to wear. Taft replied, "It makes no difference to me but you couldn't put on too much to please Mrs. Taft." Nellie ordered an automobile for herself, which was even more expensive than the president's—a large, green limousine upon which was emblazoned the shield of the nation. Another of her "startling changes" sprang from her enthusiasm for exact protocol: there was to be a return to a strict "recognition of official position" during White House entertainments. Nevertheless at their first state dinner she committed an error which revealed much about her own sense of place: the president should have entered first, but she bolted in ahead of him.

The White House was Nellie's chosen domain and she intended to make her influence felt. "You could hardly turn around," Mrs. Lillian Parks (a White House staff member) complained of Nellie's energy and ambition, "without running into Mrs. Taft. She checked up on everyone." Although wives had traditionally had little to say about who would or would not be invited to official state dinners, Nellie managed to say a good deal. Archie was particularly annoyed: "Of course, she should have nothing to say as to who will or will not come to these state dinners, but she does." Nellie wanted the last say not only on the guest lists but also on every aspect of every social event. Taft eventually got the names he wanted on the invitation list, but only after a prolonged bout with the first lady. Not only was she her own social secretary, but she superintended the White House financial accounts as well. When he reached the White House every morning, Archie Butt sent a message up asking if Mrs. Taft wished to see him. She usually did. While receiving her instructions, he wrote, "I sit bolt upright in one chair and she in another." She often spoke to him about their poor financial situation, although Taft was the first president to receive a salary of $100,000 plus expenses. In addition, beginning with the Taft administration, the government began paying the wages of all White House servants. Up to then, presidents paid their own staff. Even though Nellie was a frugal manager, she never stinted in entertaining. She had hoped to make the money go as far as possible, however, and expected Butt to help her. Their savings amounted to only $5,000 but, as she announced to Archie, "We should not have that now, had not I worried over every expenditure." Taft replied, "My dear, how much do you think we have added to our income by worry and trouble?" "I fear nothing," she said, "but I have made ends meet, and you have been able to make moves when they were necessary without borrowing money." In their first year in the White House she managed to put away $34,000 and hoped to save at least $30,000 more in each of the remaining years of his term.

"The only promise I extracted from her," Taft told Butt, was that "she would not economize in dressing and, contrary to what I expected, she is keeping that promise. As you may have discovered, economy is her prevailing mood." Although she was not at first profligate in buying clothes, Mrs. Taft was soon well launched in that direction. Few women dressed with more taste.

Nellie Taft did not have many intimate friends in Washington. The lack, Butt thought, was because she was habitually buried "down deep within herself." The *Post* suggested that she had few friends because she spent most of her time running the White House, looking after Taft's comfort, and "assisting him in his work." Nellie directed her efforts primarily to entertaining on a grand scale. And of all the first ladies under whom Ike Hoover served—from Mrs. Benjamin Harrison through Mrs. Calvin Coolidge—he felt that Mrs. Taft tried the hardest to be a success and that her parties were the most spectacular. There were twice as many social affairs in the Taft administration than previously. To the *Washington Post* it seemed the Tafts "entertained continuously." They entertained more people and more elaborately than had any previous couple in the White House.

Already impressed by Nellie's wonderful executive ability, Butt expressed no surprise that everything was done on a big scale and in the best form. According to the most critical gourmets in the city, dinners at the White House under the Taft administration were the finest to be enjoyed in Washington. Nellie made sure that there was always plenty of "a very fair vintage" champagne. Butt complained about one of Mrs. Taft's innovations, however: the serving of French artichokes for a first course. If she did not stop the practice, he feared, she was going to find some guest choked to death one night, for he once saw no less than six people seated near him trying to eat the "sticky fungus stuff" and another who actually tried to chew up the leaves.

The practice of having a musical or stage performance after each state dinner was inaugurated by Nellie. Particularly memorable were entertainments featuring Fritz Kreisler, the Boston Symphony Orchestra's stringed quartet, and a performance, notably, of *A Midsummer Night's Dream* on the White House lawn. Nellie made a point of inviting artists, musicians, and writers to dinner, favoring them with Tiffany gold medals as souvenirs.

Arthur W. Dunn, citing the numerous garden parties, musicales, dances, and dinners held at the White House, including the largest congressional reception to that time, decided that "as hosts, President and Mrs. Taft were never excelled." Mrs. Taft had very fine taste, Elizabeth Jaffray said of the first lady; the teas which she held in the Red Room were models of what such affairs should be. Their daughter Helen's debut in December 1910, was a day especially to remember. A lavish evening affair followed a tea for 1203 guests. The White House was decked with masses of holly, roses, orchids, and Azaleas. The only blemish lay in the newspaper social editors' confessed difficulty in whipping up enthusiasm for "Helen pink" as a replacement for the still popular "Alice blue."

President Taft was only too happy to relax and enjoy himself socially over the elaborate meals prepared by the talented Swedish cook (formerly in the employ of J.P. Morgan) whom Nellie had hired in New York. Taft contributed to each party's success by providing the men with good Havana cigars, which he ordered in lots of five thousand directly from Cuba. He was, Irwin Hoover noted, very fond of entertaining, especially at dinner parties, and was ever ready to engage in all social festivities. Taft summed the matter up perfectly: "I would rather entertain people I don't like than not to entertain at all."

A joy to Taft but an extreme annoyance to Nellie were those occasions when Alice Roosevelt Longworth attended White House social affairs, although they soon dwindled in number at Nellie's express command. "Princess" Alice always managed to capture everyone's attention. Taft did not approve her madcap behavior, but was charmed by her beauty and her brilliant repartee. He got dreadfully put out with Alice at times, but melted whenever she was nice to him. One of the few persons Alice could not please was Mrs. Taft. She therefore sometimes took pleasure in annoying her. At a French embassy dinner in 1909 celebrating the fall of the Bastille, Alice came late as usual, knowing full well that arriving after the president was an unpardonable offense. After a flamboyant entrance, her apologies to Taft were so flagrantly absurd that everyone present could not help but laugh, including the president. He took her hands and said, "Alice, if you will only stop trying to be so respectful to me, I believe you would become so." Sweeping her arm around the room, she replied, "And then I would bore you to death as the other women do." Nellie was not amused.

Nellie thought nothing of revising established White House forms of entertaining if she felt improvements were possible. At the annual New Year's reception for congressmen, for example, she noted the declining attendance in past years and sought to discover the cause. She learned that guests disliked having to come in through the long East corridor where they were jostled by others, and then waiting in a long line to be greeted by the president. Senators, she found, had been passing their White House invitations on to friends and even to servants. Nellie forthwith issued an invitation for them to use the South entrance. She also did away with the formality and stiffness that made these receptions so boring. The congressmen were surprised and delighted. For the first time in the history of diplomatic receptions, Butt said, the guests had remained until the end. White House social affairs, the New York *Herald Tribune* reported, were, thanks to Mrs. Taft, now so enjoyable and lovely that they compared favorably with state functions in the Old World. The critical news-reports on Taft's administration were thus counterbalanced to some extent by praise of Nellie's social administration.

One joy Taft had as president was the great delight he took in seeing Nellie in the White House. It was, he knew, the fulfillment of her dreams, and he fully expected her to be an energetic first lady. He described proudly to his brother Henry how she took such an interest in presidential politics. But his greatest happiness, he confided to Roosevelt in 1910, was that she seemed indifferent to the "storm of abuse" to which he was subjected. Disappointing her by the inadequate performance of his duties now that he was at last in the White House was something he greatly feared. But she was not bothered by the controversies which arose, and that, he wrote, "has reconciled me more than anything else." Nellie particularly enjoyed listening to Taft's speeches. Butt describes one such occasion in May 1911, when Taft delivered an address to a lawyers' banquet at the Hotel Astor in New York. Nellie was looking truly pretty, he observed, happy and in good health. She joined in the applause, especially when Taft attacked the recall of judges, which for some time she had urged him to oppose openly. No doubt Nellie derived vicarious satisfaction from seeing her husband publicly present ideas which originated with her.

For Nellie, the culmination of her social ambitions was their elaborate Silver Wedding anniversary party held in June 1911. "It did not seem unfitting to me," she wrote in her memoirs, "that this anniversary should be spent in the White House or that we should seek to make it an event not to be forgotten by anybody who happened to witness it. I thanked the happy fate that had given me a summer wedding day because I needed all outdoors for the kind of party I wanted to give." And indeed, she noted, "a more brilliant throng was never gathered in this country." A virtual inundation of silver anniversary presents flowed in. "Well, I never knew there was as much silver in the world," Butt remarked to his sister-in-law. "It is hideous to see such profligacy." He felt that it would have been more dignified if the president had requested that no presents be sent, but that was not part of Mrs. Taft's plan. Chief among the gifts was a huge, two-hundred-year-old soup tureen, reputed to have cost $8,000, which Judge Gary, the steel magnate, sent. John D. Rockefeller, Jr., gave them a cabinet of splendid tea caddies. These presents prompted the scrupulous Taft to give directions that "no one see the presents, at least until certain ones have been secreted in cold storage." Three dozen sterling silver service plates were sent by the House of Representatives and a set of sterling compote dishes came from the Senate. Express wagons arrived hourly at the White House bearing gifts large and small. Forty general's wives combined to send a platinum watch, encrusted with diamonds. Vice-President Sherman gave a huge silver vase; Secretary of the Treasury MacVeagh, a silver punch bowl with a gold lining. The silver vases, almond dishes, pitchers, trays, fruit dishes, cups, and flatware were too numerous to be counted. (Years later the ever-frugal Nellie had the monograms erased from many of the items and gave them again as wedding presents.) The czar of Russia, the sultan of Turkey, the emperor of Germany, the president of France, the emperor of China, the kings of Italy, of Spain, of Sweden, and Pope Pius X—all sent greetings and gifts.

Nellie sent out six thousand invitations, and for months the White House and Washington buzzed with nothing but plans for the spectacular event. Relatives of every president since 1861 were invited. Mr. and Mrs. Robert T. Lincoln, Major General Frederick Grant, U.S. Grant, Junior, Mr. and Mrs. Chester A. Arthur, Mr. and Mrs. Harry Garfield, and Mrs. Grover Cleveland came—but Colonel and Mrs. Theodore Roosevelt sent regrets. The guests arrived, thirty-four hundred in number, to find the White House lawn a fairyland—the shrubbery around the mansion twinkled with thousands of tiny red, white, and blue electric bulbs. Paper lanterns glowed among the trees, colored lights sparkled in the fountains, and from the roof of the White House searchlights illuminated an American flag. A thousand feet to the south the Washington Monument, shining with a thousand electric lights, stood in magnificent relief against the dark sky. The White House was lit throughout with hundreds of electric lamps. Each drawing room was lined with flowers and its mantel banked with the same—the Red Room in

American Beauty roses, the Blue Room with rare orchids. Mrs. Taft's white and gold piano nearly disappeared under flowers. When the Marine Band struck up the Wedding March, twelve ushers in white came down the main staircase of the White House to open the way along the carpeted walk to the lawn. The president's aides descended next, then President and Mrs. Taft—wearing the diamond tiara he had given her—followed by the cabinet members and their wives, and finally the president's brothers and Mrs. Taft's sisters. They proceeded slowly through the White House to the rear portico and onto the lawn where they planned to receive the guests. Hundreds of military officers ranked in white uniforms looked on. Outside the White House grounds one hundred policemen and scores of plain clothesmen and Secret Service guards carefully supervised the fifteen thousand people who crowded up against the iron fence in an attempt to catch a glimpse of the spectacle.

Nellie Taft, resplendently begowned in white satin brocaded with silver flowers, stood on the South Portico with the president receiving guests underneath a huge arch of smilax and palms emblazoned with the dates 1886–1911 in silver. Nellie remained at Taft's side in the receiving line the entire evening, even though she had originally planned to retire inside early to avoid excessive strain. The State Dining Room was opened at eleven o'clock to reveal an elaborate buffet supper with champagne and great bowls of wine punch. The seventy-five-pound anniversary cake was decorated with twenty-five crystal hearts embedded in scrolls, surrounded by turtle doves, and covered with cherubs that "rose from a frosted sea."

By midnight Nellie was exhausted. She watched from a window as the dancing and festivities continued until two A.M. After the party was over, one observer proclaimed it to be "the most brilliant function ever held in that historic mansion." Ellen Slayden, wife of a Democratic congressman from Texas, had another view: It was "a prodigious affair," she wrote in her memoirs, *Washington Wife*, but the company was "promiscuous" to such a degree that it was "crude like a fair or a circus. . . . The Tafts have such excellent taste usually, and I am sorry to hear them criticized so sharply for accepting carloads of presents."

Unlike most first ladies, Nellie did not confine her influence to the social sphere. Her unprecedented role soon caused a great deal of talk within the White House, for she presumed to sit in on many of the important political conferences held in the mansion. Hoover felt that she possessed a "keen discernment" in such matters and acted as if she had been accustomed to taking part all her life. She sometimes walked in on Taft's private conferences unheralded and unannounced. "Mrs. Taft seemed to feel responsible for everything," Mrs. Parks recalled, including "her husband's success." She freely entered into political discussions at White House parties, joining the men who surrounded the president. She "seemed to enjoy that more than talking with the ladies." (Upon entering the White House she discontinued the weekly meetings of the cabinet officer's wives, which Ethel Roosevelt had inaugurated.) Sometimes when Taft was unsure of his ground she would carry on the conversation for him, with much success. And on the sly she was continually helping the forgetful Taft with names and statistics. "Mrs. Taft seemed always to be present and taking a leading part in the discussions," Ike Hoover observed. If at a large social gathering, some important politician took Taft aside for a private talk, "they would always be joined by Mrs. Taft as soon as she realized the situation." The conversation would then continue with her taking a full share in it. It was no uncommon sight, according to Hoover, to see Senator Aldrich or Speaker Cannon consulting jointly with President and Mrs. Taft. When accused of attempting to influence policy, Nellie retorted that she was only keeping the president awake. But more than one biographer has suggested that if her health had remained good and she had been in a position to advise him about the tariff and other matters, Taft's record might have been altogether different.

She would not suffer being cast in the background. When President Taft on occasion gave a stag dinner for various congressmen, Nellie, hating not to be at the center of all the political talk, arranged to have her dinner served in a lobby closely adjoining the State Dining Room so that she could hear the voices and the music through the door. A reporter once sought an interview with her for an article entitled, appropriately, "There are kings and rulers of kings, presidents and makers of presidents." She began by snapping, with a touch of indignation, "Of course you know *I* can't be quoted on any subject of importance." Her continual advice and reproaches were gossiped about in Washington circles, and it was told that she had a sharp tongue and thought nothing of rebuking her husband at public gatherings. In self-defense, Nellie countered, "I confess only to a lively interest in my husband's work, which I experienced from the beginning of our association."

Taft once expressed his amusement over the fact that they disagreed on policies so often. "Will, you approve everything—everything Norton [Taft's private secretary] brings you," she charged. And all that "Captain Butt brings to you," she added in exasperation, "and everything everybody brings to you." Taft chuckled and replied, "Well, my dear, if I approve everything, you disapprove everything, so we even up on the world." "It's no laughing matter," she answered sharply. "I don't approve of letting people run your business for you." Admonished, Taft answered, "I don't either, my dear, but if you will notice, I usually have my way in the long run." To which the shrewd Nellie retorted, "No you don't. You think you do, but you don't."

The ultimate irony of this exchange is that Taft did live long enough to have his way finally, for Harding was to sign the papers appointing him chief justice of the United States in 1921. By then, of course, Nellie had enjoyed her "full years" in the White House.

Almost immediately after Taft's inauguration, Washington began discussing Nellie's influence on official appointments, especially with respect to the White affair. The new president took his time about making new appointments and reshuffling governmental officials, but there was one noticeable exception. Ambassador Henry White in France was immediately requested to step down from the diplomatic post which he had enjoyed so much. The cause of the dismissal had its beginnings years before, at the time of the Tafts' honeymoon tour of Europe in 1886. White was then secretary of the legation in a German city. Nellie, desirous of attending a diplomatic function with European royalty present, sent Taft to the legation to secure their invitation. White unknowingly made a grave mistake for his future career when he sent the Tafts a note saying that the affair was "very exclusive," and they were not welcome. Nellie did not forget that slight, and in 1909 she had her revenge. After White's dismissal, Washington was buzzing with this tale. Delegated by Roosevelt to query Taft on the matter, Alice was reassured by the new president: "You must believe that I am big enough to forget that sort of thing." But Nellie was not. Elihu Root attempted to dissuade Taft from firing such an experienced and able diplomat as White, but he discovered him to be "inexorable." And so, Alice wrote to her father, "there was another to add to a mounting list of black marks, or betrayals, as they began to seem." Later, after the collapse of Roosevelt's and Taft's friendship, Taft regretted hearkening to his wife's command. He ruefully confessed to his brother Charles, "I had no idea that his [Roosevelt's] heart was [so] set on Harry White."

Nellie was sometimes just as influential in making new appointments. Archie Butt reported the conclusion of one discussion between the Tafts about one particular official appointment, in which, after vetoing Taft's choice for the position, Nellie said, "I could not believe you to be serious when you mentioned that man's name. I won't even talk about it."

Washington circles knew that Nellie was envious of the young, witty, intelligent daughter of the former president. And Archie, well aware of the nature of their strained relationship, once warned Alice that she was making a mistake in not placating Mrs. Taft and in underrating her influence in the administration. Mrs. Taft had informed Archie, and he confided the information to Alice, that she personally had prevented Nick Longworth—Alice's future husband—from being assigned minister to China. "I suppose the president put it on different grounds, but the real reason for his refusal was the opposition made to it by Mrs. Taft." She simply would not have it. On another occasion Nellie evened another old social score with President Harrison's daughter, Mrs. McKee. It was expected, until Nellie intervened, that she would be invited to the White House. "No, I do not want her," Nellie commanded. "She was never even polite to me in the past and I have not forgotten it."

Nellie took a lively interest in the political activities in Washington. Senate and House floor discussions exhilarated her, and sometimes she would not leave the proceedings even to take time out for lunch. When the Supreme Court opened in 1911, she went to see the new justices sworn in and therewith demolished one more antiquated custom. She demanded and secured a seat within the bar of the court—the first time a woman had ever penetrated that august circle. On most issues, Nellie was as well informed as her husband, and more liberal in her point of view. The *Washington Post* described her as "brainy, competent," and a force within the White House.

Nellie performed a vital role in less dramatic situations as well. She kept after the president to correct his embarrassing habit of falling asleep at unsuitable times, a trial for any wife, but especially for the first lady. President Taft also relied on Nellie to get him to his appointments on time. As he was fond of saying, she was his partner in every endeavor. When, for instance, Taft was visiting the invalid Justice Moody, and the Justice began giving him some excellent advice on how he should handle his relationship with Roosevelt, Taft, impressed with Moody's argument, turned to Butt and said how much he wished Mrs. Taft was in the room. He then asked Butt to go to the car and bring her up. When this was done, Taft requested the dying Justice to repeat all again for Mrs. Taft to hear.

Nellie's political advice, while often shrewd and intelligent, was not always to the president's liking. Unconcerned with political consequences, as he usually was, Taft did not very much care what others thought of his association with controversial figures, such as Aldrich and Cannon. His occasional socializing with them had alienated many progressive Republicans, as did his friendship with the industrialist Henry Frick. Once in Augusta, Nellie had prevented a golf game with John D. Rockefeller although the president was quite set on it. Another time she convinced Taft that he would get bad publicity if he were seen with J. Pierpont Morgan, even though Taft regarded him more highly than other financiers. Thereafter Morgan was constrained to make only clandestine visits to Taft. On one occasion in 1910, Morgan, dressed in yachting clothes, came to Beverly in a motorboat and slipped up to the presidential cottage and out again with no one being the wiser.

In Henry Frick, Taft found a congenial friendship that was more impor-

tant to him than fear of any political repercussions. But eager to avoid antagonizing Nellie openly, Taft took to sneaking off to join Frick and his friends
for secret poker games. The Frick house near Beverly was a perfect palace
hidden away among the trees; its marble rooms were decorated with Tur-
ners, Gainsboroughs, and Van Dycks, and frequently echoed with music
from a huge organ Frick had built at a cost of one hundred thousand dollars.

After Taft became president, Nellie continued as his cultural mentor
much as before. She had little difficulty in getting him to plays and operas,
more in luring him to symphony concerts. At a performance of Massenet's
Herodiade, the French Ambassador, who had the box next to the Tafts, kept
the interlude between acts interesting with his vivacious conversation. Thus
stimulated periodically, Taft confined his sleeping to the performance. The
ambassador's company relieved Nellie, who was always humiliated when the
president was seen asleep in the full glare of the lights during intermissions.
From February to April 1911, Taft accompanied Nellie to see *Macbeth; Where
the Trail Divides; The Maestro's Masterpiece; Becky Sharp; Seven Sisters; King Lear;
1492; A Man's World; The Piper; Aida;* and *The Man from Home*, in addition to
seven other plays, four other operas, and a wild west show. Four symphony
concerts she attended without him. She also arranged for a quartet and a
pianist to entertain three hundred fifty guests at the White House in March
and held three musicals for two hundred guests in April.

Nellie's triumphal career in the White House did not really begin until the
spring of 1910, a year after the inauguration. Just two and a half months after
achieving her long-cherished goal, Nellie was struck down by a debilitating
stroke, which caused her retirement for over a year. In May 1909, while the
Tafts and a few guests were aboard the presidential yacht on an excursion to
Mount Vernon, Mrs. Taft suddenly fainted. A shot of brandy was ordered,
and some cracked ice applied to her pulse and temples. Although Nellie
seemed to revive in a few minutes, she didn't speak. When President Taft
was told, he turned "deathly pale" and rushed to his wife's side. During the
trip home he was terrified, for no one seemed able to help her, and she did
not move. "The president looked like a great stricken animal," Archie noted.
"I have never seen greater suffering or pain shown on a man's face."

Most people who knew them well had worried about the president's health
and had given little thought about whether Nellie might be overtaxing herself. She always seemed so strong that it was natural to feel unconcerned
about her. Taft thought of his wife as "about the most self-reliant person" he
had ever met. Now however she lay seriously ill. Not even the attending
surgeon could say what might be the consequences of her attack. In retrospect everyone agreed that she had been too active during the campaign and

since entering the White House. Various diagnoses have been suggested as the cause of Nellie's debilitation, but little factual information is available, and Nellie wrote no letters reflecting on her own condition. Assuming speculative privilege, this writer believes that having gotten to be "president," Nellie crumpled under the responsibility. Ironically, seven months after the election, it was she, not her husband, who proved unable to handle the stress. Taft was being attacked in the press; the Payne-Aldrich tariff contest was heatedly going on; and the president was caught up inevitably in the power struggle within the House over Uncle Joe Cannon's autocratic rule. In facing these conflicts, Taft was happy, after Nellie's stroke, that she would be spared each day's contribution of painful news. She, it would seem, had found her husband's dependence upon her a burden, and a growing burden, especially after he became president. Just the thought of keeping him awake in company with the nation's leaders for four years must have been intolerable. The dramatic ironies multiply when it is remarked that she—his prod, his alter ego, his voice—lost the power of speech and became totally silent just when he needed her most. The roles suddenly reversed themselves, as she, unable to speak, became as dependent as a child without language or mobility.

This event in the history of their marriage is so dramatic and important it cannot be stressed enough. Nellie must have discovered, to her own great delight, that Taft could cope without her presence, without her voice. (She was not able to attend official gatherings, even informal ones, until a year after her breakdown.) She must also have been proud that her husband proved that he could be his own man, could function without petticoat government, better than she had supposed; for whatever her personal ambition may have been, we may give her this credit. She loved Taft in her own fashion and wanted him to be president, for her, yes, but also for him. Nellie is a sympathetic figure. She was as trapped by the infantile demands of her husband as he was trapped by her ambition. They both needed an escape from the mutually binding chain of their own neurotic requirements, and Nellie's stroke gave them that. Upon her recovery each was free to pursue individual ends.

Nellie must have had a keen understanding of Taft's talents. What she did not understand was that he had no talent for presidential (as contrasted, in particular, with judicial) decision making, because she had robbed him of this, or helped to rob him, as his parents had. Once she could no longer make decisions for him—and in a sense feeling she no longer needed to—she collapsed and he rose to the occasion, at least better than she could have believed possible. He even learned to love giving speeches, after, apparently, he discovered that he could talk without Nellie's direct advice and criticism. It is worth noting also that her subsequent acquiescence in what happened to him thereafter—her ceasing to be a driving woman, as it were—had much to do with her (and his) discovery of his ability to stand on his own. Fear of another stroke must have played its part to lessen her prodding, for the doctors told her to avoid tension. They announced that they would not be responsible for a relapse if she did not remain in quiet seclusion. By having reached the White House, her great work was completed; she would now leave Taft to go his own way pretty much as he saw fit.

During Nellie's illness Taft was a somber and stricken man, ever attentive to her needs and desires. Nellie's stroke left her very weak, with partial paralysis of some facial muscles and with a speech difficulty which took some time and considerable effort to overcome. During her slow recuperation, the president devotedly attended at her side every opportunity he could, always on the lookout for chances to do little things for her. Mrs. More, one of the housekeepers, reported that despite his anxiety, "he never permits himself to appear serious for a minute when he is in her room. He laughs all the time and tries to amuse her." For a time Taft worked with Nellie for hours every day in an attempt to help her regain command of her speech, and he was successful. He would say, "Now please, darling, try and say 'the'—that's it, 'the.' That's pretty good, but now try it again." Mrs. Jaffray declared that she had never seen a man so "gentle and affectionate" as the president was with Nellie during this crisis.

By August, three months after her stroke, Nellie had made progress toward recovery. She was not "an easy patient," Taft admitted, and "any attempt to control her only increased the nervous strain." But the president's face lit up with the keenest enjoyment one day when Butt informed him that Mrs. Taft was outside in the automobile waiting for him to join her for a ride. He "hurried out and gave her a kiss—several of them . . . could be heard by everyone present." Mrs. Taft was looking better than Butt thought possible, "about normal except for a certain pallor." Although she still avoided social events out of embarrassment over her impaired speech, she gradually became active once again.

Nellie was determined to enjoy her years in the White House, and she struggled hard to regain her health and master her speech problem. To what degree she succeeded, we have already seen. And Taft was overjoyed when she finally indicated that she was "quite disposed to sit as a pope and direct me as of yore—an indication of the restoration of normal conditions." But as George Mowry pointed out long ago, one of Taft's great misfortunes was the loss of Nellie that first year of his administration, for she had the kind of "burning ambition" that makes great presidents. At an Associated Press banquet in New York in May 1910, Taft, happy over Nellie's recovery, responded to a toast offered to both him and his wife by thanking the master-of-ceremonies "for including the real president in his toast." On a later occasion, he told a group of reporters, "I am no politician." Then, turning toward Nellie, he continued, "There is the politician of the family. If she had only let me alone I should now be dozing on the Circuit Court Bench."

XII

SMILES AND BLUNDERS:
The Payne-Aldrich Tariff

Although the tariff had little actual effect on big business or on the general economy in the 1890s and early 1900s, it seemed to be a monumental issue to people at the time. Standing primarily as a symbol of the power of big business, the tariff aroused people both emotionally and politically, and one of the more dramatic episodes in Taft's administration revolved around it. A high protective tariff, devised to protect American industries against foreign competition, had been supported as a major policy by the seven Republican presidents since the Civil War. During this era of high tariffs, industry had generally prospered and many businessmen believed protection was vital to their interests. Others, blaming the high cost of living on the tariff, saw it as a government subsidy, and many considered it the "mother of the trusts." By 1908 there was much sentiment throughout the country for the downward revision of tariff rates which had reached an all-time high with the Dingley Bill of 1897.

Taft was made to believe that the demands for tariff revision could no longer be ignored. During his campaign he expressed the view that production costs had been sharply reduced since enactment of the Dingley Tariff. Thus, maintaining the tariff at the former rate was unjustified: "It is my judgment that a revision of the tariff in accordance with the pledge of the Republican platform will be, on the whole, a substantial revision downward." That promise no doubt won many crossover votes from conservative

Democrats, and the *Washington Post* alerted its readers to expect a substantial change, for Mr. Taft had "pledged himself squarely to a revision that would benefit the consumer." As Taft explained to his brother Horace—a freetrader and the family maverick—the tariff could now be reduced because American inventors had become more ingenious, American businessmen had shown greater enterprise, and American laborers had become more productive than their foreign counterparts. Millions of people thus waited in confident anticipation of change.

Theodore Roosevelt, acutely aware of political danger, had shied away from the tariff issue. He warned Taft during the campaign to "move with great caution" on the tariff issue and to avoid pledges and commitments which, if not later fulfilled, would seem a betrayal. Later, Roosevelt remembered telling Taft "that he was making pretty drastic promises, and that there might be difficulty in having them kept, . . . but he was perfectly breezy and cheerful, and declined to consider the possibility of trouble ahead." Unaware of the extent to which political combat was involved with any tariff revision, Taft enjoyed gratifying the electorate with talk of a lower and more equitable tariff.

After his inauguration Taft kept his first promise and called a special congressional session to consider the tariff. His message opening the extra session on 15 March 1909 was a surprise, however, because it included no reference to a downward revision of rates. Taft merely identified tariff reform as the reason for the special session and urged expediency so that business activity would not be disrupted in the process. Indeed, many were shocked by the brevity of the message, which comprised only 324 words. Many interested groups in and around the capital soon became apprehensive, especially after they noticed that Taft had ceased discussing the matter. Alton B. Parker raised Democratic fears: "We must admit that a revision of the tariff can be up as well as down. So also must we admit that all the revisions so far made by the Republican party have been upward." Professor William Graham Sumner, a free-trade advocate and Taft's economics instructor at Yale, expressed doubt that Taft could get a significant revision. He felt that, just possibly, "when the Senate and House get through with it, the tariff will be worse than before." A month after Taft's inauguration, Henry Cabot Lodge wrote to Theodore Roosevelt, "Taft wants a tariff that will strike the country favorably . . . but he knows little of the question and the arguments and the conditions." But want of information was only part of Taft's difficulty. Above all he lacked the disposition and the will to oversee personally the tariff bill during the heated and protracted congressional debates ahead. "The great tug will begin [soon]," he said, "and one of the crises in my life."

A bill proposed by Congressman Sereno Payne passed the House easily. It enlarged the list of commodities which could enter the country duty free, as well as cut duties on such vital products as steel, iron, lumber, chemicals, and refined sugar. The struggle between revisionists and protectionists came in the Senate where Nelson Aldrich, representing big business, was determined to revise the rates upward. The wrangling began. At first Taft indicated that he had to have a downward revision or he would "veto the bill"; and he also thought the Old Guard advocates of upward revision could be defeated if he made the fight. As the *Washington Post* aptly put it, Taft "is master of the situation if he chooses to be master." But rather than exercise his power and influence, Taft began soon to incline toward a reconciliation of the disputants. In order to harmonize the opposed factions, Taft prepared a peace dinner—dubbed the "White House lovefeast" by the press—and invited conservatives Cannon, Aldrich, Payne, Clark, and progressive leaders such as Albert Cummins and Representative Fitzgerald of New York, a leader of the Democratic party. The nineteen guests gathered on the western terrace, for Taft enjoyed alfresco dining on warm summer evenings. He welcomed his guests with hearty good nature to one of the most carefully prepared meals ever served at the White House. But this occasion, like his other friendly get-togethers, was a colossal failure.

Taft never realized that friendship and politics did not necessarily mix. For him no obligation was more important or, as he said, rested "more heavily" on his shoulders than the obligations of friendship. Warned by many progressives not to trust Aldrich and his henchmen, Taft was confused. "I confess I don't know what is going to happen," he informed Nellie. "Aldrich said he expected to follow my lead in the matter—I don't know how much he means by that." He realized, of course, that he was dealing with acute and expert politicians. "I am trusting a great many of them," he wrote, "and I may be deceived." Taft got assurances that his views would have great influence on the action of the Conference Committee. "How much this means and how far they will be willing to go, I do not know," he told Horace. "But I have not found Aldrich or Cannon in any way deceptive in the dealings that I have had with them, and I believe they are acting in good faith."

The wilely Aldrich and Cannon proceeded to pack the committee with members holding protectionist views, leaving Taft to sputter helplessly once he discovered that he had been misled about the selection process. When the bill reached committee, Taft found that he had been, as Champ Clark put it, "served up." The Tariff was reduced on only six insignificant items. The prospect of drawing personal abuse Taft found to be the most unsettling aspect of the entire tariff issue. He could assure Nellie that "Your husband will be damned heartily in many quarters of the capital and elsewhere. It is most uncomfortable." The controversy also delayed his vacation. While the Senate labored over the tariff bill, Taft fretted, for he wanted to join Nellie at their summer home: "This thing is whittling my vacation down so that I doubt if I will have much more than five weeks at Beverly."

Taft's wait-and-see attitude disconcerted many who were anxious that the president take a firm stand against the protectionists. "The President has not yet begun to study the bill in detail," the *New York Times* charged, "and has given practically no consideration to rates of duty." Taft said little, since he was reluctant to antagonize members on either side of the dispute. He did express a desire to make hides, oil, iron ore, and coal duty free. But each person who visited the president's office left confident that he had Taft's ear. Some people came away convinced that he would veto anything less than a genuine downward revision, others left with the conviction that he would sign no matter what the outcome. "The truth seems to be," the *New York Times* concluded, "that the President does not yet know himself what he will do." Meanwhile, he told the reporters that he was "constitutionally adverse" to making up his mind on important subjects any earlier than was absolutely necessary.

Taft publicly claimed that he had already done all he could to convince the conservatives to accept lower rates. Now he was willing to let Congress settle the matter. It was not "up to him" to get sufficient votes in the Senate to insure the acceptance of his views on the tariff. "If the Senate wishes to assume the responsibility of breaking up the attempted revision, it may do so." The president's tariff remarks were always made with good humor, the New York *Herald Tribune* complained, without expletives or superlatives. A comparison with Theodore Roosevelt was inevitable, for during the fight over the railroad-rate bill, Roosevelt sought precise information on every schedule and personally contested every questionable provision.

When the newspapers complained about Taft's preferring to play golf than to nag Congress, he tried to justify his inaction to friends. One night at dinner, Archie Butt reported, the president explained that he probably "could make a lot of cheap capital" by acting more aggressively. "But what I am anxious to do is to get the best bill possible with the least amount of friction. I owe something to the party, and while I would popularize myself with the masses with a declaration of hostilities toward Congress, I would greatly injure the party and possibly divide it in just such a way as Cleveland brought dissension and ruin into the Democratic party." Ironically, his inaction on this occasion would later contribute significantly to the division of the Republican party during the election of 1912.

That Taft felt the pressure was evident in his weight rise, and he promised

Nellie to start dieting on the first of August, when the tariff should be settled. Although the president claimed he had no fear of vetoing an unsuitable bill, the high-tariff congressmen suspected they had little to be frightened about. "The feeling is pretty well abroad that he will not dare to veto any bill," Butt wrote his sister-in-law Clara. "I doubt myself whether he would have the grit to hand a veto to Congress." The conservative Republicans finally settled the issue, despite the opposition of Democrats and progressive Republicans, by pushing through a bill by a narrow margin which flagrantly increased more than six hundred duties—including such important ones as sugar, iron and steel products, lumber, cotton, lead. The standpatters arrogantly waited for Taft's reaction, all the time insisting that they anticipated no dissatisfaction.

What would Taft decide to do? LaFollette hurried to the White House, where he learned that Taft felt the bill was "not in compliance with the party platform." He advised the president to send the Senate committee an angry message. Taft blandly replied, "Well, I don't much believe in a president's interfering with the legislative department while doing its work. They have their responsibility and I have mine. And if they send that bill to me, and it isn't a better bill than it is now, I will veto it." LaFollette went to the White House again after Taft had received the bill. The president seemed ready for action.

> "Come and sit down," Taft invited the Wisconsin senator. "I want to talk with you about the tariff. What am I to do with this bill?
>
> "Mr. President, you ought to veto it," LaFollette answered plainly. "Instead of being a better bill, it is much worse. Hundreds of increases have been made in the Senate."
>
> Picking up a pencil, Taft asked LaFollette: "Tell me what things ought to be reduced in duty."

LaFollette recalled Taft's instructions to him: "You and your associates in the Senate go ahead, criticize the bill, amend, cut down the duties—go after it hard. I will keep track of your amendments. I will read every word of the speeches you make, and when they lay the bill down before me, unless it complies with the platform, I will veto it." Referring to his agreement with LaFollette, Taft told Archie Butt, "I fear Aldrich is ready to sacrifice the party and I will not permit it. I am not very anxious for a second term as it is, and I certainly will not make any compromise to secure one."

Taft soon regretted his commitment to LaFollette and to the platform, for the Aldrich group counterattacked and much bitterness emerged. Taft was both surprised and appalled by the "ruthless selfishness" exhibited in the tariff-making process. The insurgent leaders—LaFollette, Cummins, Dolliver, Clapp, Beveridge, and Bristow—were treated rudely on the Senate floor. "When I arise," Bristow wrote, "or other liberals do, I am treated with sneers and insulting remarks from the Aldrich coterie."

Although many felt that Taft could have done more to influence Aldrich's final bill, the public did not initially direct its anger at him. Instead, low tariff advocates looked to the president expecting him to exercise his veto power. Taft could not sign the bill, the *New York Times* made clear, "without complete abandonment of the principle to which he has committed himself." The *Washington Post* predicted an instantaneous and overwhelming popular response. Veto advocates were disconcerted, however, when Taft seemed no less friendly with conservatives than he had been before the vote. If Taft was unhappy with the bill, Aldrich and Payne commented, "he has concealed his concern successfully."

Suddenly Taft began to talk about signing the tariff bill and having done with the matter. He emphasized his satisfaction with reductions on iron ore, scrap iron, coal, and oil. He was happy too with the provision establishing a commission to study the tariff scientifically and make recommendations on future revisions. Lastly, he liked the corporate income tax provision in the bill.

Taft had supported a corporate rather than a personal income tax, much to the progressives' dismay. He was politically unopposed to a personal income tax, but he was convinced that a constitutional amendment was needed since the court had ruled earlier in 1894 that an income tax was unconstitutional. "I prefer an income tax," Taft told Archie Butt, "but the truth is I am afraid of the discussion which will follow and the criticism which will ensue if there is another serious division in the Supreme Court on the subject." After the corporation tax passed, Taft wrote, "If I had not intervened the income tax would certainly have passed both houses of Congress, and I would regard that as a great public injury, thus to involve the Supreme Court and injure its prestige, whatever its decision."

After convincing himself that the bill was not in fact a betrayal of his campaign pledge, the president told Nellie, "I hope that my attitude will have so reconciled the people of the country as to make them believe what is a fact, that the bill is really a good bill." Of that, he was not able to convince many people. Senator Jonathan Dolliver spoke for the insurgents who felt betrayed by the president; the tariff was a "fraud," a "humbug" prepared for the special interests, and a "rank interchange of reciprocal larcenies." A delegation from several large clothing manufacturers warned that the price of woolen clothing for the poor would rise 20 to 25 percent. The press condemned the tariff again for favoring industrialists and letting the heaviest burden fall on consumers.

A terrific thunderstorm broke out on 5 August 1909, as President Taft prepared to sign the bill, and one newspaper reporter quickly seized upon this coincidence "as a note of warning from the country, indicating that the bill would be received by a storm of protest." Taft announced that he had signed the bill "because I believe it to be the result of a sincere effort on the part of the Republican party to make a downward revision." Some suggested that Taft must not have read the bill. Taft had now adopted a position little different from Senator Aldrich's; this shift, they alleged, was unprecedented in the history of American politics.

To avoid criticism, the president tried to escape, by making the first of two very long trips. He was anxious to get as far away from Washington as he could. He would have gone to Alaska, the president told reporters, if it had not been for Mrs. Taft's illness, and he had not given up hope of going to Hawaii soon. The proper way to gain an understanding of the country, he claimed, was "to go to the four corners and the places between." Elaborate advance preparations were made. His private railroad cars, the *Mayflower* and *Haslemere*, were to travel over twenty-two railroad systems. The trip was scheduled for sixty-seven days and included visits to fifty-four cities. Special stops on his itinerary were the Royal Gorge, the Alaska-Yukon Exposition at Seattle, three days in Yosemite National Park, the Grand Canyon, four days on his brother Charles's ranch in Texas, and a visit with President Diaz of Mexico. Nellie remained at Beverly, but Taft took along his personal secretary, his new valet, Brooks, and of course Archie Butt. Various cabinet officers and senators planned to join him on various parts of the trip. He started out on 15 September 1909, feeling in "rare good humor" and "thoroughly happy."

His optimistic mood was short lived. It was characteristic of Taft's diplomatic sense that he now chose to eulogize the Payne-Aldrich Tariff in Minnesota, a hot-bed of the insurgent movement and a state in which antipathies against the tariff were intense. Incredulously, Minnesotans heard Taft exclaim in a speech at Winona: "I am bound to say that I think the Payne Tariff Bill is the best tariff bill that the Republican party ever passed and therefore the best tariff bill that has been passed at all. I do not feel that I could have reconciled any other course to my conscience than that of signing the bill." In summary, Taft found it "a substantial achievement in the direction of lower tariffs and downward revision."

The previous discontent with President Taft's inaction during the tariff debate was nothing compared to the public reaction after he had signed the bill and then began to praise it. The response to his speech from Minnesota to the East Coast was quick and violent. Taft's praise truly passed all understanding. "He no longer apologizes. He accepts, he defends, he is enthusiastic," the *New York Times* raged. Throughout the Midwest, Taft's already tarnished reputation declined precipitously. After Winona, the rest of his trip through progressive country was, according to the historian George Mowry, a "polar dash through a world of ice."

In retrospect, Taft's refusal to veto the Payne-Aldrich Tariff perhaps did him more harm than any other of his official acts. Although his travel, golf, and general inanition provoked irritation, the tariff caused many people who had praised him formerly to condemn him now. Taft later compounded the damage by apologetically explaining that he had just "dashed off the Winona speech hastily between stations" and had barely had time to consider it. Not even Republican faithfuls could abide such an explanation, especially after Taft, in a speech to the annual Lincoln dinner of the Republican club in New York City, again defended the bill. His opening remark, to the effect that nothing in the Republican platform had promised downward revision, was met by derisive laughter.

Because Taft's predecessor had railed at men like Aldrich and Tawney and Senator Tom Carter of Montana, when Taft proceeded to praise them, most people were amazed. In Kansas Taft publicly thanked conservative Senator Reed Smoot of Utah for his vote on the tariff. Taft purposefully neglected to invite any progressives to join him on the trip, calling them "assistant Democrats." And though, as Butt felt certain, Taft personally disliked Uncle Joe Cannon, the Speaker accompanied him on part of his trip. Taft openly flattered Cannon, perhaps because he feared future confrontations if he did not feign respect, and Cannon continued to manipulate Taft to gain his own ends.

On the tariff bill, one indignant citizen of Kansas put it this way: "We have suspended judgment until the rubber is worn out of our suspenders." And Mr. Dooley evoked many smiles throughout the country when he explained to *New York Times* readers how good the Payne-Aldrich Tariff really was.

Th' Republican party has been thru to its promises. Look at th' free list if ye don't believe it. Practically iverything necessary to existence comes in free. Here it is. Curling stones, teeth, sea moss, newspapers, nox vomica, Pulu, canary bird seed, divvy-divvy, spunk, hog bristles, marshmellows, silk worm eggs, stilts, skeletons, an' leeches. Th' new tariff bill puts these familyar commdyties within th' reach iv all.

Assessing the situation a few months later, Mr. Dooley informed readers of *American Magazine,*

We ar-re now in th' midst iv a season iv unexampled Prosperity. Hiven an' Bill Taft have smiled on us. We ar're blessed with a tariff that accordin' to Bill is wan iv th' handsomest an' most becoming loads that was iver, says he, imposed upon th' breakin' back iv a patient people.

The welcome Taft received across the country, however, was a soothing balm for his bruised feelings in Minnesota. Almost everywhere people turned out to see and cheer so unusual a sight as a president despite popular disillusionment over this one's tariff. In the Far West and the South he was greeted enthusiastically, especially in the white South, where Taft was loved because he never "pandered" to Negroes. His determination to identify only with white men during his visit in the South, Butt wrote, brought him a popularity that was "marvelous." His spirits suffered a slight dampening only when strong anti-tariff editorials from the *New York Times* were sent along with his mail. Finally, he angrily telegraphed a message telling his secretary Fred Carpenter to send no more, for they only upset him.

Taft normally dreaded public speaking, but before long, basking in the glow of warmer popular receptions, he now began to enjoy speech making. He felt so self-assured that he spoke even when no speech was expected— and at times when none was desired. Before the close of the trip, Archie reported, if anyone so much as raised his glass to toast the president, Taft would jump up and speak extemporaneously for five or ten minutes.

"I am looking forward with pleasure to my visit to Yosemite, which I will take with John Muir, the naturalist," Taft wrote to Nellie from Oregon. Yosemite did delight him, for Muir explained every view, tree, and flower along the way and told about the glacial theory of Yosemite's formation. But whereas Muir had inspired Roosevelt with a zeal for conservation of the nation's forests, he left Taft with only the memory of his fatigue from hiking.

From California he proceeded to the Grand Cayon. "It is stupendous. We must visit it together," he wrote Nellie. At El Paso Taft crossed over into Ciudad Juarez to meet President Diaz, thereby becoming the first American president to visit a foreign country. Taft next stopped at his brother Charles's 265,000 acre ranch "La Quinta" in Gregory, Texas, where he spent a few days playing golf. While horseback riding, he used the specially built extra-large saddle crafted for his visit. Then began the last portion of his trip, a swing through the South. In Savannah, Georgia, on 4 November, he enjoyed the most elaborate dinner of the trip. Augusta also prepared a grand reception. "The good will of the Southern people I cannot be mistaken about," he wrote to Nellie with satisfaction. "I am sure I have it." Taft responded to their enthusiastically cordial reception by assuring Southern politicians that he had no intention of appointing blacks to office. He would, he indicated, eliminate them altogether from politics if he could.

On 10 November Taft arrived at Union Station where his family, cabinet members, and other dignitaries greeted him after his two-month peregrination. That night he spent quietly at the White House, but the very next day he left for a three-day trip to New Haven.

Despite his triumphs on tour, Taft's problems with the tariff were not over. The uproar about revision was so upsetting that he called for a new commission to investigate and report on each tariff schedule separately, with duty recommendations based on the merits of each case. Despite the general condemnation of Taft's tariff policy heretofore, the commission plan stimulated hope that some relief might be forthcoming after all. By August 1911, Congress passed two tariff bills that lowered a few rates; one revised the wool schedule and the other added more goods to the duty-free list. But Taft, unsure about tariff matters generally and still rankling over the violent public reaction to his praise of the Payne-Aldrich Bill, decided that these new schedules were not low enough to stem the furor, and he consequently vetoed the bills. He explained his reasoning to Senator Smoot, an ardent high-tariff man, and ex-Senator Carter, who came to discuss the two bills. "It is on account of my ignorance of the question of the tariff that I am going to veto these bills," Taft confessed. "That is a very honest statement to make, Mr. President," one of the senators replied incredulously, "but it would be a ruinous one to make public." Taft continued, "They are both perfectly true statements, nevertheless. But I promise not to bring shame and disgrace to the Republican party by admitting it in my veto message."

The speech failed, nevertheless, to make the party look especially good. The overall public reaction was more subdued than previously. The *New York Times* felt Taft had destroyed all the "renewed hopes" kindled by the commission. His veto was a "serious mistake" and has made the probability of his re-election "highly unlikely." Butt noted that his explanations for the vetoes were "poorly received everywhere."

Traveling did not enable Taft to escape from the tariff imbroglio. On another trip in the fall of 1911, he chose Cheyene, Wyoming, the center of the sheep country, to explain that he had vetoed the revised wool schedule because he had "not had time to hear from the Tariff Board" and because he thought that the revised rate was still too high. Described by historian Frank Taussig as "the most uncompromising and even fanatical among protectionists," sheepmen felt dependent on a high tariff on foreign wool to keep them in business. Thus they were flabbergasted by such statements in their very midst.

In the congressional elections of 1910, the Republican party felt the first painful effects of Taft's acceptance of the Payne-Aldrich Tariff. He had tried to explain his course to the people, trusting that an honest expression of his good intentions would be received with understanding. But the voters were not receptive. To the New England Jewellers and Silversmiths Association, he first pointed to the "great prosperity" of the times and ended by asking for sympathy: "The presidency is not an easy burden, and one's spirit sometimes lags and hopefulness sometimes disappears." "However much you may have to criticize me," he urged them not to "misconstrue my motives."

The voters were more interested in performance than good intentions. Not surprisingly the average citizen could take no comfort from millionaire industrialist Andrew Carnegie's assurances that the Payne-Aldrich Tariff was "the best law ever enacted." The people were listening instead to the two southern senators who had investigated the high cost of living and put the blame squarely on the tariff. They charged that the Payne-Aldrich Tariff contributed directly to making "great fortunes for the few and great suffering for the many."

The Republicans repeated Lincoln's trite remark on tariffs: "I do not know much about the tariff, but I know this much: When we buy manufactured goods abroad we get the goods and the foreigner gets the money. When we buy the manufactured goods at home we get both the goods and the money." But the Lincoln statement did not help congressional Republicans this time. The congressional election of 1910 was a repudiation of the administration. The large Republican majority of 1908 was suddenly reduced to a minority. "Democrats Sweep the Country; Win Congress and Many States," the *New York Times* headlined on November 9. To have brought the Republican party to such a state "must be set down as the most notable achievement of Mr. Taft."

Speaking for the Republican progressives, Gifford Pinchot warned that the outcome was an "overwhelming rebuke to the reactionaries." Insurgent Republican candidates for governorships had generally won, he pointed out, while the standpat candidates were defeated across the nation. Democrats were jubilant in driving home the moral. House Speaker Champ Clark announced, "The people are tired of the present administration and . . . the tariff deception."

XIII

A MOUNTAIN OF
CONTROVERSY:
The Ballinger-Pinchot
Blunder and Other Affairs

During his first year in office Taft became involved in another serious and upsetting political dispute: the Ballinger-Pinchot affair. His troubles cut especially deep, for Nellie, who suffered a stroke in May 1909 and had remained in a weakened condition, was a source of constant anxiety. The Ballinger-Pinchot affair proved to many who were previously unconvinced that Taft was not competent in executing his duties. The effect on Theodore Roosevelt was worse: he began to think that Taft was betraying his policies. In the opinion of historian Alpheus T. Mason, the Ballinger controversy was "our most notorious public land fraud." He thinks it has been forgotten largely because it lacks some descriptive epithet such as "Teapot Dome" or "Watergate."

Taft believed in the protection of America's natural resources in principle, but the idea of activist conservation, Theodore Roosevelt's magnificent obsession, Taft once confessed, remained for him "rather abstruse." He was for it, he said at one point, because "there are a great many people in favor of conservation no matter what it means." At first he seemed to understand the dangers of indiscriminate and reckless use of resources: "As a people, we have the problem of making our forests outlast this generation, our iron outlast the next," he wrote, "not merely as a matter of convenience or comfort, but as a matter of stern national necessity." After reading a geological survey report, he recommended that Congress set aside all major water-power sites for future public development, which it did. He approved legislation for irrigation projects and the preservation of forest and mineral land. Yet he appointed as head of the Department of the Interior, Richard A. Ballinger, a businessman's lawyer who wanted to open federal land in the West to private enterprise.

Ballinger had earned a good name as mayor of Seattle by ridding the city of slot machines. He was appointed because he had some reputation as a conservationist. Secretary Ballinger said he would promote conservation in "a safe, sane, and conservative way without impeding the development of the great West and without hysteria in one direction or another." But many considered Ballinger weak and likely to comply with the demands of special interests that were ready to deplete America's mineral resources and strip her forests bare. Louis Brandeis said of Ballinger, "Wherever there is pressure, there you will find him yielding. The only cases where there can be any doubt as to what Mr. Ballinger will do is where there is pressure from both sides at the same time."

Taft and Ballinger felt that Theodore Roosevelt and Pinchot had probably acted illegally in placing so much land irreversibly in the public domain, and in reaction they decided to make some of the same land available for private ownership until clearer laws were passed. "We have a government of limited powers under the Constitution," Taft maintained, "and we have got to work out our problems on the basis of law. Now, if that is reactionary, then I am a reactionary."

Gifford Pinchot, the ardent chief forester and a dedicated conservationist, was one of the few Roosevelt officers Taft retained in his administration, and soon there was a clash between him and Ballinger. Pinchot was independently wealthy; he was a "millionaire with a mission." Years later, Harold Ickes, FDR's secretary of the interior, dubbed Pinchot "Sir Galahad of the Woodlands." He had studied foresty in Europe, entering government service in 1898 to put his considerable knowledge and unbounded enthusiasm for conservation into practice. Pinchot intensely admired Theodore Roosevelt, who accepted his homage but not without some amusement. He once explained to his son-in-law Nicholas Longworth that Pinchot had "a sort of fetish worship" for him. "He thinks that if we were cast away somewhere together and we were both hungry, I would kill him and eat him. AND I WOULD TOO!" Roosevelt exclaimed, grinning and baring his teeth in a mock-savage fashion. Roosevelt appointed him chief of the United States Forest Service.

In August 1909, Louis Glavis, a field agent of the General Land Office, accused Ballinger of allowing the Morgan-Guggenheim interests to get control of certain reserved coal lands in Alaska. Pinchot supported Glavis. When Pinchot made public the charges against Ballinger, he was, of course, criticizing the president by implication. Ballinger proceeded on his own to fire Glavis for insubordination. Very soon nationwide attention was focused on the Ballinger-Pinchot controversy. Taft wished to avoid becoming involved, but he asked Attorney General Wickersham to look into the matter, an unusual request, since he was directing one cabinet member to investigate another. After discussing the firing of Glavis with other members of his cabinet, Taft judged Ballinger innocent of any wrongdoing. After that, Taft kept the problem at arm's length. Pinchot then became outspoken in his contempt for the president's inaction. It was, he insisted, the most "critical and far-reaching problem this nation has faced since the Civil War." Taft was convinced that Pinchot, with his fanaticism and disappointment at his decision in the Ballinger case, planned to resist, thereby compelling Taft to dismiss him, which would lead to further controversy. Earlier Taft had described Pinchot "as a good deal of a radical and a good deal of a crank." Unable to consult Nellie, still recovering from her stroke, Taft announced to Butt, "this is something I will have to decide for myself."

After trying unsuccessfully to conciliate both Ballinger and Pinchot and their respective supporters, Taft decided to stand by Ballinger "at whatever cost." Ballinger convinced Taft that the whole controversy was engineered by the progressives to make the administration look bad. Publicly Ballinger called it a "deliberate conspiracy, organized by Mr. Garfield and Mr. Pinchot to blow me out of office." "I will not resign," he stated adamantly. Six months after the scandal broke, Taft wrote with rare mockery to his brother Horace, "G.P. is out again defying the lightning and the storm and championing the cause of the oppressed and downtrodden and harassing the wealthy and the greedy and the dishonest." Still on the defensive, he added, "If I were to turn Ballinger out, in view of his innocence and in view of the conspiracy against him, I should be a white-livered skunk." Horace, in reply, tried delicately to suggest that calling Pinchot a conspirator would stimulate mutual name calling. But once Taft's sense of loyalty was engaged, he could be stubborn.

Still, the whole matter irritated and depressed him. "The president has been in a pretty low frame of mind," Butt wrote to his sister-in-law Clara. "His mood is due entirely to some muckraking stories . . . concerning the Guggenheim coal lands." Taft recognized his own limitations in dealing with the alleged scandal: "Of course, Roosevelt would have come back at those preferring the charges and would by now have them on the run," he told Butt, "but I cannot do things that way. I will let them go on and by and by the people will see who is right and who is wrong." Taft added irritably, "I get rather tired of hearing from his friends that I am not carrying out his policies." With rare insight, he concluded, "There is no use trying to be William Howard Taft with Roosevelt's ways." Gradually he was coming to accept his own identity as the national and party leader and began to raise his independent colors.

In weighing Pinchot in the balance with Ballinger, Taft was weighing also the consequences of any action he might take. If he let Pinchot go, how much would it hurt Roosevelt? As Butt wrote, "I believe he loves Theodore Roosevelt, and a possible break with him or the possible charge of ingratitude on his part is what is writhing within him now. He can't say to his advisers, 'What will Roosevelt think?' His very question would be misunderstood even by the members of his cabinet." Taft wrote to progressive Senator Jonathan Bourne, complaining that everyone was "full of despair and predicting all sorts of evil" and that everyone was advising him differently. Yet, he made it clear, "I have done nothing that I would not do over again." He was taking first steps toward defining for himself what Taft would and should do, regardless of Roosevelt.

After Pinchot made public a letter to Jonathan Dolliver, the progressive Iowa congressman, confessing his insubordination and ascribing it to his defense of the public interest, Taft regarded the admission as unparalleled audacity. Late in the evening of 7 January 1910, he made his decision to dismiss Pinchot. Conservationists and liberals in general were outraged, and Pinchot rushed to describe Taft's action to Roosevelt as a betrayal of his conservation program. "We have fallen back down the hill you led us up," he reported, thanks to "a most surprising weakness and indecision" on Taft's part. The news stunned Roosevelt. And reports that Mr. Roosevelt had sent for Pinchot to join him in Europe depressed Taft.

Taft might have settled the matter by firing Ballinger as well. Instead, without consulting his cabinet, he released a letter supporting Ballinger. When Wickersham complained of this precipitous action, Taft hurriedly composed a letter of explanation and apology for each of his cabinet members. Unfortunately he was never able to satisfy all parties concerned, and he ended by pleasing very few. His actions in this episode further damaged his prestige and widened the fissure in the Republican party. Because the Ballinger-Pinchot charges were to come under the scrutiny of a congressional committee, Taft several weeks later appointed a subordinate, Oscar Lawler, to draw up an official indictment of Glavis and Pinchot. This record Taft then signed. When news of the record leaked out, Taft foolishly denied its existence. General Clarence Edwards, who was playing golf with Taft and Archie Butt when news of the leak broke, recalled that "Mr. Taft declared at once and with emphasis that he didn't know anything about it." A short time later, Taft threw down his club complaining that the game was ruined. He called Lawler a "damned scoundrelly stenographer," whose testimony was "a lie, or to say the least a perversion of the facts." He then suddenly turned about face and confessed that the story was true. Afterwards, when Taft tried to explain his reversal to *Times* reporter Oscar Davis he insisted that on the golf course "he had just plain forgotten all about the memorandum," which might very well have been true. Later he issued a statement declaring how "anxious" he had been "to write a full statement of the case," but as he had six or seven speeches to write in preparation for his western trip, he was unable to give it the time it required. "I therefore requested Mr. Lawler to prepare an opinion as if he were president."

A storm of protest followed. This "white washing enterprise," *Hampton's Magazine* reported, was "the gravest demonstration of moral dereliction." *The Nation* charged the president with "monumental and almost incredible blundering"; his clumsy behavior has resulted in a "deplorable and mortifying mess." Taft's "good nature and kindliness" were fine qualities, *The Nation* conceded, but a president needed "a great deal more strength in dealing with situations like the Pinchot-Ballinger imbroglio." The *New York Times* argued that this crisis further pointed up how "loosely, inadequately, and poorly organized" was Taft's administration.

Although the congressional investigating committee report exonerated both Taft and Ballinger of any official wrongdoing, it underscored Ballinger's lack of enthusiasm for conservation. Ballinger, counterattacking, said that he had "no apologies to make to the American people," and that he had merely thwarted "certain overzealous persons" in their attempt to convert the public domain into a great national preserve. Republican leaders, sensing that Ballinger was now a political liability of some magnitude, advised Taft to ask for his resignation, since the party had already to go into the 1910 congressional campaign with the tariff albatross wrapped round its neck. But Taft resisted. Ballinger had suffered enough, he claimed, "without having the dagger driven into his heart by me." In private Ballinger offered three times to resign, and each time Taft refused to accept his offer. And so the awkward situation dragged on. Knox told Taft that by refusing to accept Ballinger's resignation he was "pulling at the beard of death." Even Nellie, who had by now recovered sufficiently to see what was happening, lost patience with him. In March 1911, almost a year after the trouble started, Taft finally bowed to Nellie, his brother Charles, and his cabinet, and reluctantly accepted Ballinger's resignation. (Ironically, the Taft administration's overall record of keeping land from public sale was almost as good as Roosevelt's despite the Ballinger-Pinchot blunder. But few critics noticed this fact at the time.)

To the consternation of some conservationists and the incredulity of others, Taft appointed as the new secretary of interior Walter L. Fischer, a good friend of Gifford Pinchot and a man whom he earlier had branded one of the "foul conspirators" in the Ballinger affair. Confused and dismayed, Ballinger wrote to Taft a few months later: "The circumstances of the appointment of Mr. Fischer as my successor in view of his attitude toward your enemies and my enemies, was, I frankly confess, hard to bear." Taft had been mortified by the furor and the unpleasantness arising from the charges and the countercharges during the whole affair, and thought the appointment of Fisher would heal wounds. Instead, as usual, he only succeeded in confusing all interested parties.

Understandably, Taft's spirits sagged by the end of his first year in office. At a Yale Club dinner in March 1910, he declared that he had "suffered all the pangs and trials of Job." A month later, he spoke gravely at a fraternity dinner at the Raleigh Hotel: "Brother Bridgeman [the toastmaster] offers me a recipe for acquiring twenty-five successive terms. I thank you, Mr. Bridgeman, but the first term is enough for me. Judging from the trouble and the worry of getting through the first year of my first term, the contemplation of twenty-five terms, or more than one, is more than I can stand. It will require all the energy, philosophy, strength of character, and every other thing which the Psi U fraternity teaches to carry me through one term."

Despite his minor pangs, Taft generally maintained a smiling face in public. Taft's smile and laugh were constantly noted by all those who knew him. To be exposed to his smile, Archie Butt said, was like having "a huge pan of sweet milk poured over one." Roosevelt, knowing its infectious quality, had advised him to smile constantly during the campaign. That he had done. "The famous smile that won't come off," the New York Times called it. His laughter, the Washington Post reported, was "like the roar of a storm." Seemingly "gregarious, ebullient," the picture of "expansive charm," Taft had the typical exterior of many obese people whose social graciousness camouflages inward suffering and anger.

During the campaign of 1908 reporters quickly perceived how Taft often dodged political questions behind a screen of laughter. Newsmen frequently found themselves "headed off by the secretary's laugh." Whenever the president was in public, the Washington Post noticed in particular, he was heartily smiling or laughing almost continuously. William Allen White, a very fat man too, once described himself in words which equally apply to Taft: "My answer to argument all my life has been a grin or a giggle . . . , anything to avoid an acrimonious discussion."

Whether trying to placate quarreling Republican factions or to reassure office seekers and other suppliants, Taft relied on his famous smile. Increasingly he resorted to jokes, making his points indirectly. When, for example, a committee of the newly elected Democratic Congress sought to embarrass Taft by digging up an old scandal in the State Department, he answered them with an anecdote about the man who was asked by a waiter whether he wanted oxtail soup. "Oxtail soup," the waiter explained, "was merely soup made from the tail of the ox." "Neighbor," the patron replied, "don't you think that's going a hell of a long way back for soup?" In a confrontation once with Senators Smoot, Dixon, Nelson, Hughes, Chamberlain, and Borah, who came to protest the bill legalizing the withdrawal of land from the public settlement, Taft stood them off with an impenetrable wall of smiles. Flushed with anger, Senator Borah finally said to him, "Then, Mr. President, as we are to understand it, you are going to do as you damn please without consulting the interests of those states mostly affected." Although Taft was smiling at the time and continued to smile, Butt noticed the little glint in his eyes which always telegraphed anger. Taft then launched into an anecdote about an old schoolteacher who, determined to have order in his school, singled out the ill-behaved son of the most cantankerous farmer in the area and expelled him from class one day. The farmer, stalled in his angry demands to have his son reinstated, finally said, "It appears to me, then, that you expect to run this school as you damn please." The teacher calmly replied to the farmer: "Your language is coarse, your manner offensive, but you have grasped my idea." With that, Taft excused himself and went out, still smiling.

In contrast to his much happier days as secretary of war, Taft soon considered newspaper and magazine writers to be his implacable enemies. It was primarily Taft's extreme sensitivity to adverse criticism which caused him so radically to change his disposition toward the press, not, as two of his recent biographers believe, his "indifference toward his public image" or his failure "to evaluate properly the propaganda value of the journalistic estate." Roosevelt, in contrast, had been his own best press agent. He had met with newsmen frequently and possessed a splendid comprehension of news and its value. Once in the White House, Taft could not bear to read many of the newspapers he had formerly liked since most were often critical of him. Butt noted that Taft culled clippings only from papers supporting his policies. After the Hearst papers censured him for vetoing the wool bill, he took them off his reading list. "Last night after dinner, when he asked if the New York papers had come," Butt recalled, "Mrs. Taft handed him the *New York World*." "I don't want the *World*," he said. "I have stopped reading it. It only makes me angry." "But you used to like it very much," said Mrs. Taft. "That was when it agreed with me, but it abuses me now, and so I don't want it," he replied. He also quit reading the *Washington Times* and such western papers as the *Kansas City Times* and *Star*. On another occasion, Nellie, disturbed by his hypersensitivity, tried to point out his folly in ignoring all critical papers: "You will never know what the other side is doing if you only read the *Sun* and the *Tribune*." Taft answered simply, "I don't care what the other side is doing."

In May 1910, Taft remarked in an address to the Grand Army of the Republic, "I am glad to have been hammered this first year, because the next three years will be pleasant, no matter what the newspapers say about me." Even to Republican groups, Taft talked either of not running in 1912 or of being defeated if he did, causing much consternation among party regulars. "To be a successful latter day politician, it seems one must be a hypocrite," he complained. "That sort of thing is not for me. I detest hypocrisy, cant, and subterfuge. If I have got to think every time I say a thing, what effect it is going to have on the public mind . . . I had rather not be president."

Taft began to make bitter and angry comments in private about the insurgent leaders, calling them "cantankerous, vicious, malignant, black flags, and demagogues." He proceeded to withhold patronage from the progressives as a punishment for what he conceived to be their obstinacy and disloyalty. In this design he was abetted by Vice-President Sherman, who told him, "Mr. President, you can't cajole these people. You have to hit them with a club. My advice is to begin to hit. I would send for Hitchcock and shut off the appointments of postmasters." "I hate to use the patronage as a club unless I have to," Taft replied. "It is your only club," Sherman reassured him. "You have other weapons, but the appointing power is your only club." Taft was always susceptible to bad advice, and he did as Sherman advised. It was not long before news of his retribution plan was out, and he was roundly condemned. Representative George Norris of Nebraska censured Taft publicly on behalf of other progressive Republicans.

By the end of his second year in office Taft had come full circle by now trying to placate the insurgents. But unlike the Old Guard, the progressives openly disdained him. Robert M. LaFollette, the leading progressive, who blamed Taft for aborting their first attempt to defeat Cannon in 1908, now turned cold toward any overtures from the White House. Just as earlier he had invited Cannon, Aldrich, and Payne to the White House, Taft in December 1910 called the important insurgent Senator A.B. Cummins of Iowa in for what the *New York Times* called a "harmony talk." Most insurgents were not eager for a reconciliation and showed little disposition to receive Taft's olive branch. The president, they insisted, could not be friends with them while continuing to surround himself with reactionary and standpat influence. As he tried in vain to avoid factious contention, Taft found himself again in the middle. The progressives avoided him, and conservatives still eyed him with distrust. In 1910 Henry Adams reported to a friend Wall Street's unhappiness with Taft. They professed to prefer their old enemy Theodore Roosevelt to Taft, for "at least he did what he said, while Taft talks to everybody in their own sense," and is wholly unpredictable.

Without question this isolation was one of the most tragic consequences of Taft's presidency. He had cast aside his Old Guard supporters before lining up a new set of friends. As Ray Stannard Baker commented later, President Taft had "alienated the most virile, free-thinking, and courageous group of men in our political life: Cummins, Pinchot, LaFollette, Dolliver, Beveridge, Norris."

More and more the president was referred to as "Taft the Blunderer." Deeply unhappy, he continued to gain weight, to vent his frustration in outbursts of temper, and rapidly to grow both older and sadder. Taft had a massage every morning which, with his daily outdoor recreation, should have improved his condition, but it was not long before he was complaining about his health and would not even venture out. "Last week he suffered from pain in one foot and gave out that he had strained it," Butt reported, but when the swelling affected the other foot, Taft could no longer "hide the fact that it was gout." Butt noticed lines coming into Taft's face, "deep, deep lines, which I had never noticed before." He told his sister-in-law that Taft "looks much older than he did six months ago and has lost much of his joyous and happy manner. . . . I can see him aging every day," whereas Mrs. Taft, despite her stroke, looked ten years younger since coming to the White House and became "more gracious and kinder toward the whole world."

Battered after the tariff difficulty and suffering from the Ballinger-Pinchot embarrassment, Taft would take no part in the battle against Cannonism when it flared up in the House once again in 1910. He was traveling through Pennsylvania in March when the attack came. The insurgents and the Democrats, far from despairing after their defeat the previous March, had regrouped for a new offensive. Taft remained impervious to all the dispatches which poured in urging him to return to Washington to stand by the regular organization and preserve it from a second defeat. When he did return to the White House, he still hoped to remain friends with both sides by making no comment and taking no part in the fight. To Butt he laughed roguishly and said, "Well, Archie, I think they have got the old fox this time. It would be funny, if he got the best of them after all." Cannon's enemies were ready to close in, and this time the old fox would not escape.

The actual toppling of Cannon came in a deceptive manner and at an unexpected time. On 17 March 1910 in the House the decennial census was casually being discussed when Nebraska progressive George Norris drew a tattered paper from his coat pocket and quietly addressed the Speaker: "I present a resolution made privileged by the Constitution." Cannon, caught off guard, replied, "If it is a resolution made privileged by the Constitution, the gentleman will present it." Norris then read his resolution providing that the House, rather than the Speaker, appoint all members to the Rules Committee, which determined what legislation would reach the floor, and excluding the Speaker from membership in the committee.

Immediately an uproar broke out on the floor of the House. Champ Clark recalled, "We all realized that the decisive battle was on, none more thoroughly than . . . Cannon, who . . . carried on a filibuster from the chair for three wearisome days and two more wearisome nights." The first night the stalwarts used every parliamentary ruse to save Cannon's power, including a motion to recess, which failed along with all the other motions. Meanwhile absentee congressmen were arriving hourly by train to join the fracas. Finally, Cannon could postpone the vote no longer. "Boys," he said grimly, "it looks as though we're beaten, but we'll die game."

The galleries were jammed with reporters and spectators by the time Norris made his final plea on behalf of the resolution. It would return popular government to Congress, he declared. The vote on 19 March was 191 to 156 against Cannon. Every Democrat and over thirty Republicans supported the Norris resolution. In a magnanimous gesture to ease the blow to the proud Cannon, he was permitted to stay on as Speaker.

After his overthrow, Cannon became vindictive toward Taft, for he felt the president had been involved. One incident on an April evening in 1911 revealed the depth of his feeling. Uncle Joe came to the theater and took his place a few seats from the president's box, but refused to look once at Taft. Taft smiled toward him for a time and tried to catch his eye and bow. Finally, the audience noticed Cannon's sullen snub of the president. Taft turned red and never looked at him again. Butt felt mortified that a president should have ended up in such an embarrassing position. Although Taft made no mention of the incident afterwards, his remarks about Cannon became increasingly bitter.

The president got his revenge a few months later. Arriving at the Dover House in Maryland to dine with Secretary Knox, Taft discovered Cannon there with a group of congressmen. All of Cannon's party came out to greet Taft, all except Uncle Joe. As the evening progressed, Cannon, after drinking much wine, came into the president's dining room, waved his hands, and made a sweeping bow to Taft, greeting him pleasantly. Taft looked up, without a word or a smile, and went right on talking, ignoring Cannon entirely. Uncle Joe "shambled rather than walked out of the room, looking greatly humiliated."

Frustrated in his efforts to maintain party solidarity and perplexed at what was happening around him, Taft took refuge on the golf course and contrived whenever possible to flee the capital altogether. The *Times* observed with dismay that the Republican party was rapidly becoming "demoralized." Theodore Roosevelt, returning from Africa in 1910, though proclaiming himself only an impartial onlooker, expressed deep concern about the gulf in the Republican party. "One of the heaviest counts against Taft," he wrote to Gifford Pinchot, "is that by his actions he has produced a state of affairs in which the split is so deep that it seems impossible to heal it, and the most likely result is that the people will say 'A plague on both your houses' and will turn to the Democrats." Roosevelt thus early predicted the direction the 1912 election would take.

XIV

ACHIEVEMENTS
AND REVERSALS:
The Record

The poignancy of Taft's situation became especially clear when in December 1910 he appointed Edward Douglas White to be the new chief justice for the Supreme Court. "It does seem strange," he confided to Justice Moody, "that the one place in the government which I would have liked to fill myself I am forced to give to another." As he signed the document, he grew wistful: "There is nothing I would have loved more than being chief justice. I cannot help seeing the irony in the fact that I . . . should now be signing the commission of another man." Often he referred nostalgically to the "delightful" life of a judge, who was "not exposed to criticism." Walking by the west entrance of the Capitol one day with Butt and John Hays Hammond, Taft stopped and looked up at the bronzed statue of Chief Justice John Marshall: "Would you rather have been him than president?" Hammond asked. "Of course," Taft answered quickly. "I would rather have been Marshall than any other American. . . . He made this country."

Taft's reluctance to put another man in the position he coveted led him to procrastinate more than usual, with the result that he ineptly handled the filling of the Supreme Court vacancy. Taft once remarked to Archie Butt, "I don't know the man I admire more than Hughes. If ever I have the chance I shall offer him the chief justiceship." His sentiment about Charles Evans Hughes was well known, and when the vacancy occurred Hughes and others expected the president to act as he had previously indicated. "I don't see how he can but name Hughes for the chief justiceship," Butt thought, for "he is already committed to Hughes. In fact, he wrote to him, saying . . . that he would make him chief justice and offering a place on that bench, but withdrew it as a positive statement in a postscript." Newspapers announced it as "practically certain" that Hughes would be the next chief justice. But when the time arrived to fill the post Taft temporized. Hughes grew embarrassed: "I thought that if the president was not going to appoint me he should say so frankly and proceed promptly to appoint someone else."

Suddenly, Taft chose Associate Justice White. Republicans were upset because White was an ex-Confederate Democrat. Six members of the Senate Judiciary Committee visited the White House to learn Taft's reasoning. He explained that he had changed his mind about Hughes because of his judicial inexperience and because he felt Roosevelt might be annoyed by a Hughes appointment. Hughes's biographer, Merle Pusey, perceptively suggests that Taft might have feared appointing so young a man as Hughes, who was forty-eight, since it might preclude his one day realizing his own lifelong dream. Hughes was, under President Hoover, finally appointed chief justice, but not until William Howard Taft was dead, having already served nine years in that position.

A different problem arose just a few months later, in the spring of 1911, over the resignation of the famous advocate of pure-foods legislation, Harvey Wiley, the chief chemist for the Department of Agriculture. A public furor soon erupted. The enemies of pure-food legislation had leveled the trivial accusation that Wiley had employed several pure-food experts at a slightly higher per diem rate than the nine dollars set by Congress. Taft considered the charges inconsequential, but nonetheless, to avoid a wrangle, he did not come to Wiley's defense. In private he expressed annoyance that Secretary of Agriculture Wilson had left himself open to the charges, declaring that this showed "how poor a secretary he is." But he did not go beyond simply saying that the charges against Wiley were not serious enough to cause dissension. Butt saw the trouble coming: "If the president yields to pressure and sacrifices Wiley, the trouble which followed the removal of Pinchot will be as a zephyr by the side of a storm which will follow Wiley's removal. . . . The general belief is that Wiley stands between the people and a national belly ache. . . . In some places he is almost deified." Uncle Joe Cannon derided Wiley by saying that if he is allowed to have his way, "everybody would be afraid to eat anything for fear of being poisoned." Taft accepted Wiley's resignation, but won no admirers and ended by antagonizing both groups.

Not only was Taft seldom aroused to take sides in a political battle, but he rarely strove for the passage of any particular piece of legislation. He expressed constitutional scruples about interfering in the legislative process. "I have no disposition," he told Aldrich, "to exert any other influence than that which it is my function under the Constitution to exercise." On one measure, however, Taft made an exception; he pushed a reciprocity agreement with Canada calling for the removal of tariff barriers between that country and the United States. His uncharacteristically strong feelings on this issue may have been inspired by the legal nature of treaties. They required the kind of courtlike considerations and negotiations he liked best. From the projected agreement he anticipated an expansion in the sales of United States manufactured goods as well as greater purchases of Canadian raw materials. Both Taft and Secretary of State Knox believed that by enlarging the free list of food products coming in from Canada the treaty would also reduce the cost of living. On their side, newspaper owners and their editorialists for once heartily approved the provision removing duties on newsprint and wood pulp. Although the agreement was expected to be popular with most Americans, many farmers, especially wheat farmers, were unalterably opposed to the free importation of Canadian foodstuffs, fearful they would depress prices in domestic markets. Some Republicans from northwestern states and some New Englanders opposed putting fish on the free list. Because it would reduce duties on manufactured goods from Canada, industrial protectionists also lobbied against the treaty, mostly on principle, not wanting to see precedents set. The Democrats seemed happy with the idea and planned to support Taft. Taft knew that more tariff wrangling would revive still smoldering animosities, but he persevered in this instance. In light of the previous tariff fiasco, Taft told his brother Horace, "I should like to have this scalp dangling at my official belt even if I am to wear it only four years." "I am not urging reciprocity on any political ground," he declared, and as for the farmers, "I cannot help what they feel . . . I wish to push it through." He hoped that "ultimately there will come a realization that it will help the country," no matter what the short-term effects.

Taft sent a special message to Congress in January 1911, a step rare for him, urging the prompt passage of a reciprocity treaty. Such an action "deserves and secures . . . approbation," the *New York Times* said. His new "boldness," the *Times* predicted, could secure his renomination in 1912 if he kept it up. The conservative Nelson Aldrich was away from the Senate recuperating from illness at this time, but Taft still sought his support for the bill: "How I wish you were here. A blast upon your bugle is worth a thousand men." "I feel sure we are going to be beaten in the next presidential election and then the Democracy without restraint will play havoc with . . . business." On Aldrich's recommendation the Senate Finance Committee released on 24 February 1911 the text of the Canadian Reciprocity Agreement but did not endorse it. Angered at Congress's inaction, Taft threatened an extra session if reciprocity were not passed. Unaccustomed to such aggressive methods on the president's part, many senators did not believe Taft and regarded his threat as mere bluff. It seemed incredible that Taft would call a Democratic House into extra session, for it was well-known how much he wished to avoid controversy. House Democratic leaders Champ Clark and Oscar Underwood assured him they would pass the measure in a special session, but added ominously, they might also pass "other bills" that they thought proper, "including tariff bills." Sensing the seriousness of the situation, Republican legislators warned him against the move, but Taft quickly replied, "I do not care a tinker's damn whether it injures my political prospects or not." Trying another tack, the Republicans argued that the measure was economically unsound. Taft retorted, "It may be economically rotten. But I regard it as good statesmanship." The bill was defeated in the closing hours by a filibuster led by progressive House Republicans.

Taft made good his threat about the reciprocity treaty and called for a special session of Congress to convene in April 1911. Most Americans applauded Taft's newfound "elevated and statesmanlike spirit," but Taft feared that the influence of special groups would prevent Congress from passing it. Congress moved slowly but steadily toward acceptance of the treaty, nevertheless, and Canadian-American consultation on the details of the agreement went forward. The press predicted "a solid and brilliant success" for the president if the agreement was passed. Taft even invited members of the opposition to play golf with him. Senator Guggenheim had long been anxious to golf with the president, even though he was a poor player. They talked reciprocity and Taft praised the senator's bad shots, prophesying that he might be a champion one day. By the end of the match he had Guggenheim committed to the bill. "That is the hardest afternoon's work I have had in many a day," Taft whispered to Butt on the seventeenth green. "I would not go through with it again for two votes on the bill." It was one of the few occasions on which he mixed work and pleasure.

Taft continued to lobby hard for the bill. To friends concerned about the pace he was setting on behalf of the measure, Taft explained that he was "determined to leave no stone unturned." He thought Canadian Reciprocity was one of the most important pieces of legislation in a decade, and the opportunity to secure it was finally at hand. Taft made three trips about the country to persuade Americans of the wisdom of his course. He was gratified when Congress approved it in July 1911. The Senate Democrats supported the measure overwhelmingly, while the Republicans split with 21 for and 24 opposed. But again Taft inadvertently sabotaged his own proposal. The president made two statements which, combined with Congressman Champ

Clark's demand for the annexation of British North America, eventually led to Canada's rejection of the treaty. Taft wrote to Theodore Roosevelt confidentially that the amount of Canadian products the United States would import "would make Canada only an adjunct to the United States." Precisely how this letter was leaked to the press is not clear. The letter, combined with Clark's demand for Canadian annexation, understandably alarmed many Canadians. In addition Taft wrote a letter to William Randolph Hearst thanking him for spreading "the gospel of reciprocity" in his newspapers, and Hearst was an outspoken advocate of Canadian annexation.

Prime Minister Sir Wilfred Laurier, the longtime Liberal leader, supported reciprocity, but in a national plebiscite the Canadian people voted in September 1911 to reject the treaty. Its defeat was a serious disappointment for the president. As the *New York Times* reported, the "negotiations of the Reciprocity Agreement was the most conspicuous success of his Administration." The *Times* blamed Taft for the failure, because of his letter to Roosevelt. By not sufficiently heeding Canadian sensitivity toward its giant neighbor to the south he contributed to the defeat of one of the few pieces of legislation for which he had strenuously fought.

Although Taft shirked some presidential duties and was confounded by several issues, it would be a gross misrepresentation to say that his administration was devoid of constructive accomplishment. One of his greatest successes was the Postal Savings System, which had been the subject of much debate for almost forty years. Taft urged its enactment in his December 1909 message to the Sixty-first Congress. The Postal Savings plan was intended to protect the average citizen's savings, which were so often lost in periodic bank failures. So enthusiastic was Taft for this program that he startled Washington by acting, as the *New York Times* put it, "in a fashion not employed before in his Administration," that is, he put pressure on the Senate. Disagreements over the postal savings system revolved around the use of the deposits. Taft wanted people to deposit their money with the government and earn interest, but Nelson Aldrich, Joe Cannon, and many bankers called the idea vicious and paternalistic. Cannon complained about the increasing role of government in the economic order. Taft disagreed. The country had advanced, he said, beyond the days of "the laissez-faire school which believes that the government ought to do nothing but run a police force." Aldrich offered an alternative plan to replace the national banks with a new central bank. Both Democrats and insurgents opposed it, arguing that funds would concentrate in the big eastern cities. Taft moved for a compromise to save the postal savings bill by calling in Senate leaders. He warned them that he would keep the Congress in session until December to defeat any filibuster attempts. He summoned Uncle Joe for consultation, who indicated his distaste for the Postal Savings Plan but offered his aid because it had been one of the party's pledges. "I think it a decided step toward populism," Cannon declared. "Exactly," replied Taft, "but those fellows in the Senate who are opposing this bill are not doing it for any reasons which you have given but merely to make trouble or else to freight it down with heavier populistic burdens." Toward the end of their conference, Taft asked Cannon to help get the two new battleships he had promised Roosevelt to add to the fleet. Cannon laughed and said, "Nothing illustrates better than this the difference between our last two presidents. Roosevelt never wanted but two at a time, and yet he always asked, even demanded, four a year, hoping thereby to get two. You, on the contrary, want two and ask for two."

In pursuit of his postal savings plan, Taft even sent telegrams to absent senators requesting their presence for the vote. Hearing rumors about noncooperation from Republican Senator Burroughs, Taft called him on the phone: "I thought you were an administration senator," he said. Burroughs replied, "I am an administration senator, but——" To which Taft retorted: "There is no 'but' in it. The way to be an administration senator is to vote with the administration." When Burroughs tried to explain further, President Taft angrily hung up. Jonathan Bourne from Oregon, who had earlier avoided a White House dinner, declined to come when Taft sent for him. Furious, Taft declared he would have nothing more to do with him, and he never did. Thanks to Taft's determination the insurgents passed the amended bill, which contained a compromise plan allowing deposits to be placed in local banks under the supervision of a government Board of Trustees. Taft signed the bill on 25 June 1910, and the postal savings system went into operation in 1911.

Another of Taft's favorite projects was the arbitration treaties with England and France. Taft had not premeditated improving or replacing the twenty-four arbitration agreements that Elihu Root had negotiated in 1908; he came on this issue by accident in a speech to the American Arbitration and Peace League in March 1910. "It is strange how one happens on this sort of thing," he explained later to Archie. "When I made that speech in New York advocating the arbitration of questions, even those affecting the honor of a nation, I had no definite policy in view. I was inclined, if I remember rightly, merely to offset the antagonism to the four battleships for which I was then fighting, and I threw that suggestion out merely to draw the sting of old Carnegie and other peace cranks, and now the suggestion threatens to become the main fact of my four years as president."

The speech had been unexpectedly successful. Newspaper editorials, religious and peace groups, even business organizations, expressed approval, and the president basked in unaccustomed praise. This "unanimous expression of earnest interest," as Taft termed it, moved him to press forward. He delegated Philander Knox to negotiate and draw up arbitration treaties with Britain and France.

The opposition in Congress was led by isolationist Senator Henry Cabot Lodge, who later led the fight to defeat Woodrow Wilson over American participation in the League of Nations. Taft bungled by not submitting an advance draft of the arbitration treaties to the Senate. He acknowledged his error late, explaining that "it did not seem wise to submit the matter to the Senate until after we had found that the other countries were willing to join us in such treaties." But the Senate took umbrage. Some senators began speaking of the treaties as "breeders of war rather than harbingers of peace." Lodge particularly disliked the idea of subjecting questions relating to "vital interests," the "national honor," and "independence" of the United States to arbitration, arguing that the Monroe Doctrine, United States immigration laws, and territorial claims against the United States were all inarbitrable. An aroused Taft defended the treaties by answering Lodge's complaints, and though he answered with skill, Taft was so fearful of normal political debate that he felt he had inadvertently hurt his own cause. As he wrote to Nellie, "I blundered into a speech . . . in which what I say answers some of what he says. I suppose it will add to the general disposition to kick against me which is evident in the Senate but I am in the right and I must continue it until the end." Taft continued bravely to battle for his treaties and to meet Lodge's objections head on. His stubborn perseverance, lasting over eighteen months, led finally to victory over Lodge. The treaties with Britain and France were signed in August 1911. Taft later admitted ingenuously that he had hoped "the senators might change their minds, or that the people might change the Senate; instead of which they changed me."

Taft was likewise initially uninformed about the immigration laws, yet he learned quickly. In February 1910, representatives of 350 foreign language newspapers descended upon him to protest proposed congressional restrictions. They particularly objected to the literacy test, a measure which xenophobic restrictionists hoped would block much of the immigration from south and east Europe. Other provisions of the immigration legislation under consideration included an increased head tax and the stipulation that all males over sixteen be in possession of twenty-five dollars. Taft answered these reporters' pleas with the frank admission that he did not know much about the proposed legislation but he planned to investigate. After he had acquainted himself with the literacy test bill, he vetoed it, as McKinley had done before him, on the grounds that it was unfair to deny opportunities to peoples who had had no chance for an elementary education in their home countries. Eventually the restrictionists won, however, passing a literacy test over Wilson's veto in 1917, but Taft thwarted them for a time, allowing many thousands of immigrants to seek in America opportunities they were denied elsewhere.

As a quiet administrator, Taft had learned quickly and displayed unexpected talents, which, unfortunately, went largely unnoticed in the wake of the publicity surrounding his major failures. During his years in office many postal employees were placed under civil service regulations, and Taft, ever scrupulously honest, insisted on placement and promotion by merit. He wanted the merit system extended to all important offices to increase government efficiency and economy, although he conceded his plan was not likely "to win votes and make platforms to carry elections." Had he succeeded in persuading Congress to pass such a measure, it would have been a creditable accomplishment. Taft backed away from the larger plan when Congress appropriated funds for another of his pet projects, the Economy and Efficiency Commission. He did succeed in placing thirty-five thousand fourth-class postmasters under civil service and in bringing the merit system to lower diplomatic officials as well as to twenty thousand skilled workers in the navy yards. Taft got little credit for his civil service reform, because, as Secretary of the Treasury Franklin MacVeagh observed, such a tame issue aroused little comment and evoked scant public interest.

There were other accomplishments as well. With Taft's assistance, Congress also strengthened the Interstate Commerce Commission with the Mann-Elkins Act of 1910. The act empowered the commission to suspend railroad rate hikes for up to ten months, in order to study their appropriateness, and gave it ultimate power in rate making. The measure culminated one of Roosevelt's major efforts. In the name of economy Taft abolished four hundred positions in the Department of the Treasury and one hundred in the Philadelphia mint. He reorganized the customs service and made large cuts in the military services. Because the federal government did not yet have a unified budget, Taft tried during his first year in office to centralize control of the budgetary process. He pruned an unprecedented $92 million from the original estimates and sent the first modern budget to Congress. Later he admitted that trying to achieve economy through the budget process had been naïve, and so in 1910, Congress, at his behest, appropriated $100,000 to create the Commission on Economy and Efficiency to study federal administration, budgeting, and efficiency in all departments. In June 1912, he sent their report, plus his own special message—entitled "The Need for a National Budget"—to Congress. Thus Taft began the process which, with the passage of the Budget and Accounting Act of 1921, resulted in a unified budget office. This measure shifted the balance of control over financial policy away from the legislative and toward the executive branch.

During Taft's administration the Department of Commerce and Labor, created under Roosevelt in 1903, was divided into two departments; the Federal Children's Bureau was established; Arizona and New Mexico were admitted to statehood; the Sixteenth Amendment (Income Tax) was passed; and the Seventeenth Amendment enacting a reform long desired by Populists and progressive Republicans, the direct election of senators, was finally adopted. Taft, however, was lukewarm about the direct election of senators, one of the major reform acts of his administration, and he vetoed Arizona's and New Mexico's admission because of their constitutional provision for the recall of judges. He signed the resolutions only after the recall clauses were removed. Finally, during Taft's presidency Roosevelt's conservation policies were regularized and his Food and Drug Acts were strengthened.

Taft did not actively seek the passage of most of these new measures, but saw his term as a time to perfect the existing governmental machinery and to consolidate Roosevelt's prior reforms. New legislation was initiated not by Taft but by Democrats working with insurgent Republicans. The momentum of the Roosevelt years and the strong sentiment in the country for a more active government helped their adoption more than did any role Taft played. Personally, the president's most congenial work lay in studying the various pardon cases which reached his desk. He took great delight in writing his opinions. He was also extremely proud of the six new Supreme Court appointments and numerous lower court selections he made.

Moreover Taft aggressively prosecuted the trusts, again because of his constitutional and legal interests—he liked to get involved in issues which came before the courts rather than the legislature. More trust prosecutions may be attributed to Taft than to Roosevelt, though of course the two major Supreme Court decisions during these years, against the Standard Oil and the tobacco trusts, had been initiated under Roosevelt. When Taft first learned of the Supreme Court's decision against the Standard Oil Company, he appropriately echoed an old Roosevelt cry: "Bully for that!" He soon began to have reservations, however, and to fear that the commercial structure of the country might go to pieces if trust busting went too far: "I want to read the business interests of this country a lecture, but it should have some warning before the law becomes too drastic." Butt, knowing how much Roosevelt had desired further antitrust proceedings, worried that Taft might lapse into total apathy on this matter. Ironically, the administration's action in prosecuting the United States Steel Company was the most direct cause of the breakup of his friendship with Roosevelt.

Big businessmen increasingly objected to the court's interpretation of the Sherman Antitrust Act and the executive branch's commitment to file suits. As Archie Butt put it, "President Taft will do anything if he has the law on which to base his act. The law to President Taft is the same support as some zealots get from great religious faith." Although he insisted that he wanted the law "enforced to the letter," Taft was often ambivalent. Not long after Attorney General George Wickersham began his numerous prosecutions, Taft began to feel that he was "too energetic." Wickersham was, after Secretary of State Knox, the most independent and powerful member of Taft's cabinet. Taft believed he was its "most brilliant member." But by the fall of 1911, as Wickersham instituted antitrust suits at an unprecedented rate, special business interests damned his "pestiferous activity" and labelled him "the most radical man who has held that office for years." Since Wickersham had once been a corporation lawyer, they thought him a great traitor. Wickersham's suit against U.S. Steel was a strategic blunder because it adversely affected Taft's relationship with Roosevelt and convinced millionaire businessman George Perkins to support Roosevelt in 1912. Once aware of Roosevelt's displeasure over the suit, Taft became very upset and pleaded that he had not been consulted when the decision to prosecute was made and therefore he was unable to stop it. To avoid further conflicts, Taft unequivocally told his attorney general to confer with him before any similar steps were taken in the future.

Taft's expectations that vigorous antitrust prosecution would bring him the same sort of general acclaim that "trust buster" Roosevelt had enjoyed were soon dispelled. After his second cross-country trip in 1911, he told brother Horace, "When I went West I was going into enemy country; now that I return, I seem to be coming back into the enemy's country, due to the enforcement of the antitrust law by George Wickersham's prosecutions." His friend Otto Bannard, a New York banker, took Taft sharply to task: "Your Department of Justice has offended big business, small business, stock holders and mechanics and poor people." Wickersham, Bannard claimed, "has cost you the greater part of your popularity in the eastern states, and the impression exists that he conducts an independent suzerainty, entirely free from your influence or control. . . . You should prove yourself the master of *your* departments." Indignant and puzzled by what he considered business's apostasy, Taft exploded privately to his brother Harry: "Wall Street, as an aggregation, is the biggest ass that I have run across."

Taft had studied the matter sufficiently to realize the inadequacies of the Sherman Antitrust Act, and he sent a special message on trusts to Congress in December 1911. The president called for a supplemental law to delineate unfair methods of competition and to strengthen government control through a special bureau in the Department of Commerce and Labor. But Congress made no move to act on the recommendations, partly because, as Root informed Stimson, "No one really knows what the president's position on the trust question is." Woodrow Wilson, with the upcoming election in mind, began early to jab at Taft's record, claiming that he and Wickersham were responsible for the 1911 business recession. In particular Wilson attacked Taft's indecisiveness: "One day Taft says he is absolutely going to enforce the Sherman law, but after reading the newspapers, he thinks he has excited too much of a clamor and backs off. And so businessmen naturally demand to know where they're at." Paolo Coletta, a generally sympathetic Taft biographer, concludes that in this area the president came out poorly: "Taft's efforts to revive the Sherman Act stabilized the trusts rather than destroyed them, weakened rather than strengthened the act, and failed to win [legislation] from Congress."

Taft, far more than Roosevelt, gave vigorous encouragement to foreign trade. Uncle Joe Cannon said of Roosevelt, "I think if the truth be known, [he] rather despised trade." Taft was therefore reviving McKinley in his desire to see American commercial supremacy throughout the world, hence his interest in the Canadian Reciprocity Agreement. On his 1909 tour of the United States, he said that the goal was to see "the American commercial flag . . . made to wave upon the seas as it did before the Civil War." Taft's extensive travel, to the Far East during his governorship of the Philippines and to Panama, Cuba, and Rome on special missions, gave him greater first-hand knowledge of world affairs than any recent president had possessed. Yet he handled foreign affairs much like domestic matters: he set broad policies and then left their implementation to the secretary of state. He strongly believed in delegating power. Taft so esteemed Philander Knox, his secretary of state, that he tended to rely on him too heavily: "I want you to know that the arrangement of the State Department is to suit you, and you can take any course you see fit. . . . Whatever you do will satisfy me." "The comfort I have in your management of the State Department I cannot exaggerate," he later wrote. Knox took this delegation of power seriously. As his deputy Francis Huntington Wilson put it, Knox "had it tacitly understood, that, outside of Congress, no official from the president down was to say or do anything that touched upon foreign relations without his approval in advance." Archie Butt observed how cleverly Knox influenced Taft and how "shrewd" he was "in getting his ideas incorporated in the speeches of the president." So unlike the "imperial" presidents of the second and third quarters of this century, Taft, according to Wilson, "practically never interposed in any matter of foreign relations."

Knox was a good lawyer, but a poor statesman. In addition, Knox, much like his chief, left the actual administration of his department to subordinates, especially to Francis Huntington Wilson, his first assistant secretary. Like other ambitious administrators, Knox bothered little about the routine things in his department, but took a keen personal interest in major policy-making decisions. Wilson, too, unfortunately, was a poor diplomat. Taft disliked Wilson, who considered himself Knox's alter ego. "What Knox sees in him," Taft once said to Butt in exasperation, "I do not see." "I would like to sit on Wilson and mash him flat," a remarkable statement, indicating the pleasure Taft sometimes took in his own "weight."

The most successful aspect of Taft's foreign relations policy was the arbitration of several long-standing fishing and hunting disputes, especially with England. Again the legalistic arbitration appealed to him. American and British sealers, who had been restricted in their hunting in the Bering Sea, feared that Russian, Canadian, and Japanese sealers would destroy the species. Prodded by the anger of conservationists, Taft sent to Congress in March 1910, a special message on the matter. The result was a conference held in Washington the following year, at which the British, American, Japanese, and Russian representatives agreed to follow an "international game law" in order to preserve the seal herds.

Other disputes were solely with the British. One involved fishing rights off Newfoundland, over which England and the United States had quarreled for eighty years. In his 1909 message to Congress, Taft declared that a settlement was long overdue. He then dispatched Elihu Root to the Court of Arbitration at The Hague where an agreement shortly took shape. Another British-American quarrel, dating back to 1783, concerned the boundary line between Maine and New Brunswick in Passamaquoddy Bay. In May 1910, that issue was resolved through arbitration.

In the Far East, Taft and Knox subscribed to the "Open Door." Their interest, however, was not the protection of China but the development of overseas markets and the wish to gain financial influence. "What I am especially anxious to secure in China is the investment of American capital," Taft confided to his wife. Again, the president set the policy and left the details to his secretary of state, who formulated a plan for American commercial expansion with the unification of all Manchurian railroad lines as the first step. Japan and Russia immediately protested American involvement, forcing Knox to back down. Not only did little come of Knox's railroad efforts, American exports to China actually declined under Taft. He failed to gain a strong economic foothold in China or an Open Door in Manchuria.

Roosevelt's earlier intervention in Panama and Santo Domingo had left United States relations with Latin America troubled. Taft and Knox proceeded to aggravate the ill will by aggressively seeking commercial advantages in Central America. Taft outlined his policy for Knox as "the same . . . entered on by Mr. Root and Mr. Roosevelt." He listened to men like Senator Stone, who urged that "we ought to exercise supervision over all Latin American countries."

The most flagrant example of American intervention occurred in Nicaragua. Infuriated when two Americans were executed during the revolution against dictatorial President Zelaya, the secretary of state instituted his "Hard Knox policy" by withdrawing recognition of Zelaya's government and ordering naval vessels to stand by on alert. When disorder increased again in late 1911, Taft and Knox sent in twenty-seven hundred marines under the pretence of protecting American lives and property. The marines proceeded to engage Nicaraguan soldiers at Leon and occupy the capital and other major cities. Such incidents brought Pan-Americanism to a halt during Taft's administration. The fourth Pan-American Conference in 1910 was concerned chiefly with ways to curtail American commercial penetration, influence, and intervention.

Taft proved more successful in handling a difficult Mexican incident and in maintaining neutrality despite much provocation. Fearful about the fate of business's billion-dollar investment in Mexico, Taft, who had met President Porfirio Diaz in 1909, expressed confidence in the dictator. "I can only hope and pray that his demise does not come until after I am out of office," he wrote to Nellie. He finally took charge of American policy toward revolution-torn Mexico, rather than leaving it strictly to Knox. When some insurgents crossed over into the United States to commandeer horses and supplies, Taft spoke with reserve about the "exceedingly delicate and difficult situation created along our southern border" and the need "for taking measures properly to safeguard American interests" in Mexico. He decided, without consulting his secretary of state, to dispatch two thousand troops to border points and to order warships to San Diego and Guantanamo Bay. Infuriated over this presidential interference in his domain, Secretary Knox, who had been on vacation when the crisis arose, announced that he intended to resign from the cabinet. The president pooh-poohed the idea. He then sat down to write a long letter hoping to pacify Knox, who was still vacationing in Palm Beach, Florida. There were rumors that the whole cabinet might "buck" over Taft's act. Some resented his moving troops without holding a meeting or consulting with more than Secretaries Meyer of the navy and Dickinson of war.

Incredibly, Secretary of the Navy Meyer had sent warships to Mexican ports without authorization from the president. When Taft learned that part of the American fleet had assembled in the gulf off Tampico and that the Mexicans naturally expected an invasion, he swore that he had never given such an order. Either Meyer had misunderstood him—or was acting on his own. Immediately he sent orders to remove the ships from Mexican waters. This display of American muscle, however, shored up Diaz temporarily. But the revolution continued, and Diaz was overthrown by Victoriano Huerta in February 1911.

Despite pressure from American businessmen who had suffered losses in Mexico, Taft assured Congress he would not send troops into Mexico except at its direction. To a friend he confided, "I am not going to intervene in Mexico until no other course is possible, but I must protect our people in Mexico as far as possible." When Butt inquired about his intentions, Taft answered, relying on one of his favorite metaphors, "I am going to sit tight on the lid, and it will take a good deal to pry me off." Taft continued to resist pressure for more intervention in Mexico by "sitting tight," in that way helping to prevent a second war against our strife-torn neighbor.

The army and navy, indispensable to foreign diplomacy, were, not surprisingly, of little interest to President Taft, and his desire for economy resulted in a slight decline in the position of the American navy as a world power. Secretary George Meyer practically excluded Taft from his department's affairs. Charles P. Taft complained to Archie Butt, "Only today the president wanted to appoint a solicitor in the Navy Department where there is a vacancy, and Meyer had the impudence to say he would not have any politician in the department." Secretary of War Jacob Dickinson failed to arouse Taft's interest in much-needed organizational reform. The army lacked sufficient officers, specially trained men, as well as adequate transportation, for no automobiles or trucks were yet employed. Additional funds could not be allocated, Taft insisted, because he wanted to economize.

In summary, the preoccupation of the Taft administration with trade expansion, and the discussions about intervention in foreign countries on behalf of business interests, led to cries of Dollar Diplomacy. Democrats and progressive Republicans found one more reason to unite in opposition to President Taft. Seeking to explain his policies and justify himself, Taft made things worse by some impolitic statements. In reply to charges of Dollar Diplomacy, he said his policies were "substituting dollars for bullets."

In attempting to refurbish Taft's presidential reputation, Paolo Coletta defensively argues that his legislative record does not "wholly warrant" the characterization of a "gigantic symbol of standpattism." Because Taft's conception of administration was "mechanistic" and he was unable to give managerial "leadership and spirit," he finally "retreated to a defense of conservative constitutionalism." Taft exercised little leadership over Congress and therefore failed to drive his programs through. He could not keep his party united. It was tragic that the reforms Taft sought "rebounded against him and split his party." Coletta nonetheless concludes that, all in all, Taft "was not a bad president but a rather good one."

Arthur Wallace Dunn has written that "it is difficult to write of President Taft's four years in the White House without seeming to be severely critical. He did so many things which made him unpopular." Even his devoted friend, Archie Butt, commented, "It is hard not to be critical when one sees mistake after mistake being made which may as well be avoided." Butt felt that in many ways, "he is the best man I have ever known, too honest for the presidency, possibly, and possibly too good-natured or too trusting or too something."

During his years in the White House Taft unquestionably matured as he learned anew to assess his own potentialities and to forward them himself. After achieving the presidency for Nellie and having nearly completed a term in the office, he became more self-concerned than he had ever allowed himself to be in the past. Despite his blunders and problems, Taft had come to approve of himself ethically and morally—quite independently of both Roosevelt's standards and Nellie's demands. Taft entered the White House at age fifty-one and underwent a good deal of mellowing as he moved toward the final stage of his professional life. He had reached the point where he could approve of his own course in life, even though it had meant and would mean breaking free from a life pattern which, having served him for so long, was clearly becoming unsatisfactory. Power and the call to leadership gave him a new sense of identity and independence. He liked this new-found self enough to want to continue its development—in the presidency. This meant the growth of a genuine ambivalence toward re-election. For the first time his attitude was not wholly negative. Yet too much had happened that could not be reversed. Republican domination was about to end, and with it Taft was to undergo a personal loss which meant more to him than the party ever did or could: the friendship of Theodore Roosevelt.

XV

THE END OF A
BEAUTIFUL FRIENDSHIP

That William Howard Taft was meeting with little success as president did not go unnoticed by his mentor, Theodore Roosevelt. Even before Taft took office, Roosevelt expressed reservations about his hand-picked successor. While on his hunting trip in Africa, Roosevelt received numerous reports about Taft's problems, yet he insisted that he would not attempt to impose his opinions on Taft. He gave not the slightest hint of wishing to run again, and "earnestly hope[d] that Taft would [retrieve] himself yet." Any failure of his administration would be as keenly felt, he said, "by me as by himself or his family."

Soon Roosevelt became enraged by news of Taft's courting the conservative faction of the Republican party. As president, Roosevelt had skillfully used conservative Republican leaders for his own political ends without being drawn into their camp. Such maneuvers, Roosevelt acknowledged, were beyond Taft's capacities or inclinations. The difference is, he said, that Mr. Taft "gets their assistance at the price of going their way." Even though Roosevelt had deftly avoided the tariff issue and had left the politically sensitive task of revision to his successor, he nonetheless was indignant when Taft did not sufficiently influence the protectionists in Congress to get an honest revision. Taft, Roosevelt charged, "sat supinely by and allowed his friends, Aldrich and Cannon, to produce a bill" which betrayed the party pledge. The Ballinger-Pinchot affair further annoyed Roosevelt, for Gifford

Pinchot was one of his closest friends. "For a year after Taft took office . . .
I would not let myself think ill of anything he did," Roosevelt confided to
Henry Cabot Lodge in May 1910. "I finally had to admit that he had gone
wrong on certain points." Certain it was that Taft had gone his, not Roosevelt's, way.

The rumors that all was not right with the Roosevelt-Taft friendship
moved nearer to confirmation after 1911. But matters had been disturbed for
some time prior to that. Shortly after his inauguration Taft had written in
an article for *Colliers* magazine entitled "My Predecessor" that "the relationship between Mr. Roosevelt and myself has been one of close and sweet
intimacy. It has never been ruffled in the slightest degree." He seems to have
been trying to quiet rumors of a cooling in their friendship, but he was also
giving voice to his own most sincere thoughts. To his brother Charles, Taft
wrote, "I am determined if . . . a rupture is ever to be brought about that it
shall not be brought through any action of mine. Theodore may not approve
of all I have done and I don't expect him to do so, but I shall try not to do
anything which he might regard as a challenge."

Later, given the actions he had taken as president, Taft was afraid Roosevelt might misinterpret his intentions. He attempted to explain himself in
May 1910. Archie Butt wrote to Clara, "The president told me last night
that he had written a long letter to Roosevelt telling him what he had accomplished . . . and the reasons for his failures where he had failed." "I have
been conscientiously trying to carry out your policies but my methods of
doing so have not worked smoothly," Taft wrote. He told Butt that "at first
he thought he ought not to write at all; then he felt that possibly this silence
would be misunderstood, for after all he owed Mr. Roosevelt a debt of gratitude which he had to acknowledge." In distant Africa, Roosevelt avoided
making any public statements which might have reflected poorly upon Taft.
He must have taken satisfaction, however, from the commentaries that
appeared frequently on both sides of the Atlantic favorably comparing his
administration with that of his successor's. Once back in the United States
in June 1910, Roosevelt found it more difficult to remain quiet and impartial.

As we have seen, Taft had been devoted to Roosevelt and served him well.
Yet soon after Taft's inauguration a coolness arose between these two old
friends, and it increased steadily until by 1912 they were seemingly implacable enemies. What caused the breach in William Howard Taft and Theodore Roosevelt's friendship became the subject of much discussion and
debate among their contemporaries, and later, among their biographers.

Many have pointed to an incident which took place directly after Taft's
inauguration when it was said that he wrote to Roosevelt as follows: "Yes, in
thinking over the whole campaign, I am bound to say that I owe my election

more to you than to anybody else, except my brother Charley." Roosevelt allegedly was incensed; Charles P. Taft had, after all, supplied only money, whereas he had nominated and elected Taft singlehandedly. Indiana Congressman James Watson states that when he congratulated Roosevelt on putting Taft into office, the ex-president spoke of Taft's ingratitude. Watson also described Roosevelt's rage at Taft's celebrated letter: "He mentions his brother Charles in connection with me?" Roosevelt said through clenched teeth. "Does he not know that I could have beaten him, had I not been for him? Is he not aware of the fact that I could easily have taken that nomination myself? The idea of his putting his brother Charles alongside me in an expression of gratitude. . . . It is monstrous, I tell you." All this and much more Roosevelt uttered with explosive force, Watson recalled. No doubt much of Roosevelt's anger must have been directed at himself for not taking the nomination when it could have been his with a nod of the head.

Taft later confessed to Butt in August 1910 that he suspected bad feeling had started with that letter. "Something offended him in that letter," Taft observed, "but I was never certain what it was until recently, when someone . . . told me. It seems that I said that I would never forget what he and my brother Charlie had done for me. He became very angry and . . . at the same time [used] some rather objectionable terms in description of old Charlie." Jimmy Sloan, Roosevelt's secret service guard for seven years, told Butt that Roosevelt was upset before he left Washington. Coming back from a walk one night, Roosevelt said to Sloan, "Jimmy, I may have to come back in four years to carry out my policies." Ike Hoover also claimed that the relations between Taft and Roosevelt had cooled before inauguration day, for there was much apparent bitterness, he felt, between the incoming and outgoing families.

Alice Roosevelt Longworth recalled friction developing right after the election. She had resented the way Mrs. Taft and others seemed to view Taft's election as his due reward, thus ignoring almost entirely the decisive role her father played. Alice probably contributed to the friction, for she was bitterly disappointed: "No one will ever know how much I wished, in the black depths of my heart," she candidly admitted later in Crowded Hours, "that 'something would happen' and that Father would be renominated. It was against human nature, against mine anyway, not to feel that the prospect of all those great times coming to an end was something to be regretted, though most secretly." As the voting returns came in, Alice recalled, Nellie and the family compared them to Roosevelt's victory margin in 1904 and they "fairly gloated" whenever Taft ran ahead of Roosevelt's figures. Looking back on the post election activities, Alice wrote, "the stage was set for the first steps that led to the 'breaking up of a beautiful friendship.' "

Some observers think that genuine hostility emerged only after Taft had selected his cabinet. Roosevelt pointedly mentioned to Taft the men who had been the nominee's most "staunch and ardent supporters" during the campaign. And just before the election, Taft told Roosevelt that he probably would not change the existing cabinet. It soon became apparent, however, that Taft planned to nominate several replacements. One reason he stalled reporters from week to week was that he knew his cabinet changes would offend Roosevelt, a consequence he desired to postpone as long as possible. Newberry, Cortelyou, Bonaparte, Garfield, Straus would go, Taft hinted, yet he was in no rush to hurry their departure. Roosevelt was agitated and asked for a clarification: "Now I think it would be well for you to write them all at once that you do not intend to reappoint them. They will be making their plans . . . and I do not think they ought to be left in doubt." Much surprised, Taft said, "I learned later that Roosevelt had practically told every member of his cabinet that he was going to be retained." Roosevelt recalled, on the other hand, that Taft had expressly directed him to "tell the boys . . . that [he wanted] to continue all of them." After the election, Roosevelt added, "He never spoke to me of having changed his mind and never alluded to the subject again. He simply did not appoint the men." It seems as if Taft's instincts were properly for a new cabinet, yet he could not be direct with Roosevelt concerning the matter. His desire not to give offense or to appear ungrateful, led him, as usual, to delay the decisive moment, thus making the situation far worse than it needed to be.

Of the five cabinet members that Taft finally did replace, Roosevelt particularly resented the dismissal of Interior Secretary James Garfield. The son of the former president was, along with Gifford Pinchot, expecially close to Roosevelt. "No two men have been as closely identified with so many of the policies for which this administration has stood," Roosevelt said. Garfield felt so certain of being retained that he had renewed the lease on his house in Washington. Before making his selections, Taft further offended the progressives by conferring with several archenemies—Nelson Aldrich, Speaker Cannon, Wall Street lawyer Nelson Cromwell, and railroad magnate James J. Hill. No progressive leader was consulted. Nor was Roosevelt pleased by Taft's replacement of members of his special team with corporation lawyers. Undoubtedly he felt gratified when the Senate balked at several of Taft's nominations.

Taft rightly feared repercussions from his appointments. "I presume there will be a yell against my selections on the ground that they tend to those who are subject to corporate influence," he wrote to his brother. Yet he would have the cabinet he wanted, if he could get it. Progressive commentator Ray Stannard Baker considered it outrageous that Taft's pre-election speeches were Rooseveltian in their insistence on "the need to control predatory wealth," but that he took as his advisers a cabinet of the very men who would most probably protect the corporations. Henry Cabot Lodge confided his suspicions to Roosevelt: "It was evidently the intention to get rid of every person who might keep President Taft in touch with the Roosevelt influence."

Still others date the breach as occurring after Roosevelt's return from his African hunting tour in June 1910. Taft did not go to New York to welcome the former president home but sent Archie Butt instead with a letter. Butt took the precaution of requesting that Mrs. Taft address a note to Mrs. Roosevelt as well. Butt felt that the president had acted properly from an official standpoint, though some critics considered Taft discourteous for not greeting his former chief in person. By then Roosevelt had called Taft a "well-meaning, good-natured man . . . but not a leader." "The break in our relations was due to no one thing," Roosevelt wrote, "but to the cumulative effect of many things—the abandonment of everything my administration had stood for."

Many contemporaries believed that the main cause of discord was the Taft administration's prosecution of the U.S. Steel Corporation, the most sweeping antitrust action ever brought by the Department of Justice. The government asked for the dissolution of U.S. Steel and thirty-six subsidiary companies which allegedly had combined in violation of the Sherman Antitrust law. The suit charged U.S. Steel with monopolistic behavior, in part because it had purchased the Tennessee Coal and Iron Company—a merger to which President Roosevelt had earlier given his blessing. Roosevelt thus seemed either guilty of complicity in the illegal combination or the dupe of Elbert Gary and Henry C. Frick, the company leaders who had talked him into approving the merger during the Panic of 1907. Roosevelt felt he was being made to look like a "knave" or a "fool" by the government's suit, and he immediately countered, claiming that Taft, a cabinet member at the time, had been "emphatic in his commendation" of the merger. Bringing the suit now, Roosevelt declared, was "small, mean, and foolish." Some supporters of Roosevelt suggested that the steel suit was politically motivated. Taft was defensive: "I would rather cut off my right hand than to do anything to disturb the business of this country, especially with a motive of cultivating political success." When Secretary of War Stimson next saw Roosevelt, he reported back that the colonel "was as hard as nails and utterly implacable" against the administration. Roosevelt's sister, Mrs. Douglas Robinson, discussing the situation one day with Archie, claimed that it was "too late now. If it had not been for that Steel suit! I was talking with Theodore only last week, and he said that he could never forgive." "Of course you know," Archie replied, "that the president never saw that suit until it was filed."

"Yes," she said, "and Theodore knows that, and that in his eyes is the worst feature of the case—that such a thing could have been done without [the president's] knowledge."

There is no question that Taft was distinctly uncomfortable in trying to find his own way as president and insecure in his strange, new relationship with Roosevelt. Meanwhile, Roosevelt at forty-five was certainly very young to be in effect retired, and he began to yearn again for the power he had so much enjoyed. Predictably the former president was drawn back into politics upon his return from Africa. The only obstacle in his path was the lieutenant he had guided into the presidency. Their relationship had been mutually satisfactory while Roosevelt was president and Taft his subordinate, but neither man was really prepared for the reversal in their positions and neither was able to readjust completely to his new role. Taft did not wish to give up his 'filial' ties to Roosevelt, and Roosevelt did not actually think he was giving up the presidency in electing Taft. Overseeing his protégé in office was expected to be a very different experience than the infuriating one it became.

A sickly, asthmatic child, with poor eyesight and hearing, Roosevelt had succeeded by arduous discipline to build up his weakened body in the gymnasium his father had ordered installed on the second floor of their house. With daily calisthenics and boxing lessons, the thin, owlish-looking boy slowly gained self-confidence as he grew stronger and stouter. His inner drive was a thing of formidable power. Roosevelt created a role of being fearless, then stepped inside the role and left his own fears behind. His new role would not permit him to experience fears any longer—or if he did experience them, he largely suppressed them. "There were all kinds of things of which I was afraid at first," he confessed in his memoirs, "but by acting as if I was not afraid, I gradually ceased to be afraid." He persisted in thinking that the role would make the man and therefore could not begin to understand Taft's attitudes and behavior once he was in the White House. "Manly" and "masterful" were two words he used almost constantly, and he sought out the company of rough, aggressive men. His active life was marked by one success after another. As the joke went, Pringle writes, Roosevelt's life was the dream of every typical American boy—"he fought in a war, killed lions, became President, and quarreled with the Pope." Some thought he was a perpetual adolescent, primarily because of his incredible energy and positiveness. His friend the English ambassador Sir Cecil Spring Rice wrote, "You must always remember that the president is about six." And on his forty-sixth birthday Elihu Root sent him the message, "You have made a very good start in life and your friends have great hopes for you when you grow up."

Roosevelt thrived on vigorous activity and invigorating confrontations. As commissioner of the New York City police he kept the whole force intimidated with his constant surveillance. As president, Roosevelt never allowed a moment to go to waste. On a quiet evening he stayed in his library until he had read three or four books. One of his favorite diversions was to take overweight military officers on long walks through Washington parks; he loved to hear them panting along behind him. After the triumph of getting Taft nominated and elected, it is not strange that Roosevelt soon felt anger over how Taft had wrecked such a "bully pulpit."

When *New York Herald* reporter Walter Wellman interviewed Roosevelt in Naples on 3 April 1910, en route home from Africa, he said that he felt "in no wise responsible" for President Taft and was not inclined to do anything to either help or harm him. The intimate friendship between them, Wellman concluded, no longer existed. In a long letter to his friend Henry Cabot Lodge in the same month, Roosevelt expressed dismay that Taft was working "in a totally different spirit, and with totally different results" than he had expected. "I wish to give Taft the benefit of every doubt," he insisted. "I very earnestly hope that Taft will retrieve himself yet." This would soon prove to be ever more impossible, for once in office, Taft revealed a gradually surfacing determination to become his own master and run his own affairs. To his own, but perhaps even more to Roosevelt's, surprise, he could not just be a stand-in. As he assumed the seat of power, he instinctively reacted by refusing to be pushed around any longer by those who put him where he personally did not wish to be in the first place. But since he was essentially a faithful and grateful man, many of his greatest failures and frustrations would result from conflicts between his own sense of things and his desire to please others, most notably his dearest friend, who thought he had done the greatest thing possible in obtaining for him the nomination and then the election.

As Roosevelt's ship approached the American coast, Governor Charles Evans Hughes breakfasted with the former president, after which a reception committee of three hundred arrived on a revenue cutter, which Roosevelt boarded in order to watch the naval parade underway in his honor. He disembarked in New York early on 18 June to the cheers of half a million people. Following the mayor's speech, a five-mile-long parade started up Broadway. The city was draped in flags and multicolored streamers; everywhere animal masks and teddy bears bobbed up and down among signs reading, "Oh, you Teddy!" and "Dee-lighted!" Innumerable cabinet officers, governors, clubs, and delegations from all over the country were there to greet the ex-president. As the ticker tape fell, Roosevelt stood in his carriage and waved, his teeth bared in his inimitable grin. The *Washington Post* reported that he laughed like a boy and then wept unashamedly. He had been away a year and a half and had travelled thirty thousand miles. Nothing in all his career, he proclaimed with "clinched jaws and a bang of his fist," had affected him like the fervency of this greeting.

After observing the celebration and Roosevelt's response, Secretary of Agriculture Wilson answered Taft's questions about Roosevelt's probable political plans: "Well, I am pretty sure he will not go to bed and sleep too long." Privately Wilson reasoned that Taft was "a mighty big man and a good man, and it will not do for Theodore to reckon too much on swaying the people against him. . . . Roosevelt can split the Republican party wide open now if he chooses and bring it to certain defeat, but I doubt if he could unite it on himself sufficiently to secure the presidency."

Once back home Roosevelt began to assess his opponent. He confided to Gifford Pinchot that Taft "is evidently a man who takes color from his surroundings. He was an excellent man under me, and close to me." But after being elected he "yielded to the advice of his wife, his brother Charley, the different corporation lawyers who had his ear, and various similar men." Despite all the celebrating, Archie Butt managed a few private conversations with his former chief. He told him about Mrs. Taft's illness and how hard it had been on Taft, but he elicited no sympathetic response from Roosevelt, who simply said that he had heard much about Taft's administration which distressed him. Butt's impression was that Roosevelt was "bigger, broader, capable of greater good or greater evil" than when he had left.

Although Taft was not in New York to greet the ex-president, he did extend an invitation to the Roosevelts to visit the White House. He had done so in his letter to Roosevelt in May and renewed the invitation in his home-coming letter, but Roosevelt declined: "I don't think it well for an ex-president to go to the White House, or indeed to go to Washington, except when he cannot help it." Taft was hurt.

Although Taft and Roosevelt failed to meet in the White House, they did manage a rendezvous in Beverly, Massachusetts, on 30 June. Butt stated that he had never seen "as much interest manifested over any one event in the administration of either man" as the press and public demonstrated over this meeting. Butt hoped that his two friends would be reconciled, but Secret Service agent Jimmy Sloan predicted that the meeting would come to nothing. "I know him [Roosevelt] better than you do," he told Butt. "He will come to see the president today and bite his leg off tomorrow." Senator Lodge and the ex-president arrived at Taft's summer home at Burgess Point in a big automobile. They proceeded up the roadway to the house, the horn honking in an irreverent gesture to announce their arrival. Taft, who had been in the library going over his mail, came out on the porch to greet them. According to Butt, he stretched out both hands, exclaiming:

"Ah, Theodore, it is good to see you," and Roosevelt answered impulsively: "How are you, Mr. President? This is simply bully."

"See here now, drop the 'Mr. President,' " said Taft, hitting Roosevelt on the shoulder.

Roosevelt replied warmly: "Not at all. You must be Mr. President and I am Theodore. It must be that way." Taft nevertheless continued apologetically: "The force of habit is very strong in me. I can never think of you save as Mr. President."

As this exchange took place, they walked up the steps, grasping each other's shoulders and laughing good heartedly—after having done their best to decide which of them should be president.

Taft, Roosevelt, Lodge, Charles Norton, and Butt sat in a circle at a table on the lawn. Butt felt the first meeting between the president and the ex-president since 4 March 1908 was "a little strained at first." Taft turned the discussion to New York politics, the ostensible reason for their meeting. The discussion then shifted to Europe and Africa as Roosevelt regaled the audience with anecdotes about his trip. After two and one half hours, the meeting concluded just as amicably as it had begun. When reporters asked if he would be coming back, Roosevelt seemed surprised and answered that he had no plans at present for doing so.

As the summer progressed, Roosevelt told the press that although he had not spoken a word of criticism of the Taft administration, he felt that some of the men around the president were hostile to him. Later, he admitted that he might "jump into the fight" if his policies were in jeopardy, but he would do so only with "extreme reluctance." He added, however, that if he did decide to seek the nomination, he would postpone the struggle until 1912.

When Roosevelt finally came to Washington on 24 November 1910, Taft was touring the South, but he sent his regrets to his former chief and extended a third invitation. Still later, Taft tried one last time: "I hope that the occasion will arise when we can have you and Mrs. Roosevelt under the White House roof and resume in some way our relations of yore." After that, he tried no more: "I invited him to the White House and he declined to come, giving some good reasons from his point of view possibly, but not from mine, so I am not in a position to ask again." Taft decided that he did not want to see Roosevelt again "until he has had plenty of opportunity to think the situation over." Nevertheless Roosevelt's silence piqued him and he showed it: "I don't care if he keeps silent forever," he said to Butt. "Certainly the longer he remains silent, the better it will please me."

Within a week of their former chief's return, progressive Republicans began arriving for talks at Sagamore Hill, Roosevelt's home in Oyster Bay—Joseph Bristow on 2 July, Miles Poindexter on 5 July, Albert Beveridge on

7 July. Report of these gatherings naturally nettled Taft. Robert LaFollette, one of the first to arrive, declared himself very much pleased after his conference with Roosevelt. They had talked of politics, he informed curious reporters, and especially of the insurgents' work. "I want to tell you that Colonel Roosevelt is the greatest living American," LaFollette declared and then added with deliberate slowness, "and he is in fighting trim." An hour later reporters managed to corner Roosevelt after he had just finished chopping down a few trees for firewood. Repeating LaFollette's comments, they brought a satisfied smile to Roosevelt's face. Gifford Pinchot was the next to advance, carrying with him a large bag stuffed full of documents. Pinchot parried reporters' questions afterward about what he thought of the Taft administration by looking up at the dreary sky above Oyster Bay and asking, "What do you think of the weather?"

Taft and Roosevelt's second meeting in New Haven on 19 September, arranged by Lloyd Griscom, minister to Japan under Roosevelt, did not go felicitously. Griscom asked Roosevelt if "for the sake of Republican unity," he would meet again with Taft. "The colonel," Griscom recalled, "assented rather skeptically. . . . 'If I do this, I'm pretty sure he'll use it somehow to convince the public I'm going out of my way to make friends with him.' " But Roosevelt agreed and went secretly to Henry White's house in New Haven where President Taft awaited him. After a luncheon with several others, Roosevelt suggested a private talk with Taft. They again had talked of New York politics, Taft informed Nellie later. "Roosevelt was very pleasant," he added, "and I hope that I was."

Unfortunately, the official news report about the meeting which emanated from Taft's press office, Griscom wrote, "implied the very thing against which Mr. Roosevelt had warned me—that it was he who had gone out of his way to make up with Mr. Taft and solicit the president's aid in the New York State fight." When Griscom called Roosevelt to apologize, the angry colonel boomed, "What did I tell you?" Taft denied that he had authorized the press release, but the damage was done. "Mr. Roosevelt had been publicly snubbed," and Griscom felt it was his fault.

Taft could accept, though grudgingly, Roosevelt's attractiveness to dissident Republicans, but he was needled by Roosevelt's private criticisms of his administration. On the one hand he seems to have longed for Roosevelt to take charge and direct events as in the past, but he also needed to assert his independence: "If I only knew what the president wanted, I would do it," he said to Butt, "but you know he has held himself so aloof that I am absolutely in the dark. I am deeply wounded, and he gives me no chance to explain my attitude or learn his." He continued to try to conciliate Roosevelt, asking his advice on matters such as the Canadian reciprocity agreement. But

Roosevelt, taking these advances as token gestures only, continued to grow cooler, and this left Taft more offended and confused.

Newsmen saw the telltale signs of Taft's mental anguish, and they reported gains in his weight and his missing a few day's golf at Myopia links in Beverly. On occasion he would climb into one of the White House cars and go off for a long ride in Essex County, sometimes not returning for two days. In a short time over five thousand miles were logged on such escapist spins. Meanwhile Roosevelt was hard at work at Sagamore Hill.

From 23 August to 11 September 1910, Roosevelt made a sixteen-state trip west, giving speeches which outlined his "new nationalism" policies. The ex-president received twenty-five invitations a day to speak—over two thousand in all. A huge crowd in Sioux Falls packed the ball park to hear him talk about the tariff. Roosevelt endorsed the tariff commission established by the Payne-Aldrich Bill, giving Taft the credit for it, but went on to say about the new tariff, "The people know that there are some things in it which are not right," provisions which encourage "a scramble of selfish interests. The American public does not wish to see the tariff so arranged as to benefit primarily a few wealthy men."

Through Minnesota, North Dakota, and South Dakota, his train stopped at every town, and crowds of people, dressed in their Sunday clothes and carrying flags, swarmed onto the tracks behind the train and called for him to speak. At one stop, a man jumped onto the train step, grasped Roosevelt's hand, and exclaimed with great fervor, "God bless your soul!" "By George," Roosevelt replied to the people, "I am profoundly touched. This is really most affecting." Escorted to his hotel in Fargo, North Dakota, he found one hundred little girls waiting for him, each with a teddy bear in her arms. "Never," he said, "in the courts of Europe did I see anything like this."

Roosevelt and Taft crossed trails in Minnesota in the first week of September but did not meet. Reporters noted, however, that Roosevelt was usually received more warmly than was the president. Returning through Chicago, Roosevelt declined to attend a banquet in his honor when he learned he was to sit at the same table with Illinois Senator William Lorimer, whose election had been tainted by accusations of fraud. When the invitation to Lorimer was hastily recalled, Roosevelt accepted his. At Freeport he addressed a crowd of six thousand, saying, "I don't suppose I shall ever be in public life again. But if I am, there is always the chance that some time I shall make my words good." He emphasized the fact that "no corporation, no politicians need ever support me for anything under the idea that I will pardon that corporation or that politician if it or he is corrupt." That night he attended a banquet in a hall decorated in imitation of an African jungle. The guests stood on chairs and tables, cheering and waving their handkerchiefs as Roosevelt exhorted them to "purify your politics." In Taft's hometown of Cincinnati, Roosevelt said that a "perfectly corking time" was given him by three thousand enthusiastic supporters. You can't complain, he declared, if sharp businessmen get an undue share of the nation's wealth while staying within the rules of the game. We must therefore "change the rules of the game!" he shouted to general applause. To those who feared government centralization, Roosevelt argued, "I do not want to give the government any more power than is necessary," but big business was already centralized, and the nation needed centralized authority to control it.

All of his speeches, both prepared and extemporaneous, were in fact a clarification and elaboration of the one he made in Ossawatomie, Kansas, at the beginning of his trip on the thirty-first of August. Roosevelt expounded his "New Nationalism" ideas in a format which strongly implied that they were part of an entire political platform. The "New Nationalism," he said, "puts the national need before sectional and personal advantage." New Nationalism applied old-time moralities to modern conditions. It sought governmental efficiency and control of the great corporations. "That is my whole creed," he explained. "There is no revolution in it. There is no appeal to mob rule." Among the eighteen points in his New Nationalism were such measures as the elimination of special interests from politics, more publicity about corporate affairs, laws prohibiting the use of corporate funds in politics, the revision of the tariff schedule, graduated income and inheritance taxes, direct primaries, the publication of campaign contributions, and the use of national resources to benefit all the people.

The newspapers generally called Roosevelt's speaking tour a great success. He had addressed over 250,000 people in over one hundred speeches. The Republicans were inspired with new enthusiasm. The conservatives were downcast; the insurgents, elated. Enjoying the entire sympathy of his audiences, Roosevelt preached private as well as public morality, calling for honest politics and clean living.

Meanwhile the newspapers continued to exploit the rift between Taft and Roosevelt. On 15 September 1910, several papers published a story claiming that President Taft was going to step aside in 1912 to make way for Roosevelt. Inquiries flooded into Beverly, embarrassing and upsetting Taft, who, after consultation, decided not to dignify the reports with an official reply. But realizing the need for some statement, he announced that it was too early to think seriously about a second term, one way or another. He did not intend to make a political bid in 1912, but now his tone was beginning to change. He conceded that he might accept the nomination again if the party and the people wanted him.

Roosevelt, in response to Taft's remarks, threw out a challenge two days later at the New York State Fair, where forty thousand people packed the grandstands. His opponents, he shouted, "shoot from the bushes, but you couldn't make them come into the open and fight the issue." Afterward, he said with satisfaction to a friend that he was fit for a good fight. But Roosevelt chose to remain noncommittal about running for the nomination. He had other matters to attend to, he insisted, and 1912 was too far away to worry about. Yet his actions tended to belie his purported intentions. A week later at the New York Republican convention in Saratoga Springs, where hopeful progressives surrounded him, he exclaimed, "By George this is bully! It is great to be back in the thick of the fight again!"

Underscoring Taft's inability to handle reporters, Roosevelt's jovial meeting with the New York Press Club received much publicity. Newspapermen sang "For He's a Jolly Good Fellow," and Roosevelt addressed them as his good friends, "men to whom I could appeal against their self-interest for what was decent and straight." The dinner was a round of mutual compliments and good cheer. Several of the correspondents stationed at Oyster Bay, who believed they were in Roosevelt's confidence, confided to Butt that the colonel was "certain that Taft had been trying to double cross him ever since he left the United States" after the inauguration. Time and again, they said, Roosevelt remarked that Taft had "kept the word of promise to the ear and broken it to the hope." Roosevelt felt that Taft could be renominated "by the aid of pocket borough delegates of the South, and the big monied interests of the conservative East," but then, Roosevelt gloomily predicted, the Republicans would surely lose the election.

In late September 1910, Roosevelt joined battle in the New York gubernatorial contest in an attempt to defeat the efforts of Vice-President Sherman and the Old Guard to nominate a young progressive, Henry L. Stimson. Archie Butt insisted that Taft was not part of the Old Guard's scheme to humiliate Roosevelt, but because Vice-President Sherman, the ringleader, kept running back and forth to visit Taft at Beverly, it was hard to convince the doubters. Taft's attitude was scarcely disinterested, however, and Butt became annoyed whenever Secretary Norton reinforced the president's growing vindictiveness: "Have you seen the newspapers this afternoon?" Taft asked on 17 August, the day after the Old Guard had jockeyed one of their men into the temporary chairmanship of the state convention. "They have defeated Theodore." At that Norton began to chuckle, and the president to laugh. Encouraged, Norton said: "We have got him—we've got him—we've got him, as sure as peas we've got him," and they laughed again. Disgusted over their complacency, Butt, who loved both men, barely restrained himself from saying, "Like hell you've got him. He is laughing in his sleeve at the whole kit and caboodle of you, and he'll eat you up when the time comes."

Roosevelt's continuing influence was soon demonstrated, for by virtue of his presence at the convention Stimson was nominated on a liberal platform. Stimson disliked the prospect of fighting Sherman, an old college classmate, but, as he wrote to Root, "there was absolutely nothing else to be done."

The New York campaign had shaped up very much like a contest between the Roosevelt and Taft forces. White House efforts to alter that impression were unsuccessful. A letter from Taft to Lloyd Griscom denying that he had favored Sherman or had opposed Roosevelt was released to the press; it mollified Roosevelt only a little and thoroughly enraged Sherman and the Old Guard. Then Taft's secretary issued a statement saying that the president did not consider votes for Stimson the equivalent of votes for Roosevelt, which sounded contentious to the Roosevelt camp.

Before campaigning for Stimson in New York, Roosevelt took to the hustings for Republican candidates in several other states. While in St. Louis he worried Governor Hadly and crowds of onlookers at the state fair by insisting on going up in an airplane with Arch Hoxie, a well-known pioneer pilot. "It was great!" Roosevelt exclaimed on landing. "First class. It was the finest experience I ever had. I wish I could stay up for an hour, but I haven't the time." Hoxie confessed that he had been "afraid the colonel would fall out or interfere with the motor, he was so enthusiastic." In Illinois and Indiana Roosevelt praised progressive candidates, especially Albert Beveridge, whom he pronounced to be "a man who stands for what is decent in our government." Surprisingly in New York, Stimson lost the election to Democrat John A. Dix, but Roosevelt had gained ground nevertheless. He had stumped for Stimson, and the crowds proved wildly enthusiastic for him whenever he spoke. The only reason he had returned to politics, Roosevelt told them, was to serve their interests. To the people it was a fight for honesty against Tammany Hall and the corporations.

Taft went to New York also to help Stimson, yet was ineffectual. "I don't think he is doing much," Butt wrote, "for he listens too eagerly to everyone who has a word to say against Roosevelt and gives the impression that Stimson more or less means Roosevelt." Despite Roosevelt's and Taft's help, Stimson was towed under by anti-Republican feeling that was beginning to rise across the country. "We are living in a 'great and awful' time politically," sighed Taft. Yet he preferred to look upon Stimson's defeat as primarily a voter repudiation of Roosevelt.

Roosevelt had missed Taft during his trip to Washington in November to address the National Geographic Society concerning his African journey, but he did not fail to pay a visit to the White House while in town. With Taft gone, Nellie, Horace wrote with amusement, found it "necessary to go to New York on the day of Roosevelt's arrival. At the White House Roosevelt recalled every old servant by name, even the scullery maids who stood by downstairs to see him as he passed. When he saw Alice, the kitchen maid, he asked her if she still made cornbread. Sometimes for the servants, she replied, but no one upstairs liked it. "They show bad taste, and I'll tell the president so when I see him," Roosevelt responded. Alice brought him a piece on a plate and he walked over to the office eating it, greeting the gardeners and laborers as he went. He inspected all the White House changes and sat down at the president's desk, remarking on how natural it felt to be there. It was a fine visit, Butt thought, with no envy, no jealousy, no carping. Ike Hoover, one of Roosevelt's most ardent admirers, said to Butt with tears in his eyes, "It is the only happy day we have had in nearly two years, and not one of us would exchange it for a hundred-dollar bill."

After the New York election Roosevelt set off on a Southern trip, arriving first in Hot Springs, Arkansas, to a cordial reception. Showers of roses descended on Roosevelt as he walked beneath a bell labeled "1776", and the Democratic governor honored him with praise a fellow Republican could scarcely have equaled. After a similar reception in Atlanta, where the mayor claimed he had never seen a larger crowd, Roosevelt burst forth with "By George! If I thought I could carry a single southern state I would willingly run for the presidency."

Before winter arrived, Taft felt that, despite their cordial, though restrained, meetings, Theodore Roosevelt had "thrown down the gauntlet." "I have doubted up to the present time," he told Butt, "whether he really intended to fight my administration or not, but he sees no one but my enemies, and if by chance he sees any supporters of the administration, he does not talk intimately with any of them." Taft added, "I confess it wounds me very deeply. I hardly think the prophet of the square deal is playing it exactly square with me now." Nellie was alarmed but expressed little surprise, for she had always expected a Roosevelt betrayal. She felt her husband would be defeated regardless: "Well, I suppose you will have to fight Mr. Roosevelt for the nomination, and if you get it he will defeat you [in the general election]. But it can't be helped. If possible you must not allow him to defeat you for the renomination."

Normally considerate of others despite his own personal discomfort, Taft told Butt, "You may hear me say some bitter things of our old chief at times and I fear it may distress you, but as long as I confine my criticism of him to my immediate family, you will have to put up with it." Moreover, Taft added, "I want you to know that it will be quite as distressing to me to break with him as it will be to you to see this break come." Butt's chief desire was to make peace between the two former friends, meanwhile he watched the relationship as objectively as he could. Yet he felt keen dismay when Taft got dragged into the petty schemes of the Roosevelt-haters. Taft, he said, listened to everything uncomplimentary said about Roosevelt and from the most "irritatingly insignificant quarters." Men like Charles Norton and Massachusetts Senator Murray Crane did all they could to intensify the split. Butt could not be disloyal to the "big-hearted and generous" Taft, nor could he patiently hear his former chief abused and scoffed at, especially by the "pigmies" who came each day bearing new rumors and creating defamatory jokes. The ardent Republican chaplain John Wesley Hill rejected Taft's joking suggestion for a sermon on the administration, saying that Taft's proffered epigram was not in the Bible. "But you are covered by many good and righteous texts," he added. "How about my predecessor?" Taft asked. "There are a good many texts which cover him too," Hill replied, "but they are all about hell and damnation and future punishment."

In expressing his anguish over Roosevelt's neglect of him, Taft complained, "I don't see what I could have done to make things different. Somehow people have convinced the colonel that I have gone back on him, and he does not seem to be able to get that out of his mind. But it distresses me very deeply, more deeply than anyone can know, to think of him sitting there at Oyster Bay alone and feeling himself deserted." Nothing could be done, it seemed, to stop their friendship from deteriorating rapidly as the political struggle intensified. Taft would sharply demand the newspapers as soon as he arose at 5 A.M., on the alert for evidence of Roosevelt's speaking out publicly against him. Ironically, Roosevelt's silence came to seem even more damning. "Never before," Taft insisted, "has he deemed it wise to shut himself up like a clam and suddenly grow wise and conservative." Instead of trying "to thrash it out," he "has closed my mouth by his seeming indifference to my administration, and it is inconceivable that I . . . should go to him on my knees, so to speak, and ask his approval."

Gradually Taft's unhappiness turned to bitterness: "I shall always be grateful for what he did for me," he explained, "but since he has come back he has seared me to the very soul." Unable to explain Roosevelt's attitude in any other way, Taft accepted his wife's argument that Roosevelt turned from him because he had planned all along to run for the presidency in 1912. How much this was consciously part of Nellie's tactics is impossible to say, but she could not have chosen her words better, given her interests. He now was aroused to seek renomination with more active concern and determination than he had shown in 1908 to win the election.

The newspapers printed stories, Taft felt, to embarrass him and aggravate an awkward situation. Reporters gave much space, for example, to the remarks of Colonel William Nelson from Kansas City, a progressive whom Taft had entertained at the White House. When questioned about whether Roosevelt could come back, Nelson snapped, "Come back? Why he'd sweep the country. But I don't think he will run unless he has to." Trying to explain the difference between his man Roosevelt and President Taft, he noted that Mr. Roosevelt went to visit coal miners and Taft to see J. Pierpont Morgan. Asked if Taft would be re-elected, Nelson's laughing reply was "Now boys, you must not ask me foolish questions."

Buoyed by the success of his first speechmaking trip in the fall of 1910, Theodore Roosevelt ventured on a second cross-country tour in the spring of 1911. In Atlanta he damned "half-baked reforms"; in Dallas he spoke in favor of fortifying the Panama Canal; in El Paso he demanded that Mexico maintain "order, justice, and independence." He supported New Mexico's bid for statehood and congratulated Californians on their progressive government under Hiram Johnson. He coyly assured Washingtonians that he was no aspirant for anything "because I have had everything." In Minnesota he spoke on behalf of direct primaries and the popular election of senators, and in Wisconsin he praised the "forward movement" under Governor LaFollette.

Partly to escape after a year of tension worrying over Roosevelt and partly to take his case to the people to bolster his sagging popularity, Taft set off in the fall of 1911 on his second major presidential trip—an eighteen-thousand-mile tour of twenty-eight states which lasted sixty days. As usual Taft accepted innumerable invitations to local festivities along the route. He agreed to open the Appalachian Exposition in Knoxville and to speak at the Kansas and Missouri State Fairs. In Milwaukee, he personally introduced Pauline, the White House cow, who was being exhibited at the International Dairymen's exposition. He gave speeches on the tariff, conservation, arbitration treaties, the Philippines, and the Canadian reciprocity agreements, for which he especially sought public support.

Although Taft said his trip had not been "entered into with malice aforethought," he did take some oblique thrusts at Roosevelt and his supporters whenever the opportunity arose. To GAR veterans at Rochester, New York, Taft said he was unalterably opposed to the "nostrums of reform" which some "demagogues and theoretical pedants" had proposed. And at Hamilton, Massachusetts, he condemned both Democrats and Republican insurgents who had wanted to revive tariff schedules. Democratic leader Champ Clark replied two days later with a warning: "President Taft will hear from me," he warned, "for I am going after him with hammer and tongs. The insurgents can take care of themselves, but I shall reply for the Democrats." Speaking to a crowd of four thousand in Lincoln, Nebraska, Taft revealed his inner conflicts over the way he felt about himself and Roosevelt: "We are big enough even when we are insulted to do what a great strong man does. . . . He holds himself in and says, 'I am a greater man because I resist the temptations to lick your pusillanimous little body.'" And in Pocatello, Idaho, he spoke affectionately of the Supreme Court, suggesting where he would much rather be: "I love judges and I love courts. They are my ideals on earth." "To question the Supreme Court's motives and attack it," he said of those critics who felt the justices had emasculated the antitrust laws, "is to lay the axe at the root of the tree of our civilization." By stages Taft came to think of Roosevelt as a danger to the nation.

For Taft's entourage the trip had been a "perfect nightmare"—numerous days of constant motion, a whirl of noise, confusion, and indigestible food, with hoards of bad-mannered citizens screaming out "Hello, Bill." Taft covered 15,270 miles by train and in automobile side excursions, 3000 more. He visited most of the states and was "yapped at by all the congressmen and ward politicians from Beverly to the Coast and back again." The train made 220 stops; Taft delivered 380 speeches; and they saw 3,213,600 "ear-splitting citizens." Everyone on the trip except the president felt as if "their nerves had disintegrated and their innards turned upside down."

While Taft toured the country, Roosevelt was busy making his speeches. To a huge enthusiastic crowd at Carnegie Hall he spoke on "The Conservation of Womanhood and Childhood," attacking the use of child labor and demanding a Children's Bureau in the Department of Labor and Commerce. He proposed a host of new reform measures, and the very mention of his name seemed to stir up excitement. Despite Roosevelt's earlier protestations that he would never run again, most pundits surmised that he would be active in 1912 because the progressives needed him to carry their banner.

At first mystified by his behavior, finally Taft began to sense what was happening. "In most of these speeches," Taft had written to his brother Charles earlier, Roosevelt "has utterly ignored me. . . . His attitude toward me is one that I find difficult to understand and explain." To Horace he wrote in late 1910, "I think he occupies his leisure time in finding reasons why he is justified in not supporting me." Roosevelt, he continued, "has determined to become a candidate for 1912. I have it on authority that can hardly be disputed." At one point he inadvertently revealed his thoughts in a savage fantasy: "If you were to remove Roosevelt's skull now," Taft told a friend as early as September 1910, "you would find written on his brain '1912.'" As a result of Roosevelt's increasingly radical ideas, however, Taft began to feel optimistic. Writing to Charles, Taft described them as "utterly impracticable, because they could never be gotten through without a revolution or revision of the Constitution, either of which is impossible."

By mid-1911, many others realized that Roosevelt was planning to contest the nomination. Taft did not want a second term, but Roosevelt's radicalism and his own maturation in office led him to reconsider. Yet the idea of a combat still disheartened him. To Charles Kohlsaat, the newspaper publisher from Chicago and close friend of Theodore Roosevelt, Taft tried to explain his views, obviously hoping that some of what he said would be repeated to Roosevelt. As he spoke, his eyes were filled with tears: "You are a great friend of Colonel Roosevelt's. Through some misunderstanding he feels hurt with me. I must have done something that displeases him very much. Knowingly I have done nothing to hurt his feelings. I may have been tactless, but not intentionally did I do anything to displease him. I owe him everything. He is responsible for my being president. I am so disturbed it keeps me awake nights." Taft brooded openly to Butt over what he might have done to forestall the break, and yet, "I could not ask his advice in all questions. I could not subordinate my administration to him." "It is hard, very hard," he moaned, "to see a devoted friendship going to pieces like a rope of sand." In reaction Taft began to pull himself together, for as he wrote to his brother, "he made me president and not deputy, and I have to be president."

On 21 February 1912, Roosevelt took public aim at Taft: "My hat is in the ring," he said. "The fight is on and I am stripped to the buff." Elihu Root knew what this meant: Roosevelt "is essentially a fighter, and when he gets into a fight he is completely dominated by the desire to destroy his adversary. He instinctively lays hold of every weapon which can be used for that end." With little heart for a battle, Taft nevertheless slowly gained resolution of his own. "I am content with one term and get through with it," Taft wrote to Horace, "but if they do not look out, as I said, they may drive me into a second term against their will."

XVI

SLANDER AND BILLINGSGATE:

The Party Splits

"I have a strong presentiment," Taft told Archie Butt on 21 February 1912, "that the colonel is going to beat me in the convention. It is almost a conviction with me." Why then did he not capitulate in advance? To his brother Horace he wrote that he would not bow out, for "I am under obligations to accept another term if it comes, and if only the nomination comes, to accept that and go through the campaign and be beaten like a gentleman." The presidency had to this extent toughened Taft's self-esteem and strengthened his resolve.

Nellie was pessimistic. Remembering 1908, she told him, "I was always hopeful then. I am not hopeful now. Things are different." "Well, you are not hopeless about the nomination?" he queried. "No," she replied, "I think you will be renominated, but I don't see any chance for the election." That prospect angered Nellie, but not Taft. So long as he could be renominated and not humiliated by his own party, he viewed losing the election with some equanimity.

As the Republican convention loomed closer, Nellie became increasingly agitated, especially enraged by Roosevelt's strident public criticisms of her husband's administration. These wrenched Taft's heart, but he was no more able to fathom the causes of the rupture than to restore the broken friendship. When various newspapers began to predict Roosevelt's nomination, Mrs. Taft grew indignant and refused to read them anymore. Still she took an "I-told-you-so" satisfaction, for plotting and opposition was what she had always expected from Roosevelt. "I told you so four years ago and you would not believe me," she said. Taft responded, not without a touch of sarcasm breaking through his good nature, "I know you did, my dear, and I think you are perfectly happy now. You would have preferred the colonel to come out against me than to have been wrong yourself."

Taft at times seemed to be no more interested personally in the contest for the nomination in 1912 than he had been in 1908. "I don't believe," Butt said, "he ever thinks about a second term or if he does, merely as something not even to be desired." As Taft himself had said at the outset of his term, "In four years I shall step down and out. . . . In my heart I have long been making plans for my future."

While Taft brooded in the White House, Roosevelt began an aggressive campaign directed at securing the Republican nomination in June. In January he sent letters to Governors Osborn of Michigan, Glasscock of West Virginia, and Hadley of Missouri, directing them to arrange for a group of governors to write public letters asking him "to respond to the popular demand." By 9 February, seven governors had signed a petition requesting Roosevelt to seek the Republican nomination, and it was made public on the twenty-fourth. Other progressives turned away from the long-time progressive leader Robert LaFollette, who had expected their support, to join the draft-Roosevelt movement. Roosevelt clubs soon sprang up across the country.

One embarrassment remained for Roosevelt and his followers—how to circumvent his 1904 statements that he would never again seek the presidency. A sufficient explanation shortly came to him: "My position on the third term is perfectly simple. I said I would not accept a nomination for a third term under any circumstances, meaning of course a third consecutive term." Also, he assumed office after McKinley's assassination, and therefore had been elected to only one term. *The Outlook*, for which Roosevelt was contributing editor, elaborated on the theme in its February issue. What Theodore Roosevelt really meant in 1904 "was something like this: 'Under no circumstances will I be a candidate for or accept another nomination unless I am allowed to become a private citizen for a while, so I can't use the patronage of my office as President to get votes for myself.' " Or to put it another way: "When a man says at breakfast in the morning, 'No, thank you, I will not take any more coffee,' it does not mean that he will not take any more coffee to-morrow morning or next week, or next month, or next year."

A direct primary, allowing the people to voice an opinion on a preference for candidates on their party's ticket, had been instituted in Wisconsin in 1905, and by 1912 ten states had primary laws, including South Dakota,

Oregon, Nebraska, New Jersey, North Dakota, and California. Prior to 1912, presidential aspirants had not campaigned until after nomination at their convention. Roosevelt entered his name in these primaries, and his supporters helped initiate others in Illinois, Maryland, and Massachusetts. Thus Roosevelt began his offensive. Yet Taft refused to respond, despite attacks on his administration from the Roosevelt camp.

Old Guard Republicans, supplying most of the support for the Taft renomination campaign, began to urge him to strike back. Taft's cabinet, in a dramatic all-night session, tried to persuade him that it was his duty to reply to Roosevelt's charges. Conservative Republicans generally were disappointed with his want of initiative. Industrialist Henry Clay Frick, who had supported Taft from "force of habit" in 1908, now gave monetary backing grudgingly. Solicited for still additional money, Frick expressed resentment at having been asked to contribute in the first place, not only because President Taft had little chance of re-election, but because the Taft administration had "utterly failed to treat many of its warmest friends fairly." Frick was especially perturbed over Wickersham's prosecution of the United States Steel Company, which included a charge against him for instigating an allegedly illegal property purchase. He was not mollified by Taft's explanation "that he did not know that such a charge in the suit was to be made." "This shows," Frick declared, "a great lack of interest in very important matters on the part of the president."

Unable to repel attack, Taft could only suffer pain. "I have a sense of wrong in the attitude of Theodore Roosevelt toward me which I doubt if I can ever get over," he confided to his Aunt Delia. "It is very hard to take all the slaps Roosevelt is handing me at this time," Taft told Butt. "Everyone wants me to answer his last attack on the peace treaties, in which he practically calls me a hypocrite."

In a speech entitled "A Charter of Democracy," delivered in February 1912, in Columbus, Ohio, his most radical address since Ossawatomi in 1910, Roosevelt outlined his position. He spoke against the evil of money in politics, insisted that property rights be subject to human rights, and pleaded for the initiative, the referendum, and the recall of judges and judicial decisions on constitutional questions. But it was Roosevelt's attack on the sanctity of judges which galvanized Taft's resolve to resist: "I can fight just as well when losing as when certain of victory," he said to his aide, "and I have made up my mind to answer that speech of Theodore's." This time Roosevelt had "gone too far."

Taft decided finally to stay in the campaign for the express purpose of defeating Roosevelt, whom he now saw as "a great danger and menace to the country." "If I could nominate . . . Hughes by a withdrawal it would give me great pleasure to bring it about," Taft said. "Whether I win or lose is not important," Taft said to Charles Thompson, a *New York Times* reporter, "but I am in this fight to perform a public duty—the duty of keeping Theodore Roosevelt out of the White House. I believe I represent a safer and saner view of our government and its Constitution." Not letting down the party was one of Taft's two chief concerns. Perhaps the major one was protecting himself against the pain of rejection by the party. Taft defined these feelings to his wife: "If we lose the election I shall feel that the party is rejected, whereas if I fail to secure the renomination it will be a personal defeat."

Reporting that Taft would be the first president ever to stump in a primary, the *New York Times*, which strongly opposed Roosevelt, happily noted that Taft's underdog position and the "radical" pronouncements of Roosevelt had finally activated the president. Taft's friends knew "with what reluctance he took even those defensive measures." "He has drawn the line now," Taft said, and "I hope we can keep the fight from becoming personal." His campaign manager, Representative William McKinley, a high-tariff conservative Republican from Illinois, told the press, "President Taft is in the fight to stay." Old Guard Republicans were delighted to read the headlines: "Taft to Hit Back at Roosevelt Soon!" He was now apparently ready to fight, but no one could say for certain when he would strike a blow.

Taft's brothers sought to cheer him through the ordeal. Charles deplored the despondency in his letters, insisting that the primaries would come out "splendidly." "In my opinion," he wrote, "there won't be a grease spot left of Teddy when he gets through with this campaign." Taft took heart momentarily, replying that Roosevelt might be defeating himself because he had become "so violent that some people fear that he is losing his reason. Others say he is drinking."

Exhausted by his constant service to Taft and emotionally distraught because of his divided loyalties, Archie Butt thought he needed a vacation— far away. "No matter how much we may love the colonel, we must remain true to the president," he decided. Sometimes he felt "like a human oil can" as he struggled to keep things going smoothly. As Taft's aide he had no specific authority, yet he found himself in possession of considerable power because of his immense personal influence, even though "I don't want it," he insisted, "and it bores the life out of me." Roosevelt sent word via his daughter Alice that Butt should consider leaving his present job before the convention and election. Archie, however, thought this would be cowardly, even though it was increasingly clear that Taft could not be elected, and perhaps not even nominated. It wrenched Butt's heart to think of the old days at the White House and "how these two men seemed to love one another" in contrast to the enmity that had since grown up between them. Roosevelt's and

Taft's "laughs would mingle and reverberate through the corridors and rooms." Now he felt tired out, and his doctor advised a rest. Taft encouraged him to take a European vacation. Finally Butt booked passage to Italy on the S.S. *Berlin*, hoping that "a little holiday in Rome" would cure his fatigue. He looked forward to the trip, yet felt a foreboding, which he referred to as his "presentiments." He informed Clara that "if the old ship goes down you will find my affairs in shipshape condition."

Before he left, Butt made one last visit with the Roosevelts at Sagamore Hill. They were still "the same dear people." The fireplaces were provided with logs Roosevelt had chopped while exercising; the dogs were following him all over the house; and Mrs. Roosevelt "was moving in and out like some delicate shuttle," keeping everything going smoothly. Roosevelt greeted him with "the same cheery handshake," saying "This is bully!" Afterward, Butt was struck by the fact that although Edith Roosevelt sent her love and said thanks for the little sofa Taft had sent her, never once did the colonel mention the president. On his way home, Butt stopped at the house of Harry Taft, where the president and Mrs. Taft were visiting. Obviously everyone was "itching" to know what had happened at Oyster Bay, but as Butt did not mention Roosevelt, they did not ask.

After only a month in Europe, Butt decided to return early to Washington to give much needed personal support to Taft, who was readying himself for the final battle with Roosevelt over the nomination. He prepared to sail on the sleek new 882 foot British oceanliner *Titanic*, which was to sail its maiden voyage on 10 April. Shortly before midnight on 14 April the *Titanic* struck an iceberg. There were only twenty lifeboats for 2,207 passengers. At 3:10 A.M. the ship fired all its remaining distress rockets before sliding to the bottom of the North Atlantic taking 1503 of its passengers to a cold, watery grave. Fellow passenger Marie Young, a former music tutor of Roosevelt's children, described her final view of Archie Butt: "Archie himself put me into the boat, wrapped blankets around me, tucked me in as carefully as if we were starting on a motor ride . . . as if death was far away instead of being but a few moments removed from him. . . . He stepped upon the gunwale of the boat, and lifting his hat, smiled down at me. 'Goodby, Miss Young. Luck is with you. Will you kindly remember me to all the folks back home?' "

She recalled looking up at him as he stood at the railing, hat in hand, brave and smiling.

When Taft learned of the disaster, he frantically ordered two cruisers to intercept the *Carpathia*, which was bringing the 705 survivors home, and wire him of Butt's fate. When the sad news came, Taft felt deeply. "He was like a member of my family, and I feel his loss as if he had been a younger brother," he mourned. "I cannot refrain from saying that I miss him every minute, and that every house and every person suggests him. Every walk I take somehow is lacking in his presence, and every door that opens seems to be his coming." In remembrance of Butt and his traveling companion, the artist Francis Davis Millet, who went down with him on the *Titanic*, Taft had a memorial fountain built on the south White House grounds.

After weeks of silence, Taft chose 25 April as the date and Boston as the place to hit back at Roosevelt. Taft avoided Roosevelt's criticisms of him and responded to his "radical" pronouncements; he hoped to keep their exchange limited to subjects like judicial recall. The White House released this statement: "The president's blood is up and the battle will be waged without quarter, except that . . . Taft will permit no resort to personal attacks on Roosevelt." William Allen White relayed a personal message to Roosevelt on 3 March. "He said that nothing would induce him to say . . . anything against you personally," White wrote, and "that you had made him president, . . . and that he could never forget the old and happy relations of intimacy . . . that he could not help hoping that when all this turmoil of politics had passed, you and he would get together again and be as of old."

That his own self-image was at stake, Taft ingenuously admitted in the Boston speech, his first of the campaign: "I am here to reply to an old and true friend. I do not want to fight Theodore Roosevelt, but then sometimes a man in a corner fights. . . . I don't like to fight. I am a peaceful man. I would a good deal rather go around the corner and avoid trouble, but he has got me up against the wall and if I have any manhood at all I have got to fight." He spoke for two hours refuting Roosevelt's charges one by one. Repeatedly the anguished president told the crowd, "This wrenches my soul." He never could hide what he was feeling, and he made no attempt to do so now. He insisted, "Neither in thought, nor word, nor action have I been disloyal to the friendship I owe Theodore Roosevelt." The present speech, he lamented, was one of the most painful duties of his life, and he was making it only because he owed an obligation to the Republican party. "If in this contest there were at stake only my own reputation," Taft asserted, with a sincerity not ordinarily seen in political speeches, "I would without the slightest qualm and without care as to the result continue my silence." It was his duty to counter Roosevelt's radical demands "in the name of the Constitution of the United States." "I represent a cause," Taft concluded, "and so must rise to the occasion."

Roosevelt appeared to be delighted over Taft's being stirred into action. Always at his best during a campaign, he delivered the following night what the *Times* called a "merciless denunciation of President Taft." Roosevelt charged that the president, owing to a "quality of feebleness," had yielded to the bosses and the privileged interests. In doing so, he had, of course, repudiated all that Roosevelt stood for. Some of his remarks were sure to hurt Taft personally. "It is a bad trait to bite the hand that feeds you," Roosevelt said on one occasion. The president certainly meant well, "But he means well feebly." It was a "vitriolic attack" Sumner Curtis noted, but the people responded, yelling, "Hit him again, Teddy: Hit him between the eyes: Sock him: Put him over the ropes!" Mark Sullivan said afterward of Roosevelt's speech: "It was appalling, terrible, yet also Titanic." A *Life* magazine reporter, referring to the allusion to Taft's ingratitude, commented caustically, "What was it that Mr. Roosevelt's since-bitten hand fed to Mr. Taft? It was us, our country. . . . *WE* were that dog biscuit, for which Mr. Taft was [to be] so grateful."

After this bitter preliminary to the 1912 campaign, Taft came to see himself as "the only hope against radicalism and demagoguery." The political issues which Roosevelt raised in each new address were alone enough to anger him, but when his old friend made personal attacks it hurt him unbearably. Fortunately he was spared the even harsher things that Roosevelt had been saying privately for some time to mutual friends. Roosevelt told Elihu Root that Taft was "merely a fool," but the terms he used in public were cutting enough; he called Taft an "apostate," a "flubdub," a "floppy-souled creature," a "puzzlewit," a "fathead," and a "man with brains of about three guinea-pig power." Taft had "yielded to the bosses and to the great privileged interests," Roosevelt asserted repeatedly; he was "disloyal to every canon of decency and fair play," and he was "useless to the American people." When Taft accused Roosevelt of becoming a "socialist"—Roosevelt just laughed and slapped his knee, exclaiming, "That's just what I'm doing: stealing their thunder! . . . The Republican party would have died of dryrot if we had not made this fight," he charged.

Amidst all the vituperation, Mr. Dooley asked his readers: "I wonder who ar-re th' professors iv personal abuse at Yale an' Harvard. They're good men who iver they ar-re." Mr. Dooley delighted in the slander and billingsgate, calling it very "pleasant and homelike. . . . Iverybody callin each other liars and crooks not like pollyytical inimies, d'ye mind, but like old friends that has been up late drinkin' toghether."

For Taft the widening gulf between them was a cause only for weeping: "I hope that somebody, sometime, will recognize the agony of spirit that I have undergone," he said to one gathering. Once between speeches on the presidential train, Taft "slumped over with his head between his hands" and told Louis Seibold of the *New York World*, "Roosevelt was my closest friend." And then he bowed his head and covered his eyes and cried.

The effect of the strain on Taft became evident when he said the wrong thing in the wrong place on even more numerous occasions than he had in 1908. He continued the campaign by declaring his new-found resolution to fight, but the metaphors he chose were singularly inept: "I was a man of straw, but I have been a man of straw long enough." At Hyattsville, Maryland, Taft shouted to the crowd, "I'm a man of peace and I don't want to fight. But . . . even a rat in a corner will fight."

Generally Taft began by assuring his audience that if it were only his "personal ambition" that was at stake in the election, he should not "bother" them. "I am here as part of a trip which I have undertaken most unwillingly," he would assert, "but merely from a strong sense of duty." The only reason that he was opposing Roosevelt, he insisted, was "because of the wild constitutional principles that he is advocating." Roosevelt's seeming disrespect for the law, especially his demand for judicial recall, provoked Taft most. In the climax to one of his more impassioned speeches refuting Roosevelt's dangerous ideas, he said, "One who so lightly regards constitutional principles and especially the independency of the judiciary, . . . could not safely be entrusted with successive presidential terms. I say this sorrowfully, but with the full conviction of truth."

Taft insisted at the New York Republican Club's Lincoln Day dinner in February that Roosevelt and the progressives "would hurry us into a condition which would find no parallel except in the French Revolution." And then he added a phrase which succeeded in irritating Roosevelt: these extremists were not really progressive, he said "they are political emotionalists or neurotics." Progressives of one stripe or another seemed to be everywhere he turned: "We now have Progressives, Halting-Progressives, Ultra-Progressives, Progressive Conservatives, Conservative Progressives, and Theodore Roosevelt."

"I can get along with one term," he honestly confessed to an audience in New Jersey. "A second term is not essential to my happiness. . . . I have proven to be a burdensome leader and not one that aroused the multitude." Taft's reluctance to tangle personally with Roosevelt and his lack of enthusiasm for another term disappointed many of his Old Guard supporters. The *New York Times* concluded sadly that he had been "over-persuaded to enter the . . . ante-primary campaign." As Taft himself put it on 29 May 1912, "I have been through . . . an experience that I do not care to repeat."

Taft's public utterances, so little apposite as they usually were for a presidential contender, were highly provocative to political commentators and cartoonists in search of just such incongruities for their material. Teddy Roosevelt often was pictured as a ranting, gesticulating campaigner, whereas the "stodgy, soggy" Taft was pictured reclining in a big chair with his feet up and a benign expression on his face. For the benefit of *New York Times* readers, Mr. Dooley described "Taft the scrapper" to Mr. Hennessy: "I'm a fighter. Don't ye make anny mistake about that. I ain't anny longer th' bale iv hay me pridicessor says I am. I've been crooly threated by this man. I can't get back at him too hard or he might threat me worse, but I'll put up me hands in front iv me face anny how." And a week later:

> He is light awn his feet as a ton av pig iron, and as quick t' anger as a slab av cold mush. When ye jab th' hippypotamus wid a pitchfork he on'y gives a grateful smile an' says, "Thanks, tickle me wance more." An th' behemoth dashes afther TR wid all th' agility av cold molasses runnin' up hill. As a speeder a wanlegged snail cud best him.

Mr. Dooley said that William McKinley, Taft's campaign manager, to rouse Taft told him that Roosevelt's "eatin th' Constitution an' by-laws alive an spitten' th' bones in yer face." When that got no response from Taft, McKinley implored, "If ye can't do annythin' else, sthand awn yer hind legs an' mek a noise like a steam roller."

Even those editors and pundits who had declared for the president were disappointed by Taft "the scrapper." As much as the *New York Times* deplored Roosevelt's presence in the race, the editor conceded in print that in contrast to Taft "everybody must admit that he is a somewhat awakening and inspiring agitator." With Taft as incumbent and therefore the leading contender for the nomination, many people had reason to fear a party defeat in the 1912 campaign. "I do not know," Henry Adams remarked sardonically, "whether Taft or the *Titanic* is likely to be the furthest reaching disaster."

Straw-vote contests showed the people's choice. The first, in North Dakota, LaFollette won; in New York, Taft scored a victory. LaFollette won again in Wisconsin, but all the rest of the primaries went to Roosevelt. Roosevelt and LaFollette had visited seven of the states holding primaries, and Taft six. LaFollette was soon out of the race for delegates. Only Roosevelt's candidacy aroused popular enthusiasm. Disappointed over losing California to Roosevelt, Taft wrote to a friend, "One of these days the people of California are going to wake up to the bunco game which has been practiced on them by the pseudo reformers."

As president, Taft had one big advantage over Roosevelt—federal patronage—and the Taft men proceeded to use the advantages of incumbency especially in the South, where they quickly secured a number of delegates. Nonetheless Roosevelt, winning in Illinois, Pennsylvania, California, Ohio, New Jersey, and Nebraska, had 281 delegates pledged to him against Taft's

71. Roosevelt was just 80 votes short of a majority when the convention opened on 16 June.

The Republican National Committee met in Chicago on 7 June, prior to the convention, to consider delegate challenges resulting from the primaries. Of the 53 committee members who had been selected in 1908, 40 were for Taft. By 11 June the committee had assigned 101 disputed delegates to Taft and 1 to Roosevelt, with 152 to go. Roosevelt denounced their "steamroller tactics" as outrageous. From Oyster Bay he thundered, "Again and again we have sent to the penitentiary election officials for deeds not one whit worse than what was done by the National Committee at Chicago yesterday." When the Indiana delegates were assigned to Taft, he denounced it as "a fraud as vulgar, as brazen, and as cynically open as any ever committed by the Tweed regime." Yet it was difficult for Roosevelt to substantiate his case. Even his friend and supporter Senator William Borah admitted, "There have been many frauds at the primaries, I don't say there were not. But there is no evidence of that fact presented. . . . Under the circumstances, I could not vote to sustain the Roosevelt delegates." Knowing that the people had declared for him, Roosevelt decided personally to challenge the Taft delegates at the convention, particularly the Southern ones, chosen prior to his entering the race.

To smooth the way for this strategy, Roosevelt, Senator Joseph Dixon of Montana, Gifford Pinchot, and other staunch supporters began barnstorming the country to inform the people that the Taft delegates were "stolen goods," acquired by outright "theft." The *New York Sun* satirized their effort by parodying a Rooseveltian harangue:

> The bestial nature of the indecent hordes of pirates, second story men, porch climbers, gun men and short card dealers who oppose me is now perfectly manifest. . . . This strikes at the very foundation stone of pure democracy, for it misrepresents me. . . . This despicable effort to confuse and obscure the public mind I denounce as a machination of the special interests in their loathsome campaign for the submergence of childhood, motherhood, womanhood and Abraham Lincoln.

And Mr. Dooley, after considering Roosevelt's charges, commented, "Yes sir; th' republic is doomed to destruction again."

Roosevelt's egotism and aggressive personality provided a fund of ammunition for his enemies. J. Sharp Williams of Mississippi, outraged over Roosevelt's "radicalism," rose in the Senate to offer a new Apostles' Creed:

> I believe in TR, maker of noise and strife, and in Ambition his only creed (My Lord). He was born of the Love of power and suffered under William Howard

Taft; was crucified, died and buried. He descended into Africa. The third year he rose again from the jungle and ascended into favor and sitteth on the right hand of His Party, whence he shall come to scourge the living and the dead.

I believe in the Holy Outlook, the big stick, the Ananias Club, the forgiveness of political activities, the resurrection of political ambitions and the third term everlastingly.

As Otto Bannard wrote to Taft of Roosevelt just before the convention opened, "We hold the fort, and he is the guerilla." Determined, however, not to "permit a system of naked fraud, of naked theft from the people to triumph," Roosevelt decided to go to Chicago himself. He arrived the morning of 15 June to a tumultuous greeting, sporting a big, new black felt hat fit for throwing into a political ring. At the train station Roosevelt did not even attempt to speak to the clamorous throng. So pressing was the crowd in the hotel lobby that Roosevelt's glasses flew off and were lost underfoot. To address the crowd, Roosevelt climbed out of a hotel window and stood on a parapet: "Chicago is a bad place for men to try to steal in. The Politicians will be made to understand that they are the servants and not the masters of the plain citizens of the Republican party." "It is a naked fight against theft and thieves, and thieves shall not win. . . . The receiver of stolen goods," he proclaimed to his rapt audience, "is no better than the thief!" That night he repeated to reporters his felicitious phrase of two weeks earlier: "I'm feeling just like a bull moose."

On 17 June, the night before the convention, Roosevelt held a meeting in the five-thousand-seat Auditorium Theater, to which twenty-thousand people tried to gain entrance. Those privileged to get in heard Roosevelt say, "What happens to me is not of the slightest consequence: . . . this fight is far too great to permit us to concern ourselves about any one man's welfare." Sounding the overtones of religious righteousness which the bolting Bull Moosers would soon adopt, he concluded, "We fight in honorable fashion for the good of mankind: fearless of the future; unheeding of our individual fates; with unflinching hearts and undimmed eyes; we stand at Armageddon, and we battle for the Lord." William Jennings Bryan, covering Roosevelt's speech for a Democratic paper, wrote in amused response to the colonel's outrage over the "stolen" delegates assigned to Taft: "The Arabs are said to have 700 words which mean 'camel'; Mr. Roosevelt has nearly as many synonyms for theft, and he used them all [to-]night."

The Republican convention in Chicago was engineered by Old Guard Republicans who, though dissatisfied with Taft, were intent on preventing Roosevelt, now more radical sounding than ever, from getting the nomination. "There is no doubt," Samuel Eliot Morison wrote, "that Roosevelt had the overwhelming support of the rank and file of the party, but the bosses were with Taft," and they had control. Taft again took almost no active part in organizing the convention or securing the nomination. When the Republican convention assembled, the headlines read: "President Taft Silent." The only sound that could be heard from him was a club hitting a golf ball. "My office is empty," he wrote. "My usual callers are in Chicago and all is quiet on the Potomac." Despite Taft's reluctance to act on his own behalf, conservative Republican leaders felt he had done nothing sufficiently dire to justify breaking the long-standing precedent of renominating the incumbent. And it was on that issue that progressive and Old Guard Republicans promptly split.

In his application for a ticket to the Republican convention, William Jennings Bryan promised, "I will agree not to say anything worse about Taft and Roosevelt than they say about each other—a promise I feel sure I can live up to." And Mr. Dooley wanted to "get a seat somewhere [so] that I can see th' struggle f'r human rights goin' on but fur enough away so I won't be splashed." Victor Rosewater, editor of the *Omaha Bee*, called the convention to order, standing at a rostrum protected by barbed wire concealed under the bunting on the railings around the platform. As he began, one-thousand policemen with nightsticks strolled around the hall, prepared for any eventuality. Rosewater was a small man with a thin voice. "We never did hear Victor Rosewater," George Ade recalled later. "We didn't even see him." As he prepared officially to accept the Taft delegates, Senator Penrose added his warning: "Victor, as soon as you've made that decision, jump off the platform, for someone is going to take a shot at you sure."

With the announcement, pandemonium immediately broke out. The Pennsylvania delegates shouted, screamed, and jumped about like madmen. Nicolas Murray Butler, president of Columbia University and a Taft supporter, leaned over to ask Senator Penrose how such people had ever gotten to be delegates. Boss Penrose replied, "Oh those are the corks, bottles, and banana peels washed up by the Roosevelt tide." Despite the turmoil, Rosewater announced the election for chairman, a crucial position and therefore hotly contested by Taft and Roosevelt supporters. Delegates for Roosevelt wanted Wisconsin's governor, Francis McGovern; Taft delegates, Elihu Root. As the vote for chairman proceeded, progressive Governor Hiram Johnson shook his fists in the direction of the Taft delegates when he announced California's votes for McGovern: "We deny the right of any moribund national committee to choose our chairman for us." Amid cries of "steamroller," Rosewater finished the roll call and proclaimed Root the winner, 588 to 502. Attempting to express his gratitude to the convention, Root was interrupted by laughter, catcalls, and the noisy exodus of several hundred Roosevelt men. He finally had to sit down and wait fifteen minutes until the commotion calmed down. Then, amidst more jeers and catcalls, he began the keynote address. The crowd listened to his appeal for harmony in "stony silence." Although he generously praised the Taft administration, Root told a friend after the convention, "I care more for one button on Theodore Roosevelt's waistcoat than for Taft's whole body." But Root was dedicated to keeping the Republican party together.

The reception was no better for other regular Republicans. When Representative Sereno Payne approached the podium to speak, someone in the top gallery shouted out above all the din, "Where's Aldrich?" This reference to the Payne-Aldrich Tariff started all the Roosevelt supporters "yelling and shouting and guffawing and catcalling" for several minutes. Roosevelt, with a special line to the coliseum, was taking the proceedings in from his suite at the Congress Hotel.

The second day of the convention was highlighted by the competition between Chairman Root and reform Governor Herbert Hadley of Missouri, who gave what Roosevelt called "a first-class speech about the packing of the delegates." The speech set off more wild cheering and another demonstration. William Jennings Bryan quipped, "If you didn't know where you were, you might think you were at a Democratic convention." The following day Root recessed the convention early because the Committee on Credentials was not yet ready to report on the remaining contested seats. The disappointed crowd began a "We want Teddy" demonstration that was only quelled when the police emptied the hall. In Washington the news about Taft on this day was that he and his son Robert were golfing at Chevy Chase.

On the fourth day of the convention, Root signaled the band to play until the committee report was ready. As expected, the Roosevelt protest was defeated. With Old Guard conservatives in control of the convention machinery, the seats in dispute were awarded to the Taft delegates. Roll call after roll call resulted in the Taft delegates' credentials being sustained, causing a Roosevelt man to yell, "I make the point that the steam roller is exceeding the speed limit!" When two contested California seats were assigned to Taft men, lawyer Francis Heney launched into a harangue ending, "If President Taft accepts the votes of these two men in this convention he will be guilty of high treason."

Governor Hiram Johnson then rose in an attempt to clarify the issues. The matter was much larger than the two seats in question, he began, "The whole proposition of 'Shall the people rule?' is involved. . . . The struggle is on, North, East, South, and West, for direct primaries, and the people all over the country will soon be given the right to choose their own representatives rather than let the bosses choose them." Roosevelt had won the California primary by more than 70,000 votes, yet the committee gave the two contested seats to Taft (making the score 542 to 529).

George Perkins, an important Roosevelt supporter, equally incensed over the stolen delegates, remarked that he felt "very much as a man does toward someone who has murdered his parents or outraged his sister." That night the colonel told his delegates, "I am proud of the manner in which you are fighting in the face of the steam roller. I love a dead game sport." Suddenly he instructed them to take no further part in the convention's proceedings. His benefactor, businessman Frank Munsey, then announced Roosevelt's third-party plans: "Mr. Roosevelt will be nominated for president by a new party. He refuses to have anything more to do with the Republican Convention. . . . He would not now take a nomination from that body if it were given to him."

The fifth day of the convention began as the final Taft delegates, from Mississippi, Tennessee, and Washington were seated to hisses and boos from those who remained from Roosevelt's camp. Relieved that the end was in sight, Root shouted, "Unless you let that steam roller run on for a while there isn't any chance of our getting home for Sunday."

The colonel sent one final word about the "stolen" delegates in a message which Henry Allen of Kansas delivered in an angry speech. A clear majority of the delegates honestly elected to this convention were chosen by the people to nominate me," Roosevelt had written. "Under the direction, and with the encouragement of Mr. Taft, the majority of the National Committee, by the so-called 'steam roller' methods and with scandalous disregard of every principle of elementary honesty and decency, stole 80 or 90 delegates." As Allen finished reading, fist fights, which the police broke up, erupted in several places on the floor. When order was restored, former vice-president Charles Fairbanks read the traditional, conservative platform, which condemned judicial recall, praised international peace and arbitration, advocated a reasonably protective tariff and a civil service based on merit, and called for an investigation of the high cost of living. It was followed by scant applause.

There were times during the convention when, despite all the precautions taken by the Old Guard chieftains, Taft's nomination hung by a thread. Taft was willing to step aside in favor of Supreme Court Justice Charles Evans Hughes, given Roosevelt's elimination, but Hughes would not enter the contest. The spectators stayed to hoot as the delegates on the floor, amid a wilderness of vacant chairs, went through the final motions.

Thanks to the Republican machine, Taft, whose name was placed in nomination by future president Warren G. Harding of Ohio, won the dubious honor of the official Republican nomination. Roosevelt had requested that his name not be placed before the convention. Harding's speech, which began with a eulogy of Taft, was the signal for more turmoil. Above the din, Harding shouted, "President Taft is the greatest progressive of his time," occasioning even more hisses and boos. The commotion which followed his speech was sufficiently threatening to lead James Watson to tell former governor of Kentucky William O. Bradley, who was to second Taft's nomination, "I am afraid for you to try. I think you had better quietly slip away and go down the back stairway and over to your hotel." Bradley left immediately without even trying to second Taft's nomination. In his place, John Wannamaker and Nicholas Murray Butler made seconding speeches. LaFollette's name was then placed in nomination, the vote began, and the first ballot resulted in 561 for Taft, 187 for Roosevelt, 41 for LaFollette. The convention "did its duty," Lloyd Griscom stated; "the Republican party had to choose him as their candidate, or else admit publicly that he had been a failure." But as Watson pointed out, "More personal animosity was engendered, more individual hatreds stirred and fanned high, more bitterness was aroused" than at any other gathering he had ever attended.

Mr. Dooley aptly satirized the convention as having been "a combynation iv th' Chicagofire, Saint Bartholomew's massacree, the Battle iv th' Boyne, th' life iv Jessie James, an th' night iv th' big wind." A reporter, joking with William Jennings Bryan, told him to be careful or the Democrats would nominate him for a fourth time at their convention. "Young man," Bryan replied, "do you think I'm going to run for president just to pull the Republican party out of a hole?"

Roosevelt and his enthusiastic followers bolted the convention and formed a third party called the Progressive or "Bull Moose" after Roosevelt's earlier exclamations to newsmen, "I'm feeling like a bull moose!" On the night of Taft's nomination Progressives met near the coliseum in Orchestra Hall, where Theodore Roosevelt, standing under a huge portrait of himself, told his cheering supporters, "If you wish me to make the fight, I will make it, even if only one state will support me." The Progressive convention was duly convened 6 August in the Chicago Coliseum, with the image of a bull moose hung over the entrance. Two thousand delegates and alternates attended, among them William Allen White, George Perkins, Jane Addams, Hiram Johnson, Albert Beveridge, and Gifford Pinchot. Most of the music consisted of hymns, and the New York delegation marched up and down the aisles singing "Onward Christian Soldiers." Indiana Congressman James Watson insisted that he had never seen such idolatrous devotion in his life as that manifested by Roosevelt's adherents. The next day Roosevelt arrived to deliver his hour-long speech entitled "Confessions of Faith." In his keynote address, Senator Beveridge proclaimed, "We stand for a nobler America; we stand for an undivided nation; we stand for a broader liberty, a fuller justice; we stand for social brotherhood as against savage individualism; . . . we stand for equal rights as a fact of life instead of a catchword of politics; . . . we battle for the actual rights of man."

Hiram Johnson of California was chosen as Roosevelt's running mate. The Progressive party platform, written by Gifford Pinchot, was entitled "A Contract with the People." It enumerated a wide variety of reform measures including tariff revision, stricter regulation of industry, direct election of senators, the recall of judicial decisions, woman suffrage, presidential primaries, a minimum wage for women, the graduated income tax, an end to child labor, and the initiative, referendum, and recall. The Progressive convention then adjourned to "Praise God from whom all blessings flow." After it was over many Roosevelt followers massed outside of the Congress Hotel in the park across Michigan Avenue to cheer him. For two solid hours in the rain and the deep mud they shouted with a rhythmic cadence, "We want Teddy! We want Teddy!"

A reporter for the *New York World* regretfully assessed the probable impact of all this on Republican chances in 1912: "If Mr. Hughes had been nomi-- nated for president instead of Mr. Taft, there would be no Roosevelt third-term candidacy, no Progressive party, no wreck of the Republican organization, no certainty of Republican defeat." "The only question now," said Chauncey Depew about the shattered Republican party, "is which corpse gets the most flowers."

XVII

TAFT'S TRIUMPH IN DEFEAT:

The Campaign of 1912

When the Democrats met for their convention in Baltimore in June 1912, most were confident that the man they nominated would become the next president of the United States. The leading candidate was Southern-born Woodrow Wilson, former president of Princeton University and now the reform governor of New Jersey. His most formidable rival was Speaker of the House Champ Clark from Missouri. Congressman Oscar Underwood of Alabama and Governor Judson Harmon of Ohio were also in the running. Wilson had the backing of progressive Democrats; Clark, a regular party man, appealed to the middle-of-the-road organization Democrats. Roosevelt hoped the Democrats would choose a moderate or a conservative, and he was, as his son Kermit told reporters, "praying for Clark." Before the balloting began, William Jennings Bryan launched into an attack on Wall Street, Tammany Hall, and conservative Democrats, pleading for a progressive nominee who would show that the Democratic party "is true to the people."

The balloting began with Clark ahead, Wilson second, and other contenders receiving a smattering of votes. It went on for some time before there was a winner. Mrs. Taft was so concerned about the outcome that she broke all precedent by attending the convention. The forty-third ballot gave Wilson 602 votes to Clark's 329, but he was still 120 short of nomination because of the two-thirds rule. The deadlock was broken when Underwood and then Harmon withdrew from the race and their delegates were released. The forty-sixth ballot, on the seventh day of the convention, 2 July, made Woodrow Wilson the Democratic nominee.

Wilson and his running mate, Indiana Governor Thomas Marshall, received notification of their nomination at Wilson's summer home in Sea Girt, New Jersey, where they celebrated before a crowd of ten thousand people. Senator-elect Ollie James of Kentucky struck just the right note when he said to the crowd, "A former president charges the present president with being friendly with certain trusts, and failure to prosecute them. The present president charges the former president with being friendly with certain other trusts, and failure to prosecute them. We believe both." Clearly, the Democrats planned to allow Taft and Roosevelt to offset each other. Roosevelt's program was based on the assumption that strong and active central government was necessary for reform; Wilson, a confirmed Jeffersonian, articulated the view that the government which governs least, governs best. Yet the "New Nationalism" of Roosevelt and the "New Freedom" of Wilson were not very dissimilar. There were differences, of course. Roosevelt maintained that there were good and bad trusts, whereas Wilson claimed that excessive size in business was bad in itself. Roosevelt charged that the Democratic platform was not progressive at all, but both were in fact forward looking compared to the regular Republicans. And compared with Taft, both men had definite plans for at least limited change.

While the Republicans feuded at their convention, Taft remained in Washington and totally isolated himself from the ominous party split. Once the campaign was underway he learned and fully felt what divided personal loyalties within a party could mean emotionally and politically. Alarmed by Roosevelt's dangerous views in declaring his third-party candidacy yet buoyed up by the regular Republicans who supported him, Taft agreed to stay in the campaign and oppose his old friend. The only thing that concerned him immediately was his acceptance speech for the nomination. "I am now 'up against' a speech," Taft complained to Nellie on 21 July 1912. "I have got to evolve something to say and it comes hard for me. . . . Hilles is sensitive because Wilson gets a column every day, and so does Roosevelt, on political subjects, and there is no news from me except that I play golf. I seem to have heard that before. It always makes me impatient, as if I were running a P.T. Barnum show, with two or three shows across the street" to compete with.

His nomination speech was a heavy burden weighing him down, a task made more difficult by the fact that Nellie was away on vacation. "When I am away from you," he confessed, "I am always missing something, and I feel a bit aimless as well." Pondering which issues to discuss in his speech, Taft had, he told Nellie, been advised by a friend to remark on the high cost of living: "I told him if I were to be made responsible for the price of eggs and the activity of hens, I would simply lay down my office."

Nellie had wired him from Beverly that she would be there for the notification ceremony, adding, "Not over 75 to luncheon." He nevertheless went ahead with arrangements of his own, replying to her telegram: "We will have lobster Newburg, capon and a ham, have enough for 400 guests on buffet. I know you want to keep them down to 75 but we cannot do it, my dear. I have got to be more generous." The ceremony was held in the East Room, with 400 present; Mrs. Taft sat just below the speaker's platform. Elihu Root began the program by turning toward Taft and declaring defensively, "Your title to the nomination is as clear and unimpeachable as the title of any candidate of any party since political conventions began." Taft then launched into a ponderous, ten-thousand word oration, in which he carefully avoided the names of Roosevelt and Wilson, referring to them only as "gentlemen." He ended with the tortured query, "So may we not expect in the issues which are now before us that the ballots cast in November shall show a prevailing majority in favor of sound progress, great prosperity upon a protection basis and under true constitutional representative rule by the people?" Before anyone present could raise a question, Taft had left the room, reappearing only when the buffet luncheon was served.

"The truth is," Taft confided to a friend, "I am not very happy in this renomination and re-election business. . . . I am not going to squeal or run away. But after it is all over I shall be glad to retire and let another take the burden." So Taft just drifted along with the campaign. He expected to lose and secretly hoped he would. But it was nearly certain also that Roosevelt would not win, and that was now his main objective.

Although Taft dreaded "the awful agony of a campaign," he felt it a duty to his Republican friends and to the country to counterweight the "socialistic" advances of his opponents. "Personally, I have no desire to continue as a candidate," Taft told his secretary. "I had no desire to do so when I went on the stump, but the fear of Mr. Roosevelt's success made it necessary." Taft had sincerely come to feel that Roosevelt was "really the greatest menace to our institutions that we have had in a long time." Roosevelt and his Progressive followers were demanding federal regulatory agencies and social and political reforms which Taft believed unconstitutional. "Mr. Roosevelt has planned," he asserted, "a vast system of state socialism, a government of men unrestrained by laws."

Taft was a conservative man, but the issues of the campaign soon forced him into, if not a reactionary, at least a decidedly "status quo" position. "I wrote a piece about him for *McClure's Magazine*," when he was a presidential candidate in 1908, William Allen White wrote, "portraying him as a sane liberal and I really believed it. So did millions of followers of Colonel Roosevelt." By 1911, as George Mowry puts it, Taft was sounding "the fifty-year-old shibboleths of organized reaction." Taft himself openly acknowledged his conservatism: "I have no part to play but that of a conservative and that I am going to play." Since he believed that the world was "fallible and full of weakness, with somewhat of wickedness in it," Taft felt that "reforms that are worth having are brought about little by little and not by one blow." Yet he bristled at being called an extremist, a label which Roosevelt and Wilson gave him. "Though I am a conservative," he proclaimed, "I am not a reactionary or a trilobite."

"I have no doubt we should be badly defeated," Taft confessed to Nellie. He characterized Roosevelt to her as "so dangerous and so powerful because of his hold upon the less intelligent voters and the discontented." Occasionally he believed he might not be humiliated in November, especially since his secretary Charles Hilles assured him that a defeat was improbable. "I meet a lot of people who are very confident that there is coming a wave of public opinion in my favor," Taft wrote to Nellie, "but I have not yet felt its effect." "We are badly in need of friends for carrying on this campaign," he told her candidly, and "we have had great difficulty in securing anybody who would stand up for us in California." On the reluctance of Republicans to help with campaigning, he said, "Whether it is because they think it is a losing game or not I don't know. . . . Sometimes I think I am going to be re-elected, but generally the conditions calmly considered are not favorable."

In private Taft became more bitter in the expressions he used to characterize Roosevelt. "As the campaign goes on and the unscrupulousness of Roosevelt develops," he wrote on 26 August, "it is hard for me to realize that we are talking about the same man . . . we knew in the presidency." Roosevelt was now "the fakir, the juggler, the green god's man, the gold brick man." Envious of the enthusiasm and loyalty that Roosevelt so easily inspired, Taft grumbled, "He is to be classed with the leaders of religious cults. . . . He is seeking to make his followers Holy Rollers!" To Nellie, Taft claimed that Roosevelt's followers were no better than "fanatics," "dreamers," and "opportunists." But still, he maintained, "I have not any feeling of enmity against Roosevelt or any feeling of hatred"; "I look upon him as I look upon a freak almost in the Zoological Garden"; "So far as personal relations with him are concerned, they don't exist—I do not have any feeling one way or the other."

Taft's fear of Roosevelt, which had become "almost pathological," in Donald Anderson's words, has startled other biographers, especially because, as Henry Pringle writes, Roosevelt was by no means "radical" in 1912. It is not hard, however, to account for his violent reaction when we understand that

Taft transformed his general anger and anguish into a belief in Roosevelt's extreme political danger to the nation. Despite all that had gone wrong during his administration, Taft thought he had been faithful to Roosevelt's policies. When Roosevelt turned against him, Taft's emotions, his dependency and love for Roosevelt the parent figure, could only change into intense perplexity and pain. No moderate position was possible. Taft changed from loving and idealizing his former chief to fearing him. His confusion found expression in a deep hatred for Roosevelt's ideas, ideas that supposedly threatened the Constitution of the United States.

When many businessmen, whom he thought his allies, went over to Roosevelt, he raged to his brother Charles that they were "fools, like some of the voters. . . . They don't see their real interest. They do not see beyond their noses." What hurt him most was the increasingly apparent disloyalty of some of his closest friends, particularly members of his cabinet, first during the primary and then during the fall campaign. "One of the discouraging things," he informed Horace, "is that I have to do it nearly all myself. Men do not seem to be willing to come forward, even those who recognize the crisis." His entire cabinet had proved reluctant to work for his renomination, and even Vice-President Sherman seemed ready to desert Taft if Roosevelt got the Republican nomination, hoping thereby to remain on the ticket as the colonel's running mate. "I find that my cabinet, and especially Wickersham and Fisher, are not sufficiently sympathetic with me in an effort to help me out politically," he wrote to the Taft family's long-time friend Mabel Boardman, a Cleveland socialite. Stimson, still a good friend of Roosevelt's, had earlier agreed to make a speech for Taft but complained when it came due, "I am in a hell of a fix."

Postmaster General Frank Hitchcock worked openly for Roosevelt's nomination. Informed of Hitchcock's activities, Taft listened, but refused to believe it. Friends advised the president to purge Hitchcock from the cabinet, even though he had great influence over the southern delegates. When Hitchcock and Taft conferred one afternoon in January 1912, some observers thought that Taft had finally taken the long overdue step, but when they emerged, Taft called in the press to affirm his belief in Hitchcock. Taft's secretary, Charles Hilles, was distraught and stormed in to see Taft. Hilles was seen sitting by Taft, "looking like a thunder cloud, and the president's eyes were red, and it certainly looked as if he had been weeping a little."

In the primary campaign in Ohio Taft had approached Root to speak on his behalf, but Root replied that he "was not at liberty to make speeches upon the issues into which this primary campaign has drifted." He explained that he had been privy to many matters in the Roosevelt administration and could not speak without "betraying confidence and disloyalty" to his former chief. He tried finally to soften the blow by pleading age and poor health. Meanwhile Secretary of State Knox reluctantly agreed to make a few speeches for Taft, but he delivered them in a perfunctory manner. With friends and subordinates reluctant to speak on his behalf, the party drifted toward not just defeat, but possible chaos.

"I do not expect to take any part in the campaign," Taft announced in the middle of August. As in the 1908 campaign, he played golf more persistently than before. Concerned Republican regulars dispatched a committee to the White House to admonish Taft and urge him to take a more active part in the campaign. "I see many people are complaining that there is not energy enough," he admitted. The *New York Times* sarcastically noted that Taft's announcement that he would not leave Washington to campaign was especially surprising when it was recalled how much "the President loves the Executive pleasure of traveling." He planned, the *Times* added, "a porch campaign, with some intervals on the golf links." Taft tried feebly to defend himself: "I have been told that I ought to do this, ought to do that, ought to do the other; that I ought to say this, ought to say that, ought to say the other; that I do not keep myself in the headlines; that there is this or that trick I might turn to my advantage. I know it," he added in frustration, "but I can't do it."

As Taft retreated, the real contest was left to Theodore Roosevelt and Woodrow Wilson. Wilson praised Taft as a delightful person but condemned him as an "unserviceable president" and an uninspiring campaigner. The Republicans, Wilson charged, were a "Know-nothing, Do-nothing party which had allowed the ship of state to drift about for four years without a pilot." Taft was "sitting on the lid," and the time had come for active leadership. The Republicans had not had a new idea for thirty years, he charged. It was Roosevelt that Wilson went after in earnest, faulting him for too often promising but not delivering the millennium.

Disgusted with Taft's inaction, Roosevelt announced that he was dropping Taft from any further consideration during the campaign. Replying to an enthusiast in Massachusetts who shouted "Tell us about Taft," he sneered, "I never discuss dead issues." Roosevelt now had his turn to discover how William Jennings Bryan must have felt in 1908 when Taft refused to enter the fray. Turning his guns on Wilson, Roosevelt characterized him as "a vague, conjectural personality, more made up of opinions and academic prepossessions than of human traits and red corpuscles." He did not deny that Wilson was a good man but denied vehemently that he had "any special fitness for the presidency." In the course of his campaign Roosevelt visited thirty-four states, with only occasional jibes at Taft. Upon seeing people wearing Taft buttons during his stopover in Springfield, Missouri, he quipped, "They are the appropriate color of yellow."

The most dramatic event in the campaign came on 14 October in Milwaukee when a crazed New York saloonkeeper, John Chrank, who believed that "any man looking for a third term ought to be shot," actually acted on his beliefs. As Roosevelt was standing in an automobile to acknowledge the crowd's cheers, Chrank shot him with a pistol point blank at a distance of only a few feet. The colonel sank down onto the seat, but insisted immediately to Wisconsin progressive Henry Cochems that the shot had only "pinked" him. Despite the bullet in his chest, very near his heart, he exclaimed that the "chances were twenty to one that it was not fatal." His secretary Elbert Martin, a former football player, tackled the would-be assassin; the crowd cried "Lynch him!" A Texas Republican leader wished to dispatch him with his revolver, but Roosevelt insisted that Chrank be remanded to the police. Later he admitted, "I would not have objected to the man's being killed at the very start, but I do not deem it wise or proper that he should be killed before my eyes if I was going to recover." Chrank lived to explain at his trial that McKinley had appeared to him in a dream and said to him, "This is my murderer; avenge my death."

The force of the bullet had been greatly diminished by fifty pages of a speech manuscript in Roosevelt's breast pocket, but the bullet nevertheless reached a place near the heart. Despite the pleading of his friends, old "Rough and Ready" insisted on delivering his speech as scheduled: "It may be the last one I shall ever deliver, but I am going to deliver this one." "I will make this speech or die," he dramatically informed his doctor. Accordingly, he gave a portion of the one-and-a-half-hour address he had planned, despite interruptions from the audience imploring him to desist. "I give you my word," he answered, "I do not care a rap about being shot, not a rap. . . . What I do care for is my country." The mock-heroics, however foolish, electrified the nation, as he knew they would.

Taft regretted the publicity Roosevelt got. His friends were "attempting to make all they can of the shooting," even "charging it to the vituperation of my supporters," he said. Nonetheless he wired his "heartfelt sympathy" to Roosevelt and his family, and Roosevelt politely responded. To his brother Horace, Taft wrote, "I have never been so disgusted about anything he has done as at the speech he made to his audience after the shooting."

Before election day, Taft said, "If I cannot win I hope Wilson will, and Roosevelt feels that if he cannot win, he hopes Wilson will." When the results were in, Taft and Roosevelt, having split the regular Republican vote, were roundly defeated. Taft won only two minor states. The Mormon machine pulled Utah through, and in Vermont "it was practically a capital offense to vote a third-party ticket." The electoral vote was 435 for Wilson, 88 for Roosevelt, and 8 for Taft. "What I got was the irreducible minimum of the Republican party," he confessed to a *New York World* reporter. Roosevelt, he consoled himself, had gotten votes of the "labor, socialistic, discontented, ragtag, and bobtail variety." Reporters found Roosevelt "all buoyant and good-humored." He had expected to pull off a miracle and win, but in defeat he took satisfaction in Taft's defeat, for Wilson, as he well knew, represented sound progressive elements within the Democratic party.

With the election, the ordeal between these former friends was over, and Taft was deeply relieved. There is no evidence to support Paolo Coletta's assumption that Taft "hid his bitterness" when he said that he "was not greatly disappointed." Taft spoke from his heart, without guile, when he said, "The people of the United States do not owe me another election. I don't carry in my heart the slightest resentment against the people or any bitterness of spirit with respect to their view of my administration." And despite his political defeat, the 1912 presidential campaign was for Taft a real psychological triumph in terms of personal growth. By standing up to Roosevelt in the preprimary fight, he succeeded in casting off most of the child in him and became more his own man. His years in the White House, however painful and full of problems, had matured him and prepared him to resist Roosevelt. In a sense Roosevelt compelled him to grow up. By 1912 he was ready for the greatest emotional battle of his life. He entered it ambivalently, but with a stubborn determination. Taft felt that Roosevelt had in some way betrayed him. He knew he would almost certainly be defeated in the election, yet he decided in the most truly aggressive fight of his life to defeat his "father-friend" for the nomination.

Taft eagerly waited for the fourth of March, when Woodrow Wilson was scheduled to begin his term as the twenty-eighth president of the United States. He accepted defeat generously and good-naturedly, and much to his relief the press began to treat him less harshly. The reporters assessed Taft as a pleasant, well-meaning man who had been caught up in a situation which he could neither understand nor control. He had been a weak president, they admitted, but a good sport.

Although magazines like *The Nation* insisted that Taft "brought his fate upon himself," all were impressed by the calmness, the stoicism, and the good humor with which he accepted his defeat, and many now came to his defense. Journalist William Allen White tempered his criticism of Taft considerably, claiming "that in the main the president has been doing the right thing in the wrong way." Taft, many thought, deserved particular praise for being a "constitutional president"; in no way had he overstepped the prescribed bounds of the executive. Although there was considerable disagreement about the extent of his accomplishments, most commentators agreed that he had tried to enforce the laws impartially and had rigidly abstained from profit seeking or political advantage for himself.

Political obituaries noted that Taft's accomplishments were often obscured by the outbursts following some unfortunate remark or act by the well-intentioned but mistake-prone president. His chief failing, the independent *New York Globe* charged, was his inability to satisfy the progressive wing of the party, which had been responsible for his nomination in 1908. If he had done so, a split in the party probably would not have occurred.

Happy that the end of four hard years in the White House was in sight, Taft made an assessment of his accomplishments in a letter to his wife: "I am content to retire from it with a consciousness that I have done the best I could. I have strengthened the Supreme Bench, have given them a good deal of new . . . legislation, have not interfered with business, have kept the peace, and on the whole have enabled people to pursue their various occupations without interruption." He admitted, however, that it was "a very humdrum, uninteresting administration, and it does not attract the attention or enthusiasm of anybody."

Several months remained to serve between defeat in November and the inauguration of Wilson in March 1913. Taft looked forward to the relief from his duties, and he showed none of the depression or pessimism often associated with a rejected chief executive. Instead, he acted like a man freed of a great burden. His old friend John Hays Hammond seemed surprised to discover that Taft was "genuinely glad that he did not have to assume the burden of another four years in the White House." Taft assured his friends, "Don't for a moment suppose that I am cast down or humiliated, or in any way . . . suffering from disappointment. The truth is I am glad that it is all over. . . . The nearer I get to the inauguration of my successor, the greater relief I feel."

Taft's personal feelings of triumph amidst political defeat furthered a subtle change in his relationship with Nellie, a change that had commenced with his becoming president. As he gained in maturity, his dependency on her gradually subsided. He spoke as lovingly as before, but his actions showed that he had finally become the master in his own house. At the same time Nellie felt less compulsion to direct her husband's life and may finally have been glad to relinquish the burden of supporting his immaturity. Disheartened, of course, over the prospect of leaving the White House, she nonetheless realized that she had derived great satisfaction and joy from three of her four years as first lady.

Taft's chief worry about the Democratic victory concerned the "untold mischief" he learned the new administration might do in the Philippines. "It is dreadful to think that Jeffersonian theorizing and the mouthings of demagogues should condemn eleven million of people to a kind of anarchy," he wrote to Horace. Nevertheless he was more sanguine over the actual Democratic victory than the possibility of Roosevelt's success, for to him, Roosevelt had become "the most dangerous man that we have had in this country since its origin." At the same time, he felt that the Democrats after demonstrating how incapable they were of running the government would make the Republican party certain victors in 1916. Even if Wilson enjoyed eight years in the White House, Taft was confident that he would "not attempt greatly to change our fundamental law."

On 4 March, the last day of his term, associates marveled over "the cheerful optimism" Taft displayed, in marked contrast to his mood on his own inauguration day. "I'll be glad to be going," he told the president-elect, "this is the loneliest place in the world." Wilson appeared solemn and stiff; Taft, cheerful and relaxed. Viewing them on their drive to the Capitol for the inaugural ceremonies, Francis McHale wrote that one might have mistaken Taft for the president-elect for he was "smiling and radiant."

After the inauguration Taft and Wilson returned together to the White House. By about two o'clock, some two hundred guests were beginning to assemble in the East Room before they entered the State Dining Room for the inaugural luncheon. Both men alighted quickly, walked rapidly through the entrance door, and stopped just over the Seal of the President of the United States. Both seemed rather embarrassed. Although President Wilson had invited Taft to the luncheon, he obviously had not expected Taft to accept. An aide approached to inform Wilson that the luncheon party had gone into the dining room. The new president turned gallantly to usher Taft in, but Hilles, Taft's secretary, suggested pointedly to the ex-president that there was not enough time; his train would leave at three thirty and he had to meet Mrs. Taft. This plan was quickly prearranged by close friends of the Tafts who were appalled when they learned that he expected to attend the inaugural luncheon. They were unaware, of course, that for Taft, Wilson's inauguration was a ceremony of liberation, and he was in a mood to celebrate.

President Wilson looked ready to bid him good-by, but Taft was determined to have lunch. Surely there was time enough for him to eat a sandwich, he protested. Given the plaintive way he said it, Ike Hoover recalled, everyone who heard him felt sympathy. Nothing more was said, and they proceeded to the dining room. It was very sad to observe Taft among the celebrants, Hoover felt. When word came that Mrs. Taft would wait for him no longer, an embarrassed Hilles reminded the ex-president that he had to leave at once to make the train. He practically had to drag Taft away nonetheless.

Nellie Taft's mood was quite different from her husband's on the final day of his term. Sometimes hopeful that Taft would miraculously be re-elected, she had begun to make tentative plans for a second term. Taft's chief regret about defeat was its likely effect on Nellie. "I felt more sorrow at Nellie's disappointment and your's," he confessed to Horace, "than I did [for] myself." After the election Nellie became downcast, she seemed physically weaker and looked worse than she had since her illness in 1909. Although she tried to enjoy to the utmost the last few weeks of her husband's administration, she seemed to grow apathetic as the last day grew nearer. Feeling warm and sympathetic toward President-elect Woodrow Wilson, Taft had decided to invite the Wilsons to stay at the White House on inauguration eve as Roosevelt had invited him in 1908. Nellie was, however, not feeling convivial and sharply vetoed her husband's plan. Consequently, Taft intensified his own efforts to ease the transition for the incoming first lady. It is difficult to avoid speculation about what his reaction was when he received Mrs. Wilson's thank you note, in which she said, "I am naturally the most unambitious of women, and life in the White House has no attraction for me. Quite the contrary."

According to Irwin Hoover's account of their departure day, Mrs. Taft wandered aimlessly around the second floor of the White House. The atmosphere was funereal. The suggestion by one of the staff that the Tafts might possibly return one day "brought a real smile to her sad and forlorn face." Although she was scheduled to meet her husband at eleven that morning, Mrs. Taft postponed the final moment. An automobile waited in readiness for half an hour. The staff, meanwhile, just stood by and waited for her to leave. They could not begin any preparations for the Wilsons until she had gone. Finally at 11:30 Mrs. Taft arose from her desk, where she had been finishing letters to Robert and Charles, put on her hat and furs, and came down in the elevator. She was visibly affected. Attempting to hand Ike Hoover the letters, she dropped all the magazines she was carrying. She walked out the door without saying farewell to anyone. The servants who witnessed her departure were moved to sympathy: "Her feelings were so evident that practically no one even attempted to say good-by."

William Howard Taft had two careers, as a judge and a politician, and not even his political career ought to be judged wholly by his four years in the White House, for he served Presidents Harrison, McKinley, and Roosevelt, outstandingly. As governor of the Philippines, he played a remarkable role in the history of those islands. It is perhaps an unfair bias of historians to automatically think of the presidency as necessarily the highest achievement in public life. Certainly such an evaluation will not do when we consider Taft. The law was Taft's career, and he succeeded at last in achieving his "heart's desire" when he became chief justice of the United States. For him the presidency was just an unhappy interlude on the way to the Supreme Court. Therefore in evaluating his career we need to recognize the fundamentally judicial nature of the man and how it not only influenced his conduct as president but also survived the presidential years to make him a successful candidate for the chief justiceship. In short, much that Taft did wrong or poorly was often a consequence of his virtues. His basic fairmindedness, his constant adherence to principle, his reverent awe of constitutionality, all these characteristics contributed greatly to his success in the Court.

Had he joined the progressive wing of the party in fact and in spirit following the footsteps of Roosevelt, it would not after all have been, in his case, politically the best thing to do. He would have permanently cut himself off from the more conservative elements which contributed to the Republican party's recapturing political dominance in 1920 and with it his own capturing of a seat on the Court a year later. It is entirely possible that Taft intuitively sensed that joining the progressives would do him no good in fulfilling at some future date his life's dream. His entire behavior as president becomes more explicable and defensible in light of the basically judicial nature of his professional instincts. We may say that his instincts were correct, and taking the presidency, as he took it himself, simply as a step rather than the high point of his career, we can justifiably emphasize his success and not his failure. It must be remembered that he did achieve the goal of his life and that the maturing years in the presidency contributed to the success he enjoyed when he returned to his beloved bench. Also, it would be a significant historical mistake and a great unfairness to Taft to judge him a failure on the basis of only four years in so long and distinguished a public career as he enjoyed. The longer view his entire career affords allows us the perspective we need to balance the record. His dream of making a significant contribution within the courts was not an unrealized and frustrating fantasy. The final nine happy years of his life were spent in the halls of justice, which to him had always been his idea of heaven.

In taking such an outlook on the man and his life, the psychological perspective is indispensable. In the first place, by understanding more perfectly his attitudes toward becoming president and how, caught in a vice between Nellie and Roosevelt, he became president, we can see the part the presidency played in his life more as he saw it himself and not as custom and historical bias dictates. Once in the White House he conducted himself very much as if he were a judge, just as he might be said later to have conducted the chief justiceship as if he were a president. He slacked off in the presidency in part because he did not like being the one who gave the final orders. He could not be strong in such a role. Why the years in the White House were bad years for Taft can partly be seen in the very concerns which interested him most and by those actions in which he took the greatest pride. He particularly favored treaties, for example, and, as we have seen, he was especially proud of winning approval, in this country at least, of the Canadian Reciprocity Treaty as well as the general arbitration treaties with England and France. He devoted much time and interest to filling the five Supreme Court vacancies which occurred during his term. He enjoyed reviewing appeals for clemency and writing his opinions. And earlier he had enjoyed being governor of the Philippines much more than he expected to because he became involved in writing laws, providing a constitution. Being a strict constructionist, he was not by nature inclined to interfere with legislative activities. He left Congress to conduct its own affairs. That is one reason he did not play a strong role in helping his party's congressmen overturn Joe Cannon. He tended not even to interfere with his cabinet members; the delegation of responsibility and authority for him truly meant just that. He believed in the separation of powers not only between the president and Congress and the judiciary but also between himself and his subordinates. He was not greatly upset when businessmen turned against him because of his attorney general's antitrust suits; he had too deep a faith that justice would be vindicated in the courts. His faith in the law and its processes was unlimited.

It is to Taft's credit that he cared deeply about personal relationships. If Taft had married a supportive wife and one whose ambitions coincided more perfectly with his own, it is safe to say that he would never have become president. Yet as president he matured into independence. As he foresaw, he had his own way at last. Having done all he could for Nellie and finding himself in a position of ultimate power, Taft grew and matured as he never had before. Butt was able to write such informative letters home because Taft was able to confide in him in a way he never really could in Nellie. Once Nellie had achieved what she wanted she went pretty much about her business, leaving Taft free to find himself as he could. He was able to begin to live his own life. What he liked most in the presidency were the nationwide traveling tours where he was, in a sense, on his own. These trips allowed him to get away not only from Washington, but also from Nellie. His golf game was more than just a source of recreation. Despite the attacks it provoked from the press, Taft did not give it up. Instead he used it as an instrument for realizing and demonstrating his independence. By putting his golf game above his presidential duties, he gave notice to everyone that, as he put it, "I'm not going to be pushed around anymore."

Although much that Taft did and said as president does not make sense politically, it makes sense personally, when taken in light of Taft's interior life. Many of his public statements that subjected him to ridicule—such as his having never wanted to be president—may be seen as actually addressed to Nellie: the truths he could not tell her personally, she was able to read in the newspaper. Theodore Roosevelt and Nellie formed a complex relationship with Taft, who possessed something which the other two loved and needed. Roosevelt wanted a successor who would further the causes he had fought for and yet not surpass him. Astute as Roosevelt was, he could not possibly have gauged the degree to which Taft would assert himself once he came into a position of full power. In many ways Taft failed politically, but he was still young in his career, which continued more than twenty years after he left office. As president and with the ever-present company and support of Archie Butt, Taft was no longer subject simply to the criticism that drove him against himself. Released from presidential pressure, he was free to grow. There were considerable external demands to be met, of course, but they could not affect him in the same way. He had gained the power to say no and to run away when he had to. And he could do so pretty much with a clear conscience.

Despite his belief in conservation, for example, Taft's inept handling of the Ballinger-Pinchot controversy convinced many people that he had betrayed Roosevelt's policies and proved his incompetence as chief executive. First he tried to conciliate, and when that failed, he simply procrastinated, hoping that the feud would fade away. He bore himself similarly in relation to the Payne-Aldrich Tariff fiasco, which caused him finally to flee the capital for a time. Biographers and historians concerned with the political Taft have time and again confronted puzzles that do not resolve themselves in strict political terms. What must be accepted is that in many respects Taft simply will not make sense politically. With an understanding of his various dependencies along with his new self-image when he became president, we can make sense of why his break from Theodore Roosevelt naturally followed. Whatever new directions his life took in 1908, Butt was there to reinforce them by always agreeing with him and encouraging any project or recreation he initiated. Without this time of coming to terms with his identity, his assuming a determined opposition to Roosevelt in the 1912 primary campaign would have been impossible. He came out of the presidency in many respects a new man. It is altogether fitting that his distinguished career should have been crowned by appointment to a post that he valued even above the presidency of the United States.

EPILOGUE

All signs of testiness and petulance left Taft once he completed his term as president. Relaxed and content for the first time in years, Taft exclaimed, "You don't know how much fun it is to sit back . . . and watch the playing of the game down there in Washington, without any responsibility of my own." Those years in the White House, his daughter Helen said, "were the only unhappy years of his entire life." "Had you been re-elected," his friend Mabel Boardman wrote to him, "I don't think you could have lived through another four years." But Taft had now to confront the problem of supporting his family. Although Nellie had managed to save $100,000 during their tenure in the White House, it would not last forever. His first thought was to return to Cincinnati and a private law practice again, but he was reluctant because he had not practiced since he was a young man and then he had not been notably successful. But "my profession is my means of livelihood," he acknowledged, and "I don't see that there is anything left for me to do."

Meanwhile Taft received a timely offer of a Yale professorship of law. The most remarkable coincidence in 1913, as a Washington press's Gridiron Club skit put it, was that at the very moment Professor Wilson became President Wilson, President Taft became Professor Taft. The post paid $5,000 annually, which, when combined with savings and extra income from lecture fees, proved sufficient. Preparations for Taft at Yale included the construction of oversized chairs for his office and lecture rooms and the special tailoring of academic robes, since no standard size was large enough. When first offered the Kent Chair of Constitutional Law, Taft replied that it would not be adequate, but that perhaps a "sofa of law" would do.

Within eight months, Taft gave visible signs of the change which had come over him by reducing from 350 to 270 pounds. All his life he had mistakenly equated weight with his own masculinity, feeling that bigness translated into manhood. That he could successfully diet now was a reflection of his increasing maturity. He dismissed his valet, for now he was able to dress himself and tie his own shoes. The ex-president set up an academic office in his brother Charlie's hotel, The Taft, coached the freshman debating team, and recreated generally at banquets, dances, smokers, and ballgames.

The students were at first thrilled to have a former president of the United States as their teacher. But when the novelty wore off, they began to take advantage of his rather naïve assumption that all students were honest and purely dedicated to the pursuit of knowledge. Apparently Taft never did perceive the devious ways his students steered him in almost any direction they pleased.

Altogether Taft spent eight years at Yale, though he was often away addressing clubs and various civic associations. Nellie seems to have enjoyed these years as well. New Haven offered a lively assortment of people and cultural events, and for the first few years she was busily, though guardedly, completing her memoirs, *Recollections of Full Years*, which was published in 1914. He was gratified to find her still interested in his work, and she approved of the money lecturing brought in. For fees varying from $150 to $1000, hosts could select from a list of thirty lecture subjects, including "Duties of Citizenship" and "The Initiative and Referendum." Nellie studied "the various contracts" to make sure the terms were correct. For their anniversary in 1917, Taft sent her flowers with a card reading, "1886–1917, With love and gratitude for 31 years of unalloyed happiness."

When World War I erupted, Taft was, like most Americans, anxious that the United States remain uninvolved. "Our business," he insisted, is "to maintain neutrality as far as we possibly can." Unlike Roosevelt, whom he considered a warmonger, Taft sincerely hoped that President Wilson would "save us from war." Although Taft disagreed with many of Wilson's policies, he was deeply sympathetic with the individual who occupied the presidency: "The task of the president is a heavy one"; "He is our President. He is acting for the whole country." Taft therefore supported him. As it became increasingly likely that the United States was going to enter the war, Taft began to fault Wilson for not giving more attention to preparedness. Once America became a belligerent, however, Taft swung his support to the Wilson administration. He accepted a post as joint chairman of the National Labor Board, which arbitrated disputes between employees and management. During his fourteen months' service, Taft softened his formerly hard line on labor rights as he learned more about the working conditions and wage levels of the lower classes.

After the war, Taft waited in vain for Wilson to appoint him to the peace commission in Versailles. He had high hopes because Wilson's confidant and chief adviser, Colonel House, had recommended the ex-president. But Wilson, now increasingly estranged from House, had no intention of taking either Taft or Elihu Root with him to France. Wilson wanted no one of national stature on the commission to share the limelight. Succeeding in France to a greater degree than skeptics thought possible, Wilson returned home with a treaty based on his fourteen-point peace plan, which included his special project—a League of Nations. Taft did not bear grudges, and used his influence to help promote the treaty with Republicans in Congress. When Wilson was defeated in the Senate, in large part because of his stubborn refusal to accept any compromise version of the treaty, Taft felt that the amended treaty was still a good one since it ensured American participation in the League. But Wilson, gravely ill from the battle, vetoed the amended treaty against the advice of most of his associates. Taft correctly assessed the problem: "The truth is he has [so] insisted on hogging all the authority . . . trusting no one, that he has broken himself down." Had Taft still been president, a compromise would have been found. If Taft was on most occasions too pliable, Wilson was nearly always too rigid.

After the bitterness of the 1912 campaign, it was not until 1915 that a reconciliation between Taft and Theodore Roosevelt came about. Their first meeting—at the funeral of a mutual friend—was an anxious moment for both men. Taft said to a friend in advance of the meeting, "I don't know how he will conduct himself, but I shall try to be pleasant." Still feeling the injured party, Taft added, "It is the man who has done the wrong who finds it difficult to forgive the man whom he has treated badly." According to William Lyon Phelps, Roosevelt gave no sign of recognition until Taft approached, held out his hand, and said, "How are you, Theodore?" Afterward, Taft described their reunion, "It was a bit stiff but it was all right. . . . It was pleasant enough, but it was not cordial or intimate."

The next year another meeting took place, arranged by Elihu Root, at the Union League Club in New York. Taft felt that it was a good idea because "a very considerable part of the low-minded press . . . had given the impression that if Roosevelt and I met, he would curse me and I would curse him, and each would kick the other in the stomach." The meeting over, Taft was disappointed, although the press described it as an amiable reunion.

Learning that Roosevelt was going west in 1916 to campaign for Charles

Evans Hughes, the Republican candidate for president, Taft wrote, "I am glad of it. The farther he goes away the better." Taft and Roosevelt's relationship grew almost amicable, however, when they united in opposition to Wilson during the 1918 congressional campaign. But as Taft put it, a similar attitude toward Wilson was their only basis for reconciliation: "I think [he] is the chief bond between us." They were never again intimate, yet Taft was happy that additional steps toward reviving the friendship had taken place before Roosevelt died in January 1919. To a mutual friend he wrote, "I want to say . . . how glad I am Theodore and I came together after that long painful interval. Had he died in a hostile state of mind toward me, I would have mourned the fact all my life. I loved him always and cherish his memory." In the words of Sylvia Jukes Morris, Taft stood at the snowy graveside of his old friend, "and remained longer than anyone else, his head bowed, his face wracked with emotion, weeping profusely."

Taft continued to long for a position on the Supreme Court. But because of his being an ex-president he, and other concerned parties, felt that only the chief justiceship was a reasonable aspiration. He was pessimistic as to his chances. To a friend who tried to assist him in 1914, he wrote, "I am pleased . . . to have you suggest my competency to fill the chief justiceship, but it will never come." Nellie too had altered her views and now was hopeful that he would achieve his goal. The position of the chief justice had one clear advantage over the presidency: it lasted for life. Taft now feared she would be disappointed if he did not obtain the post. He did not mind her "hoping and continuing to hope," he wrote, so long as she suffered no disappointment: "I love you, my dearest, and I want you to be happy, to be happy myself."

A vacancy on the court opened in 1916, and Wilson chose the first Jewish appointee, Louis Brandeis. Taft was shocked, for to him Brandeis was a veritable radical. Chief Justice Edward White, aged seventy-one, showed no signs of retiring; and Taft, though discouraged, was properly resigned: "If the position, which I would rather have than any other in the world, is not to come to me, I have no right to complain, for the Lord has been good to me."

Taft's opportunities improved, however, when Senator Warren G. Harding, the smalltown Ohio politician who had put Taft's name in nomination at the convention in 1912, became the Republican candidate for president in 1920. Taft considered Harding "a man of marked ability, of sanity, of much legislative experience and . . . a regular Republican of principle," rather than a "trimmer" like Roosevelt. When Harding won over the Democratic nominee, James Cox, Taft wired his congratulations.

After his election, Harding invited Taft to a strategy breakfast in Marion,

Ohio. Taft as usual reported all the culinary details to Nellie: "They were very cordial. . . . They had waffles and creamed chipped beef . . . coffee and toast. They offered me eggs, but as I saw this was extra, I declined." Harding afterward took the ex-president into his study for a confidential chat. There he suddenly blurted out, "By the way, I want to ask you, would you accept a position on the Supreme Bench because if you would, I'll put you on that court." Taft, slightly startled, admitted that it had been and still remained "the ambition of my life." Harding had an opportunity a few months after his inauguration. White died in June 1921, and Taft was named chief justice of the United States, a position which was, he said, "the crowning joy and honor" of his life. His reverence for the court had always been plain: "I love judges and I love courts. They are my ideals; they typify on earth what we shall meet hereafter in heaven under a just God."

"It was a great pity," Arthur Wallace Dunn wrote, that "a splendid jurist was not allowed to carry out the ambition of his life" in the first place. It was Taft's profound misfortune, Dunn continued, to be "taken from the bench and thrown into the complexities of politics." As a judge, James Barber has noted, Taft always found the bench "comfortable and secure, stable and safe, honorable and respected." "The chief justice goes into a monastery," Taft declared, "and confines himself to his judicial work." "It is the comfort and dignity and power without worry I like." In the solitary atmosphere of a monastery, Taft could be happy; there as far as his work was concerned he would not need his wife at all. The bench, Taft came to know with a special relief, is "the only place in the country that is free from severe criticism by the press." The only ex-president ever to serve as Supreme Court Justice, he sat as William Allen White has put it, like "one of the high gods of the world, a smiling Buddha, placid, wise, gentle, sweet."

Although the chief justice had incessant labor and great responsibility, he could hardly wait to begin his duties. Up at five-fifteen every morning and adhering to a heavy daily schedule, he worked with energy and determination, clearing his docket as he had never been able to clear his presidential desk. "The truth is that in my present life I don't remember that I even was president," Taft wrote with satisfaction. The critics, too, forgot Taft the president, for as Norman Hapgood said, "All the world knows that he made a splendid chief justice."

Only reluctantly did Taft leave his duties each day: "I am never free from the burden of feeling that whenever I attempt to do anything else I am taking time from my judicial work." He wrote an average of thirty opinions per term, compared with twenty or less for the other justices. Next to Nellie and the children, the Court "is the nearest thing to my heart in life," he wrote. His weight continued to fall, and soon he was down to 259 pounds. "I don't hesitate to say," he wrote to his former cabinet officer, Jacob Dickinson, "that I would rather have been chief justice than president." Best of all, his success on the Court erased most of the bitter memories of the White House.

Moving toward the twilight of his life, he finally began to find what he had always wanted. He was not working now for his parents or for Nellie. In the final quarter of his life Taft made choices that pleased him for once, and most likely escaped many of the emotions—the "angry child," the dependency, and the needfulness—that in the past proved to have diminishing returns. He began to invest in himself.

It was during these years that Taft sustained his most open disagreement with Nellie on political questions. On the issue of prohibition, his views became increasingly puritanical as hers grew "wetter." "The truth is that Nellie and I differ on prohibition," he admitted to Horace. "We might as well face that, because I am utterly out of sympathy with her and she with me." But his pride in her continued, as did his love and admiration. "She is youthful and she is very active, and her figure is such as to make some of the younger dames a little impatient about it," he wrote to their daughter, Helen, in June 1929. "She goes without hesitation everywhere, accepts all the invitations that she wishes to accept, goes out at night when there is anything that is attractive to her." In 1924 she took a four-month tour of Europe.

When in 1920 Andrew Carnegie died and left the former president $10,000 in his will, Taft felt that he ought properly to refuse it. Nellie was of a different mind. "Mrs. Taft wishes me to do it and she is an interested party," he wrote in agreeing to accept the money.

Not generally considered a truly great chief justice, Taft nevertheless gave a distinguished performance as Court administrator. As a judicial architect, Alpheus T. Mason asserts, he was without peer. Still Taft's primary concern on the Court was to protect private property. The decisions he wrote weakened the Clayton Antitrust Act: he permitted injunctions in secondary boycotts, made unions liable to lawsuits, and invalidated Congress's tax on interstate products made by firms employing child labor. Not surprisingly, he was often at odds with Justices Holmes, Stone, and Bradeis. Taft had nevertheless conquered his initial distaste for Brandeis after seeing some portion of his remarkable abilities.

Scholars have found it paradoxical that as chief justice Taft held almost opposite constitutional views about the power of the office from those he had held as president. He had a relatively narrow, strict constructionist understanding of his powers when he was president, views which often made him reluctant to act. "The true view of the executive function is, as I conceive it, that the president can exercise no power which cannot be . . . traced to some specific grant of power," he wrote in 1915. And again, "His jurisdiction must be justified and vindicated by affirmative constitutional or statutory provision or it does not exist." Yet he took a very broad view of the chief justice's role, "investing the office," Mason believes, "with prerogatives for which there were few, if any, precedents." Pushed into the presidency against his inclinations, Taft's attitude toward the office was passive and negative. Once on the Supreme Court, however, he set to work to make a mark of excellence in his chosen field. Justice Brandeis once said to Felix Frankfurter, "It's very difficult for me to understand why a man who is so good as chief justice, in his functions of presiding officer, could have been so bad as president. How do you explain that?" "The explanation is very simple," Frankfurter replied. "He loathed being president and being chief justice was all happiness for him."

Taft's final ambition was to see the Supreme Court removed from its assigned rooms in the Capitol Building to a new building of its own, for much needed "breathing space." "In our conference room the shelves [are] so high that it takes an aeroplane to reach them," he complained to one senator. He was opposed by his own colleagues, Justices Fuller, White, and Brandeis, who considered a "marble palace" superfluous. Taft finally prevailed, securing $1,500,000 from Congress for the site, but he did not live to move into the new Hall of Justice, not completed until 1932.

Taft suffered two heart attacks in 1924, the first in February—on the day of Woodrow Wilson's funeral—the second at the end of April. Back at his strenuous routine in 1925, he wrote to his son Charlie, "I have to be careful, and when I wake up in the morning and get dressed and come to breakfast, I thank the Lord for another day." But as he approached seventy, Taft began to fail in health. "My heart has a great burden to carry and has given symptoms that I hearken to," he informed an old friend. It was time to slow down, but Taft did not resent it, for he felt that he had done a creditable job as chief justice: "Up to date [1926] I have written more cases than any of them during the five years of my service, and with the other work I have more than pulled my weight in the boat." "I am older and slower and less acute and more confused," he confessed, but "as long as things continue as they are . . . I must stay on the Court in order to prevent the Bolsheviki from getting control."

During these years Taft expanded his recreational reading to include detective novels. Nellie made selections for him from the circulating library, where she drove every Saturday morning from their house on Wyoming Avenue. With his health declining, he had an electric elevator installed, which he used to reach his office on the third floor of the house. He took much delight in pushing the control buttons and acting like a conductor, bowing deeply to Nellie when she entered. Visitors to their house noted that of all the numerous momentos and pictures displayed, there was none of Roosevelt in view, and that Taft rarely mentioned his name.

As chief justice, Taft no longer golfed or rode horseback but he still walked abroad on occasion. Arriving at the Capitol each weekday morning, he showered, had a massage, and took his place on the bench. Whereas some of his colleagues often dozed in court, Taft was now always alert to everything going on. And despite the exacting duties of his office, he seldom lost his good nature. Although Nellie socialized a good deal, Taft increasingly declined to go out. He adhered rigidly to his diet, having hard-toasted bran bread for breakfast and dinner, with small portions of meat and vegetables at midday.

Taft's health suffered a downturn in June 1929, after a visit to his brother Charles's home in Ohio. Recuperating at Murray Bay, he continued to work many hours at his desk studying the two hundred cases which the Supreme Court was to consider in the fall. He forewent his seventy-second birthday celebration on 15 September, which had long been a gala event at Murray Bay. He returned to the bench in October, presided over the annual conference of circuit court judges, and reviewed the improvements in the federal courts. But friends noted with alarm that his mind was growing weary and his chuckle growing fainter.

When Taft's brother Charles died in December, Taft insisted, against his doctor's advice, on going to Cincinnati for the funeral. He returned so weak he had to be hospitalized, and he subsequently declined into an all but helpless state from cardiovascular collapse. Robert went to Washington in February 1930, to announce his father's retirement from the Supreme Court. Oliver Wendell Holmes, who was presiding over the court in his absence, wrote warmly, "We call you chief justice still—for we cannot give up the title by which we have known you all these years and which you have made dear to us. . . . You showed us in new form your voluminous capacity for getting work done, your humor that smoothed the tough places, your golden heart that brought you love from every side and most of all from your brethren whose tasks you have made happy and light."

One month later Taft lapsed into periods of unconsciousness. The blinds of the house were drawn and a policeman patrolled the sidewalk to assure quiet. In a house a few doors away, reporters waited, catching glimpses of Taft's old friends and associates coming and going. President Hoover called to cheer him, but although Taft smiled weakly in response, no one knew whether he even recognized Hoover. As the end drew near, the only word that came from his lips was an occasional "darling" whenever Nellie came to his bedside. He died at home on 8 March 1930, in his seventy-third year. President and Mrs. Hoover, out driving at the moment of Taft's death, hurried to Nellie's side to offer their sympathies. Robert and Charles came from Cincinnati, and Helen from Bryn Mawr. Nellie bore the shock with "fortitude," according to reporters on the scene. Although President Hoover offered the East Room of the White House for the funeral, Taft had demanded a simple Unitarian service. He became the first president to be buried in the Arlington National Cemetery.

The tributes to Taft were warm and generous. They dwelt not on his "indifferent record" as president, but rightly emphasized instead his second career in the Court, calling it the most "unprecedented comeback" on record. William Howard Taft, his obituaries agreed, "was human in every ounce of his great frame and every impulse of his generous spirit."

Taft left Nellie a $475,000 estate, including their Washington and Murray Bay homes, and she lived on for thirteen more years. Her greatest satisfactions came with the success of her three children. Robert, after graduating first in his Harvard Law School class, turned down a clerkship with Justice Oliver Wendell Holmes to begin, on his father's advice, the practice of law in Cincinnati. In 1923 he became a senior partner of Taft, Stettinius, and Hollister. He also successfully began his political career in the Ohio House of Representatives, where he served from 1921 to 1926. He was elected to the United States Senate from Ohio in 1938 and served there until his death fifteen years later. Nellie lived to see in 1940 the first of his three attempts to obtain the Republican presidential nomination. As a congressman, he enjoyed a long and distinguished political career and became known as "Mr. Republican." Like his father, Robert was a "man of integrity who believed strongly in loyalty to political associates and party regularity above all else." And like his father, his dry, detailed, fact-filled speeches dismayed supporters and opponents alike.

But Robert Taft in personality resembled his mother far more than his father. He also looked more like her, even staring the way she did, with his gray eyes slightly bulging. Like her, he did not laugh easily, appeared rather stiff and solemn, was content to remain alone a good deal, and acquired a reputation for reserve, if not coldness. He married Martha Bowers, a woman much like his mother—intelligent, independent, and ambitious. During courtship he seemed so indifferent that Martha initially thought he did not care for her. The daughter of William Howard Taft's Yale classmate Lloyd Bowers (later Taft's solicitor general), Martha was, according to Robert's sister, Helen, "the most intellectual girl" in their set. Although Martha became the mother of four sons, she took a more open part in politics than Nellie had. And like Nellie, Martha had a determined, competitive spirit, was very outspoken, and cared far more for the Washington whirl than domestic matters.

–The second-born son, Charles P. Taft II, eight years younger than Robert, was completely unlike his brother, and their relationship was never very good. Given the boy's outgoing and enthusiastic nature, Taft had worried that the family would spoil Charlie irreparably. In contrast to Robert, Charlie enjoyed identifying himself as the president's son. He too went to Taft School and then to Yale, with the intention of becoming Robert's law partner. In December 1917, when Charlie went overseas to war, his father wrote, "It is hard, my darling boy, to let you go. You are the apple of our eye." Taft expressed some impatience with Charlie after his return home, however, because he seemed increasingly drawn toward reform movements. Charlie's relations with Robert in the law firm were not improved by the fact that his wife, Eleanor Chase, the daughter of a Connecticut businessman, and Robert's wife, Martha, did not get along. But they were reluctant, for the family's sake, to break up their partnership and consequently remained formally together until 1938.

Beginning as prosecuting attorney of Hamilton County, Charlie was a longtime member of Cincinnati's City Council and culminated his political career as mayor of Cincinnati from 1955 to 1957. Always idealistic, he was an active crusader in the 1940s on such issues as civic reform, slum clearance, labor relations, and the welfare of the deprived and disabled.

Nellie was proud too of her daughter, Helen, for Helen was doing what she herself might have done had she lived in a more liberated era than her own. Helen earned a B.A. from Bryn Mawr (1915), a Ph.D. in history from Yale (1924), and some years later a law degree from George Washington University (1937). The author of two books, *British Government after the American Revolution, 1782–1820* and *The Revolt of French Canada, 1800–1835*, she was variously a professor of history, a department chairman, a dean, and acting president of Bryn Mawr. In 1920 she married Frederick J. Manning, a professor of political science at Yale. More liberal than her father, Helen once made headlines in 1912 after speaking out in support of striking shirtmakers in a labor dispute. Although Nellie opposed the women's suffrage movement, perhaps feeling that only a minority of women like herself were qualified to vote, Helen, like her grandmother Louisa Taft, became an activist alongside the leading suffragettes.

It may seem strange that Nellie, who was in many ways an intellectually liberated woman and who possessed ambition and aggressiveness to an unusual degree in a woman, opposed the suffrage movement. To understand this curious circumstance, we may analogize Nellie's attitude to those blacks who do not support the Black movement, because they identify instead with the white ruling class and dissociate themselves from their brothers. Nellie did not identify with women, but with men. She considered women generally to be inferior and compared her own interests and abilities with those of the opposite sex, the ruling class. One reason she did not like to travel with Taft on his many brief excursions as judge, cabinet officer, and president was that he associated with the men while she was left to entertain what she considered a lot of dull, ignorant women. At White House gatherings she most liked mixing in political talk with congressmen and cabinet officers and most avoided becoming a fixed ornament of some female klatsch. She educated herself in world affairs and languages not to lead women out of their bondage, but to free herself from their company. The limitations and constraints other women seemed content to accept, she found intolerable. She aspired to the male's position of power and influence—not as a woman, but as an equal.

Increasingly troubled by circulatory problems in her last years, Nellie remained close to Washington. Content with her children and grandchildren, but most especially with the cherished memories of her full years as first lady, Nellie died in Washington on 22 May 1943, one week before her eighty-second birthday. She was buried beside her husband in Arlington National Cemetery. Obituary columns bluntly stressed her role in keeping Taft off the bench and moving him toward the presidency. It was Nellie, friends and acquaintances admitted, who had prevailed on Taft to forego the Supreme Court appointments President Roosevelt had offered him. She had been, all agreed, the chief generating power behind her husband's political career.

A NOTE ON
THE SOURCES

The principal source for this study has been, as noted in the preface, the extensive collection of the Papers of William Howard Taft in the Manuscript Division of the Library of Congress. Included in this seven-hundred-thousand-piece collection are addresses and articles by William Howard Taft, letter-books containing materials covering his years as secretary of war, president, and professor of law at Yale University, family correspondence, correspondence with numerous friends, such as Theodore Roosevelt, Taft's secretary of war diary, family diaries and scrapbooks, legal papers, law lectures, and a great number of documents and items from his administration entitled the Presidential Series. The Taft Papers have recently become available on microfilm from the Library of Congress.

There are in addition published collections of addresses and writings which accompany a president's career, and Taft wrote more extensively about his conceptions of the presidency than did any other president. Some of the relevant works in this category are: *The Presidential Addresses and State Papers of William Howard Taft* (New York: Doubleday, Page, 1910); *Political Issues and Outlooks* (New York: Doubleday, Page, 1909); *Popular Government: Its Essence, Its Permanence and Its Perils* (New Haven: Yale Univ. Press, 1913); and *Our Chief Magistrate and His Powers* (New York: Columbia Univ. Press, 1916).

The most important and definitive biography of William Howard Taft is Henry F. Pringle's *The Life and Times of William Howard Taft*, 2 vols. (New York: Farrar and Rinehart, 1939). Recent studies of Taft and his career include Alpheus Thomas Mason, *William Howard Taft: Chief Justice* (New York: Harcourt, Brace and World,

1964), Donald F. Anderson, *William Howard Taft: A Conservative's Conception of the Presidency* (Ithaca: Cornell Univ. Press, 1968); Paolo Coletta, *The Presidency of William Howard Taft* (Laurence: Univ. Press of Kansas, 1973). Older biographies, some of which were occasioned by Taft's presidential campaign, also came into use in the preparation of this study. They include Edward Cotton, *William Howard Taft: A Character Study* (Boston: The Beacon Press, 1932); Oscar King Davis, *William Howard Taft: The Man of the Hour* (Philadelphia: P.W. Ziegler, 1908); Herbert S. Duffy, *William Howard Taft* (New York: Minton, Balch, 1930); Robert L. Dunn, *William Howard Taft, American* (Boston: Chapple, 1908); Frederich C. Hicks, *William Howard Taft: Yale Professor of Law and New Haven Citizen* (New Haven: Yale Univ. Press, 1945); Francis McHale, *President and Chief Justice* (Philadelphia: Dorrance, 1931); Allan Ragan, *Chief Justice Taft* (Columbus, Ohio: The Ohio State Archaeological and Historical Society, 1938); and Mabel Washburn, *The Ancestry of William Howard Taft* (New York: Frank Allaben Genealogical Company, 1908).

Many insights into Taft's personality are furnished by contemporary figures. These include family members, political acquaintances, close friends and associates, White House staff personnel, and journalists. As mentioned in the preface, Archibald Willingham Butt, Taft's White House aide, is the most valuable source of information for the presidential years. Both *The Letters of Archie Butt*, 2 vols. (Garden City, New York: Doubleday, Page, 1924) and *Taft and Roosevelt: The Intimate Letters of Archie Butt, Military Aide*, 2 vols. (Garden City, New York: Doubleday, Doran, 1930) consist of letters written in diarylike form and sequence, which chronicle Taft's experiences in the White House.

Other White House staff members have compiled accounts of their experiences that are particularly useful for corroborating some of Butt's observations and for seeing Taft in a nonpolitical perspective. They include physician Charles E. Barker, *With President Taft in the White House* (Chicago: A. Kroch and Son, 1947); head usher Irwin Hood Hoover, *Forty-two Years in the White House* (Boston: Houghton, Mifflin, 1934); Elizabeth Jaffray, *Secrets of the White House* (New York: Cosmopolitan Book Corp., 1926); and Lillian Rogers Parks, *My Thirty Years Backstairs at the White House* (New York: Fleet, 1961).

Mrs. William Howard Taft's *Recollections of Full Years* (New York: Dodd, Mead, 1917) is a guarded but extremely useful account of her perceptions of her role in Taft's career. The remembrances of Taft's brother Horace Dutton Taft, *Memories and Opinions* (New York: Macmillan Company, 1942), contains some helpful material on the family background of both Taft and Roosevelt.

Important impressions of Taft and observations about his life and career are contained in the published reminiscences of numerous friends and acquaintances. The most useful of these collections are: *Henry Adams and his Friends: A Collection of his Unpublished Letters*, ed. Harold Cater (Boston: Houghton, Mifflin, 1947); *The Selected Letters of Henry Adams*, ed. Newton Arvin (New York: Farrar, Straus and Young, 1951); *Letters of Henry Adams*, 2 vols., ed. W.C. Ford (Boston: Houghton, Mifflin, 1938); Cyrenus Cole, *I Remember, I Remember* (Iowa City: State Historical Society of Iowa, 1936); Chauncey M. Depew, *My Memories of 80 Years* (New York: Scribner's,

1922); John Hays Hammond, *The Autobiography of John Hays Hammond* (New York: Farrar and Rinehart, 1935); Alice Roosevelt Longworth, *Crowded Hours* (New York: Scribner's, 1933); Robert H. Murray, *Around the World With Taft* (Detroit: Dickerson, 1909); Sir Cecil Spring Rice *The Letters and Friendships of Sir Cecil Spring Rice* (New York: Houghton, Mifflin, 1929); *The Letters of Theodore Roosevelt*, 8 vols., ed. E.E. Morison and John Blum (Cambridge, Mass.: Harvard Univ. Press, 1951–54); *Selections from the Correspondence of Theodore Roosevelt and Henry Cabot Lodge* (New York: Scribners, 1925); Ellen M. Slayden, *Washington Wife* (New York: Harper and Row, 1962); James E. Watson, *As I Knew Them: Memoirs of James E. Watson* (Indianapolis: Bobbs-Merrill, 1936); Simon Wolf, *The Presidents I Have Known from 1860 to 1918* (Washington, D.C.: Byron S. Adams, 1915).

Comments on Taft's political career are contained in the reminiscences of various political figures, particularly: Champ Clark, *My Quarter Century of American Politics* (New York: Harper and Bros., 1920); Lloyd C. Griscom, *Diplomatically Speaking* (Boston: Little, Brown, 1940); Robert M. LaFollette, *LaFollette's Autobiography* (Madison: Univ. of Wisconsin Press, 1913); Gifford Pinchot, *Breaking New Ground* (New York: Harcourt, Brace, 1947); Victor Rosewater, *Backstage in 1912* (Philadelphia: Dorrance, 1932); and Oscar S. Straus, *Under Four Administrations* (Boston: Houghton, Mifflin, 1922).

Several major journalists and political commentators of the time left published reminiscences, which include important observations on Taft in the presidency. Most revealing are Oscar King Davis, *Released for Publication: Some Inside Political History of Theodore Roosevelt and his Times, 1898–1918* (Boston and New York: Houghton, Mifflin, 1925); Arthur W. Dunn, *From Harrison to Harding: A Personal Narrative Covering a Third of a Century, 1888–1921*, 2 vols. (New York: G.P. Putnam's Sons, 1922) and *Gridiron Nights* (New York: Fred Stokes, 1915); Norman Hapgood, *The Changing Years* (New York: Farrar and Rinehart, 1930); Henry L. Stoddard, *As I Knew Them: Presidents and Politics from Grant to Coolidge* (New York: Harper and Bros., 1927); Mark Sullivan, *Our Times*, 4 vols. (New York: Scribner's, 1932); Charles W. Thompson, *Party Leaders of the Time* (New York: G.W. Dillingham, 1906) and *Presidents I've Known and Two Near Presidents* (Indianapolis: Bobbs-Merrill, 1929); Oswald Garrison Villard, *Fighting Years: Memoirs of a Liberal Editor* (New York: Harcourt, Brace, 1939); William Allen White, *The Autobiography of William Allen White* (New York: Macmillan 1946) and *Selected Letters of William Allen White*, ed. Walter Johnson (New York: Henry Holt, 1947).

The *New York Times*, the *Washington Post*, the *Herald Tribune* and the *Evening Star*—1906–1913—provide a wealth of information about the presidential years in both articles and editorials on Taft's political strategies and policies and on the opposition's views of his administration. In addition, the informal, off-the-cuff remarks of President Taft, picked up by the newsmen hanging at his heels, give a day-to-day impression of the man that we may believe to be reliable—even after we allow for some misquotation.

Political commentaries and editorials in a variety of journals supplement the newspaper accounts, especially those in the *American Mercury, Arena, Century Magazine,*

Collier's, the *Fortnightly Review*, the *Forum, Hampton's Magazine*, the *Independent, Literary Digest, McClures*, the *Nation*, the *Outlook*, and *World's Work*. Among the more important signed articles are Ray S. Baker, "The Measure of Taft," *American Mercury* (July, 1910): 365; R.E. Bisbee, "Why Mr. Taft Should Be Defeated," *The Arena* (August, 1908): 316–20, and "The President's Opposition to Effective Campaign Publicity," *The Arena* (November, 1908): 502–5; Sydney Brooks, "Mr. Roosevelt's Reappearance," *Fortnightly Review* (March, 1912): 730–46; H. Hamilton Fyfe, "Some Possible American Presidents," *Fortnightly Review* (November, 1911): 809–906; Edward G. Lowry, "One Year of Mr. Taft," *American Review* (March, 1910): 289–301; Eugene P. Lyle, Jr., "Taft: A Career of Big Tasks," *World's Work* (September, 1907): 9349–61; Wayne MacVeagh, "An Appeal to President Taft," *North American Review* (February, 1911): 161–79; Judson Welliver, "The Collapse of the Taft Administration," *Hampton's Magazine* (October, 1910): 419–31; Henry L. West, "American Politics: William Howard Taft of Ohio," *The Forum* (July, 1908): 3–6, and "American Politics: The President and the Campaign," *The Forum* (November, 1908): 413–21; and William Allen White, "Should Old Acquaintance Be Forgot?," *American Magazine* (May, 1912): 13–18.

There are a great many biographies of important political figures and events of the Taft era. Among the more useful: Claude Bowers, *Beveridge and the Progressive Era* (Cambridge, Mass.: Houghton Mifflin, 1932); Doris Faber, *The Mothers of American Presidents* (New York: New American Library, 1968); William Judson Hampton, *Our Presidents and their Mothers* (Boston: Cornhill, 1922); George Harvey, *Henry Clay Frick, the Man* (New York: Scribner's, 1928); M.A. DeWolfe Howe, *Portrait of an Independent: Moorfield Storey* (Boston: Houghton, Mifflin, 1932); Philip Jessup, *Elihu Root*, (New York: Dodd, Mead, 1938); Lewis Alexander Leonard, *The Life of Alphonso Taft* (New York: Hawke, 1920); Richard Leopold, *Elihu Root and the Conservative Tradition* (Boston: Little, Brown, 1954); Marianne Means, *The Woman in the White House* (New York: Random House, 1963); William Manners, *TR and Will* (New York: Harcourt, Brace and World, 1969); Sylvia Jukes Morris, *Edith Kermit Roosevelt: Portrait of a First Lady* (New York: Coward, McCann and Geoghegan, 1980); George Mowry, *Theodore Roosevelt and the Progressive Movement* (Madison: Univ. of Wisconsin Press, 1946) and *The Era of Theodore Roosevelt, 1900–12* (New York: Harper and Bros., 1958); James T. Patterson, *Mr. Republican: A Biography of Robert A. Taft* (Boston: Houghton, Mifflin, 1972); Henry F. Pringle, *Theodore Roosevelt, a Biography* (New York: Harcourt, Brace, 1931); Kathleen Prindiville, *First Ladies* (New York: Macmillan, 1938); Merle J. Pusey, *Charles Evans Hughes*, 2 vols. (New York: Macmillan, 1951); Phyllis Robbins, *Robert A. Taft, Boy and Man* (Cambridge, Mass.: Dresser, Chapman and Grimes, 1963); Ishbel Ross, *An American Family: The Tafts* (New York: World Publishing, 1964); Francis Russell, *The Shadow of Blooming Grove* (New York: McGraw-Hill, 1968); Nathaniel Wright Stephenson, *Nelson W. Aldrich* (New York: Scribner's, 1930); Bessie White Smith, *The Boyhoods of the Presidents* (Boston: Lothrop, Lee and Shepard, 1929); William Roscoe Thayer, *Life and Letters of John Hay* (Boston: Houghton, Mifflin, 1915).

More general historical studies used in this study were: James David Barber, "Analyzing Presidents: From Passive-Positive Taft to Active-Negative Nixon," the *Washington Monthly* (October, 1969): 33–54; David Cushman Coyle, *Ordeal of the Presidency* (Washington, D.C.: Public Affairs Press, 1960); Holman Hamilton, *White House Images and Realities* (Gainesville: Univ. of Florida Press, 1958); *History of the Progressive Party*, ed. Helene Hooker (New York: New York Univ. Press, 1958); Matthew Josephsson, *The President Makers* (New York: Harcourt, Brace, 1940); Frank K. Kelly, *The Fight for the White House: The Story of 1912* (New York: Thomas Y. Crowell, 1961); Alpheus T. Mason, *Bureaucracy Convicts Itself: The Ballinger-Pinchot Controversy of 1910* (New York: Viking Press, 1941), and *The Supreme Court from Taft to Warren* (New York: W.W. Norton, 1958); James E. Pollard, *The Presidents and the Press* (New York: Macmillan, 1947); Frank Taussig, *Some Aspects of the Tariff Question* (Cambridge, Mass.: Harvard Univ. Press, 1918), and *The Tariff History of the United States* (New York: G.P. Putnam's Sons, 1910); Rexford G. Tugwell, *How They Became President* (New York: Simon and Schuster, 1964); Norman Wilensky, *Conservatives in the Progressive Era: The Taft Republicans of 1912* (Gainsville: Univ. of Florida Monographs, 1965).

Finally, in addition to the Taft Papers, biographies and reminiscences, and the secondary historical works on the era, there is another fund of information which has proved of great assistance in my understanding Taft's particular psychological make-up—the rapidly expanding medical literature on the subject of obesity. The evidence of medical observations concerning the psychological implications of obesity, a condition from which Taft quite palpably suffered throughout most of his life, corroborates the basic conclusions in my interpretation of his personality and career. The most important articles were: Alfred Blazer, M.D., "The Obese Character," *International Record of Medicine*, 164 (1951): 24–30; Israel Bram, M.D., "Psychosomatic Obesity," *Medical Record*, 157 (1944): 673–76; Hilde Bruch, M.D., "Developmental Obesity and Schizophrenia," *Psychiatry*, 21 (1956): 65–70, and "Psychological Aspects of Obesity," *Psychiatry*, 10 (1947): 373–81; Sidney C. Burwell, M.D. et al., "Extreme Obesity Associated with Alveolar Hypoventilation—A Pickwickian Syndrome," *American Journal of Medicine*, 21 (1956): 811–18; Gustav Bychowski, M.D., "On Neurotic Obesity," *Psychoanalytic Review*, 37 (1950): 301–19; Stanley Conrad, M.D., "The Psychological Causes and Treatment of Overeating and Obesity," *American Practitioner and Digest of Treatment*, 3 (1952): 438–44, and "Phallic Aspects of Obesity," *Journal of the American Psychoanalytical Association* (1965): 207–23; Harvey E. Estes, M.D., et al., "Reversible Cardiopulmonary Syndrome with Extreme Obesity," *Circulation*, 16 (1957): 179–87; Walter Hamburger, M.D., "Emotional Aspects of Obesity," *The Medical Clinics of North America*, 35 (1951): 483–99; R.S. Illingsworth, M.D., "Obesity," *The Journal of Pediatrics*, 53 (1958): 117–30; Harold Kaplan, M.D., "The Psychosomatic Concept of Obesity," *Journal of Nervous and Mental Disease*, 125 (1957): 181–201; A. Rascovsky, M.W. de Rascovsky, and T. Schlossberg, "Basic Psychic Structure of the Obese," *International Journal of Psychoanalysis*, 31 (1951): 144–49; Thomas Rennie, M.D., "Obesity as a Manifestation of Personality Disturbance," *Diseases of the Nervous System*, 1 (1940): 238–47; Henry Richardson, M.D., "Obesity as a Manifestation of Neurosis," *The Medical Clinics of North America*, 30 (1946): 1187–

1202, and "Obesity and Neurosis, a Case Report," *Psychiatric Quarterly*, 20 (1946): 400–24; Irwin Rosenstock, "Psychological Forces, Motivation, and Nutrition Education," *Journal of Public Health*, 59 (1969): 1992–96; Alfred Schick, M.D., "Psychosomatic Aspects of Obesity," *Psychoanalytic Review*, 34 (1947): 173–83; Robert Schopbach, M.D., "Obesity: An Etiologic Study," *The Psychiatric Quarterly*, 27 (1953): 452–62; Harold Stuart, M.D., "Obesity in Childhood," *Quarterly Review of Pediatrics* 10 (1955): 131–45; and Edward Weiss, M.D., "Psychosomatic Aspects of Dieting," *The Journal of Clinical Nutrition*, 1 (1953): 140–48. The most useful books were: Hilde Bruch, M.D., *The Importance of Overweight* (New York: W.W. Norton, 1957); Philip E. Gelvin, *Obesity, Its Cause, Classification and Care* (New York: Hoeber-Harper, 1957); Rudolph Marx, M.D., *The Health of the Presidents* (New York: G.P. Putnam's Sons, 1960); Theodore Isaac Rubin, M.D., *Forever Thin* (New York: Bernard Geis Associates, 1970); and *Obesity*, ed. Roger Wilson and Nancy Wilson (Philadelphia: F.A. Davis Company, 1969).

INDEX

273